International Best-Selling Compilation
books by Ignite for you to enjoy

———————

Ignite Your Life for Women

Ignite Your Female Leadership

Ignite Your Parenting

Ignite Your Life for Men

Ignite Your Life for Conscious Leaders

Ignite Your Adventurous Spirit

Ignite Your Health and Wellness

Ignite Female Change Makers

IGNITE THE Modern Goddess

AWAKENING THE FEMININE ENERGY IN YOU AND LIVING THE LIFE YOU WERE DESTINED TO HAVE

FOREWORD BY **Regan Hillyer**
Speaker, Manifestation Coach, Entrepreneur

INTRODUCTION BY **JB Owen**
Founder of Ignite and JBO Global Inc.

PRESENTED BY

ALIDA DEL BIANCO ALLYNE HENESEY • AMBIKA DEVI • ANA CUKROV

ANA PAULA GOMES • REV. PRIESTESS ANANDHA RAY • ANNE-MARIE CHAREST

ARIADNA CRUZ GROBERIO • ARIANE BARROS • CAROLINE OETTLIN • CHARLENE RAY

ELIŠKA VAEA • ESTHER LÓPEZ • HANNA MEIRELLES • HANNAH WOEBKENBERG

IVANA SOŠIĆ ANTUNOVIĆ • JB OWEN • JENET DHUTTI-BHOPAL • JOANN LYSIAK

KATARINA AMADORA • KERRY PATON • KRISTEN APPENRODT • LAUREN CUTHBERT

MARIE MBOUNI • MAYSSAM MOUNIR, MD • NOUR FAYAD • RACHEL T GREENE

ROSE AMARU • RUQAYA KALLA • SEDONA SOULFIRE • SUYOGI GESSNER

TARA HEINZEN • UTE BENECKE • YENDRE SHEN

PUBLISHED BY IGNITE AND PRINTED BY JBO GLOBAL INC.

Published and printed by JBO Global Inc.
5569-47th Street, Red Deer, AB
Canada, T4N6L4 1-877-677-6115

Cover design by JB Owen
Book design by Dania Zafar
Designed in Canada, Printed in China

ISBN# 978-1-7923-0672-3
First edition: June 2020

Ordering Information: Quantity sales. Special discounts are available on quantity purchases by corporations, associations, and others. For details, contact the publisher at the address above. Programs, products, or services provided by the authors are found by contacting them directly. Resources named in the book are found in the resources pages at the back of the book.

Dedication

To align with the Goddess, you have to align with everything she is.

She's the lionesses of the wild, fierce and strong, yet she's the most loving expression that could ever be. She chooses herself and chooses everyone else at the same time — some call it multitasking. Others call it mother's love, the kind of love that gives everyone an equal share. She's the warmth of the womb, the safety, and the support. She's the teacher and the way. She's the flow of the river, and she's the beauty of nature — everything alive and flourishing. She's as light as a breeze and as powerful as a volcano that's known to build up new grounds. She's the daughter, the son, the mother, the father, the sister, the brother, the lover, and the friend. She's a Goddess with so many faces but only one essence: Love and Evolution. She is ferocious, savage, and untamed; a fiery hug of a loving expression.

Much love,
Dr. Mayssam Mounir

TESTIMONIALS FROM AUTHORS

"Ignite has offered me wings to soar beyond my limiting beliefs and conditioned fears. Like a gentle breeze offering a bird the gift of flight, the Ignite team has helped me illuminate the beauty of my journey, the gift of my story, and the power in sharing it with the world. For that, *MERCI!*"

~ Anne-Marie Charest

"Being part of an Ignite book has been one of the most amazing and empowering experiences. The tools and support received… the sense of community and so much sharing with other Ignite authors… and the unbeatable opportunity to share your story with the world, inspiring and igniting so many souls. It's just what the world is so much in need of."

~ Esther López

"Each time I say yes to an Ignite book, I prepare for my life to change and be transformed. The entire journey is revealing and healing! Then you get to watch your story begin to ignite and transform those who read it, which is wonderful beyond words. From start to finish, this is a journey that contains so much magic and is empowering in ways you can only begin to imagine."

~ Charlene Ray

"I was drawn to write in *Ignite The Modern Goddess* right after I had my first amazing experience of sharing my story in *Ignite Your Parenting*. I felt both fear and excitement at confronting a part of myself I wrestled with trying to embrace almost my whole life. Growing up in an Asian culture that valued boys over girls, I had bought into it with my pride in being a tomboy and over-developed my masculine qualities. I knew a deep, intimate, raw exploration was required for me to make myself whole and complete as to what it means to be a woman as defined by me and not someone else. This journey of putting my story into words allowed me to understand how I had unconsciously given away my power by disowning and devaluing myself. It has helped me to reclaim my power and I hope it inspires you to reclaim your power back as well. "

~ Yendre Shen

"Sharing my story the Ignite way was an incredible experience. During the process of writing, I found myself with a lot of other commitments at first and I was afraid that I would not be able to have enough time to birth the authentic words I knew I had within me. I received tremendous support from the whole team. The other authors were checking in on me and JB and Peter were there all the way, encouraging me and helping me believe I could do it. The result was beyond my expectations."

~ Marie Mbouni

"Being an author in *Ignite the Modern Goddess* has innovated my experience of writing inspiring content that empowers. The interaction with the editors, JB, and fellow authors combined with the fantastic 'Writer's Nest' sessions sparked the best of me in a vibrant and creative process that no other technique would awaken. I would recommend this adventure of knowledge, which is to experience 'Ignite your life' for all happiness seekers."

~ Ariadna Cruz Groberio

"The realization that is cognized through the reflection and introspection process that happens while writing your story is tremendously powerful. It will highlight your purpose and work as your North Star. That is huge! Any Ignite book you choose to share your story through will transform your life and focus accordingly. *The Modern Goddess* has a story to tell. I'm deeply grateful to be one vessel that carries her voice into our modern world. After my journey writing in this book, my connection to my Goddess grew deeper; my belief is of unfathomable measure."

~ Mayssam Mounir, MD

"Writing my chapter for *Ignite the Modern Goddess* was a fantastic opportunity. JB has a system in place that covers every step with a very detailed website guiding you, weekly Mastermind calls tracking you, and an excellent team of editors helping you with your story throughout the various stages. In the end, it was a fun, empowering, and easy experience thanks to JB and her team."

~ Joann Lysiak

Contents

HONOR

Foreword by Regan Hillyer

Speaker, Manifestation Coach, Entrepreneur

It's no coincidence you're holding this book right at this moment. Your inner goddess has called you to rise into the highest facet of your being and help your fellow sisters do the same.

As you read the stories on these pages, I invite you to go into the deeper layers of your mission. Allow yourself to tap into the purpose that goes beyond yourself and your story. When we choose to ascend and evolve together, we get to go past our limitations and create a more profound impact in this world.

You may have suffered through so much pain and disappointment before getting to where you are today. You may have experienced traumas that have been holding you prisoner in your past. You may have unhealed wounds that have started to fester and eat you up inside. You may have direct experiences of abuse, harassment, and inequality that you can't forget.

Sadly, every day, millions of women are still suffering just like you did.

Some can't wear what they want without fearing for their safety. Whether at school, home, or work, they must always keep their eyes open for predators. Other women have to submit to men's authority, even when they are the more capable one. Women everywhere have to fight for their status, especially in workplaces dominated by men with a misogynistic point of view. There exist countless more stories of heartbreaks, agonies, and injustices that many women have to withstand every day.

And I say *it's enough*. It's time for us, as a collective, to stop tolerating inequality.

Women don't always get the chance to speak up. They're told that their voices don't matter. Or worse, they're not even allowed to talk at all. This book is a space for women's voices. Inside these pages, you'll find valuable insights that will help you realign to the intuitive goddess wisdom embedded in your being. This ancient and modern-day knowledge is encoded within your cells.

Pick up this book whenever you're close to giving up or when you feel the need to go further. Let go of the setbacks you might encounter in your life and let the stories written by the exceptional women in this book pull you forward into the next layer of your highest self despite any setbacks you might encounter.

You are more than your past and you have so much to look forward to in the future. You are a goddess who has the unlimited capacity to manifest anything you desire. Many of us unknowingly became disconnected from this divine power. We grew accustomed to lowering our standards by allowing others to define who we are.

There have been many activation points when it comes to my purpose in helping women reclaim their grace. I can remember as clear as day one powerful moment that feels relevant to share with you here.

I was lying in bed at a beautiful villa in the Sacred Valley of Peru when a majestic feminine voice ringing inside my head awakened me. The sound of her voice defied logic. It echoed authority, yet it was soft and gentle at the same time.

As I tuned in deeper to the voice, a visual started to appear. I heard and saw the most divine goddess standing before me. My mind was doubting what was happening, but my soul told me to breathe and surrender.

As I did just that, the divine goddess established a connection point with me. She instructed me to travel alone to a specific island in Greece, telling me I had to complete an important assignment for the planet.

Can you imagine being woken up by a magical voice telling you to cancel your upcoming plans and travel somewhere unaccompanied? I was skeptical and perplexed. It was like a scene from a movie.

And yet...

As I talked more to this soothing, powerful goddess, she explained why I should prioritize this incredible responsibility above all else. To my surprise, my soul resonated with the instructions. All my inhibitions were gone. Excitement and pressure simultaneously overwhelmed me. I felt my mission expanding deeply within my field, while a piece of my purpose came instantly online.

I had been bestowed a mission for the benefit of all women in this world.

Easy? No.

Necessary? Yes.

And so I accepted it.

The first activation happened in Peru, and from there, I followed the voice to Greece. The goddess also initiated me to then go to Bali and Egypt.

I was to complete a series of downloads in all four vortexes to form a multidimensional energy pyramid. Afterwards, I must receive the codes and anchor them through these grid points on the earth. Only then will I be able to activate the sacred goddess inside every living woman who desires these upgrades, and helps them fully step into their true sovereign nature.

It was a lot to take in. But I knew that the divinity was there to guide my path as step by step, day by day, layer by layer, I embodied the goddess within me more and more. The journey wasn't comfortable or easy, but it went well thanks to the intuitive wisdom and guidance vested upon me.

Since then, I've been working to reach every woman in the world, intending to share with them all that I've discovered.

I know that each of us has different origins, characters, cultures, and beliefs. I appreciate your effort to understand everything I've just shared, even if it might've sounded foreign to you. Your commitment to opening your heart and soul shows how ready you are to embark on this beautiful journey beyond the ordinary.

That's why I'm so thankful to JB Owen for giving me the honor of writing the foreword of this book. We had a deep soul connection and I could feel her powerful mission codes from our very first conversation. It makes me so proud to know such a wonderful embodied goddess who is committing her time and energy to create the Ignite series for the planet. JB is an inspiration for everyone who wants to help the world progress positively, especially right at this moment when we're going through such a deep planetary shift.

Now that I'm able to reach out to you, I am inviting you to be a part of this initiative.

Several women have forgotten how, in their natural state, they could overcome anything with ease and grace. That their beauty and confidence shouldn't depend on others' opinions, for we are living embodiments of a divine goddess.

Nothing should be able to stop you from taking a stand and talking about what matters most. Because as a woman, you have the innate ability to nurture, love, and amplify the good in anything you touch — whether it be money, relationships, health, or any other area in your life. You can balance your sacred feminine and masculine energy, enabling you to intertwine and embody the best traits from both.

This book will allow you to gently challenge your limits so you can see how to ignite the goddess within your life. It will enable you to realize that everything this world has to offer can be yours, too, if you step up and claim it.

I'm in bliss knowing that you have access to this powerful body of work because it means you can now ignite the goddess that you really are. The more women recognize that we have this potential within us, the further our message will reach, and, together, the more impact we will create.

May you always remember that you are a powerful sovereign being who gets to choose not to give your power away to society's perception of normal — you weren't born for that.

You are a trailblazer that the next generation of young women will aspire to emulate.

Create your path. Follow your destiny. Be bold and embody your true nature because you are a goddess. Together as women, we get to create a different tomorrow.

Now, it's time to Ignite the goddess…

Enjoy this journey, beloved.
It's an honor to walk this path beside you as your sister.

I love you so much.
Regan x

IGN TE
THE
Modern Goddess

GRATITUDE

Introduction by
JB Owen

Founder and CEO of Ignite

Knowing the Goddess

Welcome to a book filled with marvelous wonder. In the next many pages you will find a cornucopia of beautiful stories all celebrating women who embody the multifaceted virtues and strengths of the modern goddess. You will read how the divine energy, the feminine force, the magical, mystical, and maven-like essence stepped into and transformed thirty-three amazing lives. These are not just stories, they are more like journeys; wondrous reflections of how and when the gracious goddess emerged.

To really understand the power behind this book, you must first understand the power behind the goddess. Her devoted conviction coupled with her astute knowledge, innate wisdom, and compassionate touch are just a fraction of the qualities she possesses. Known since the beginning of time, the goddess and her ethereal qualities have graced the ongoings of every human society. Her mysterious past and existential powers have exalted her to a high moral standing, regal presence, and grand gift of grace and humility.

This is just a fraction of who she is and amongst these pages, you will learn about her history, her origins, and the beliefs many have about her. You will read how she has influenced the decisions, ideas, and futures of women since the beginning of time. You will also uncover how right now, in this modern society, her qualities and virtues are alive and strong. Three unique feature chapters have been added to this book to bring background and context to her origins, ideals, and magnificence. We wanted to broaden the scope of what you may or may not know about her and give you more theory, a deeper understanding of her past, and reason to love her even more.

Then you will find the stories. The personal accounts of how she showed up and shone brightly in someone else's life. Her arrival may have been fierce and grand, or her presence may have been steady and supportive. However she presented herself in the life of every one of these dynamic women, and she did so in a way that was powerful and insightful. Her energy, her goddess greatness, was the catalyst for each of these authors to awaken and transform. She, the goddess in all her varied forms, was the instigator of a pivotal inner metamorphosis. Her otherworldly ways set a ball in motion and swirled a storm of change for the betterment of the receiver and the vital growth in her life.

Each story is varied, unique, and reflects the feminine essence and divine nature of the goddess herself. It is our hope that these stories spark that divine goddess knowing in you. We wish that you, in seeing her presence in our lives, will be inspired to make a deeper connection with her in your life. In writing these recounts of goddess reconnection, each author felt her story would touch your heart and inspire you to welcome your goddess to the forefront with a loving embrace.

Under the photos of each writer, you will see a single word — a virtue. These have been plucked from among the many innate virtues of the goddess. Each author picked their word carefully to share her multifaceted qualities and to remind you, the reader, of the vast characteristics all goddesses possess. These virtues are also in you. You are the modern-day goddess, living in a new time yet still reflecting the very essence of her greatness from eons before. More than ever, we need to call forth these virtues and implement them into our daily lives. Things like compassion, strength, and honor along with love, radiance, and peace are fused in her — and also in you.

The authors in this book believe it is in these virtues that women with their goddess energy will transform and uplift the new evolution of the planet. These virtues will be the epicenter of a more joy-filled and cohesive way of life for everyone.

BECOMING THE MODERN GODDESS

Use this book as a guide to welcome, embrace, and unleash the goddess in you. Dive into the upcoming pages, and explore the many *Power Quotes* that begin each chapter. These are the inspiring and powerful statements each of our goddesses wants to share with you. It is a phrase that encourages you to find your truth, discover your uniqueness, and bask in the glory that you divinely are. It is what you might say at your altar or whisper as you walk. They are the words you need to hear on a deep inner level and innately embody.

Power Quotes are ideas that you can use when you need some extra confidence or when the tears are flowing down your cheeks from both life's hardships and its rewards. Every Power Quote is designed to remind you of the greatness you have inside of you, of what you know you can accomplish, and how your existence is yours to harness and transform.

Next, you will see each author's caring *Intention*. These are the wonderful insights and glorious gifts they wish to bestow upon you. They are the personal, compassion-filled messages designed to awaken and inspire you. Each goddess wants to IGNITE YOU in living your most tantalizing life, and they share their intentions with the hopes of what their story can do for you.

Then, their goddess *Story* follows. It is a beautiful account of how they uncovered their goddess energy and infused that power into their lives. Their stories describe how they found their goddess gifts, unveiled her essence, seized her virtues, and became the goddess they have always wanted to be. These are their honest and authentic experiences of consciously awakening to the *Ignite* moment that resulted in a magnificent sequence of glorifying transformation.

We all have *Ignite* moments in our lives that change us, define us, and set us on a new path or trajectory. These stories are those moments told in the most loving and inspirational way. They show that we all have *life-altering* moments that not only impact us but ultimately define us and initiate long-lasting change.

Once you have finished each story, you will find a list of enjoyable *Ignite Action Steps*. These are the tangible things our goddesses did to love and embody their goddessness. Each author shares her supportive suggestion for you to try and experience immediately. These are the rituals and practices that were effective in their lives. Each suggestion is different and unique, just like you are, and each has proven to yield divine results when done consistently.

We believe actions speak louder than words; never is that more important than when it comes to becoming our true selves and loving ourselves for exactly who we are. To move closer to your true life purpose, we encourage you to explore each action step and then pick one you can do each day consecutively for 30 days. This book outlines many different action steps to try, so find the one that will create the most magnificent results for you. Each one is potentially the step that could change your life forever.

Our desire is for this book to become the beacon of light that inspires and *transforms* you. Each Goddess wishes that one of our stories has a profound impact and catapults you in a new direction in your life. We all want one line, one word, *one idea* from our stories to resonate so strongly within you that you just *have* to take action and awaken your goddess. Loving her, valuing her, and honoring who she is... is the most important thing we can share.

It is our deepest, most divine hope that one of these stories inspires you into a new conscious realization and you feel ready to transform, ready to soar, READY TO BECOME YOUR GODDESS!

WHAT MAKES IGNITE UNIQUE

Every word written in this book, every letter on these pages, has been meticulously crafted with fondness, encouragement, and a distinct clarity not just to inspire you but to transform you. Many people in this book stepped up to share their stories for the very first time. They courageously revealed the many layers of themselves and exposed their weaknesses, fears, and discomforts as few do. Additionally, they spoke authentically from the heart and wrote what was true for them, infusing love, compassion, and a desire to inspire in every word.

We could have taken their stories and aimed for perfection, following every editing rule. Instead, we chose to leave their unique and honest voices intact. We overlooked exactness to foster individual expressions. These are their words and sentiments. We let their personalities shine through so you would get a deeper sense of who they are. We focused on authenticity, honesty, and personal expression. That is what makes IGNITE. Authors serving others. Stories igniting humanity. No filters. No desire for perfection. Just realness between them and you.

Come turn the page and meet our authors up close and personal. We know you're going to love them as much as we do. Enjoy!

ZEAL

Honoring the Goddess
SHARING FROM AN EXPERT

AMBIKA DEVI

"You are the spark that lights the flame illuminating the jewel that resides upon the lotus flower of Great Mother Divine's heart!"

Every culture has a creation story that invites us to question our connection with all that is through vividly memorable metaphors. Most often they begin in chaos and the sorting of opposites. Popular pairings often include the gloaming of morning's light and the promise of release enveloping us in the obscurity of dreamtime's darkness. In the myths we are transported to places where the land meets the sea and shapelessness begins to take form. Here, we are confronted with three mystical questions: *Who am I? Why am I here? What is my purpose?*

The creatrix responsible for sorting this out is most often identified as a divine feminine force. She is a shapeshifter and can go from monstrous and destructive to suddenly nurturing and motherly. Her stories tell us how she gave birth in a variety of ways to the heavens and our Earth as we know it. Her children include time keepers and communicators, planets and stars, flora and fauna, and ultimately human beings.

It makes sense that a feminine archetype gave birth to all that is given — this is how we human beings procreate and reproduce. This is a repetitive pattern throughout history. We come from a mother and when we are tiny children it is our mother who feeds us. As we grow and develop, we identify with feminine archetypes seeking their guidance and approval.

We can see the Goddess as having many faces or as being split into multiple beings. Whatever works for each individual to make sense of this acts as a way to explain it. This is a personal preference and the lovely fact is that it does not matter. Just as the womb of a female human being is receptive and fertile, replenishing and regenerative — so are the stories of creation. The stories of the Great Goddesses echo these cycles of degeneration and regeneration in the mirroring patterns of myths and legends.

In order for us to be able to honor the idea of Goddess we must first meet her. In many cultures she is the Goddess seen as either Mother Nature or the one who gives birth to nature. My belief has always been that she is the mother of us all. She is the feminine aspect of existence.

In the west, we simply call her Mother Nature; however, in the realm of the east, she is in union of **Purusha पुरुष** *puruṣa* — the cosmos — who represents Divine Masculine — his job being to hold space for the Goddess in support of her creativity and she is the force of nature seen as **Prakriti प्रकृति,** *prakṛiti*.

The divine union of these two forces from the mystery school teachings of the Far East describes a unique union of the Sky God who must hold space for the Goddess of Nature to birth existence. In some cultures there is a specific representation that does not separate her from her partner. Such as the **Ard-hanarishvara अर्धनारीश्वर** *ardhanArIzvara* which began in the Kushan era (30–375 CE), and was later perfected in the Gupta era (320-600 CE). Appearing physically as half female and half male, the details of expression and garments explain the two sides which exist in each of *us* and in *everything*. This is an invitation to identify with the creative force of the Great Goddess and her dynamic energy as well as an honoring of her inseparable counterpart.

To me she is the mother of all mothers.

I see her in the smile of my own mother echoed in my smile. I feel her in the glowing memory of my mother's mother. I hear the sound of the Great Mother Goddess in all voices and sounds in nature. I listen to her in the rhythm of my own breath and heartbeat. I am supported by her under my feet. I am nourished by her in the food I eat and sustained by her in the sweet air I breathe. I soak and relax in her calming water. It is my hope that we all come to cherish her unconditional love and divine gifts.

In many cultures the Goddess flows in the mathematical rhythm of the number three and is known as the Triple Goddess. This can be interpreted as a variety of symbols. As Maiden, Mother, and Crone we can compare her to the life-cycle of a human woman. The maiden represents the years from birth to menstruation, mother as the reproductive years, and crone as the post-menopausal time of life. This can also be referred to as the virgin, whore, and mother archetypes.

The ancient Celts created a triple spiral symbol known as a Triskelion to emanate her regenerative powers and cycles. This symbol is believed to be associated with the Celtic Goddess Brighid and also to represent land, sea, and sky.

The word translates to mean three legs. It can be represented by a triangular set of three spirals with rotational symmetry and can also be found as three legs spiraling from a central point.

More progressions of three that can interpret the three phases or faces of the Goddess are:

- mind, body, and spirit;
- life, death, and rebirth;
- past, present, and future;
- power, intellect, and love;
- mother, father, and child;
- generation, degeneration, and regeneration.

The three worlds of many cultures tell stories of an underworld, a mundane world, and a celestial world.

In the teachings of the Far Eastern Mystery Schools there is a story of the **Devi Mahatmyam** देवीमाहात्म्यम् *devI mAhAmyam* describing the Goddess as the supreme power and creator of the Universe. Here the ancients describe a great battle between the forces of good and evil that threatened to destroy the architecture of the universe.

This Great Mother Goddess gives birth to and produces three offspring known as Gunas. The idea of **Guna** गुण *guNa* is a quality or attribute. Like everything these have proactive and challenging features and just as the Goddess herself is defined in triplicate, so too these qualities echo her continuum.

The Great Mother's faces are emulated in her three offspring. They are **Tamas** तमस् *tamas*, the stillness, darkness, and inertia. Tamas can be understood to be disorder, chaos, and destruction. **Rajas** रजस् *rajas* is motion, activity, and the ego. Rajas is driven and dynamic. **Sattva** सत्त्व *sattva* is a subtle essence and is interpreted to be spirit. Sattva is sweet, harmonious, and pure.

All of these qualities can be seen as both positive or negative, proactive or destructive. Without the others to base observation upon — they lose their magnitude and meaning. They perfectly reflect the power of the one true mother of us all.

Just as in many of the ancient tales of creation, the concept of the Infinite as Mother is supported by the **Rigveda** ऋग्वेद *Rgveda* explaining the all-compassionate mother figure as the creatrix of everything. This shows us how ancient cultures celebrated the feminine force, honored the divine feminine, and understood that we would be nowhere without it.

Looking to other cultures we find the idea of three reflected repeatedly. Ancient Greco-Roman papyri are found to address the Supreme Goddess through poem, prayer, and song asking for help from everything from healing the body of a runny nose or a migraine, to getting rid of bedbugs, or luck with betting on horse races. She is the mother of us all and therefore the requests ran and still do run the gambit of possibility.

There are specific Goddesses of many cultures who are believed to have three phases within their unique makeup. Selene, an archaic lunar deity and daughter of the Titans Hyperion and Theia, was imagined to have three faces. In many cultures she is seen as Hecate who in some stories is born each day as a maiden, lives through the afternoon as a mother, and ends each day as a crone only to begin the cycle again the following day. Relating to this idea at a very personal level enlivens our connection with her and increases our self-acceptance.

I encourage you to imagine the metaphoric possibilities. The maiden can be seen as dawn and new beginnings as well as the phase of a new moon. She can be springtime, flowers greening and growing full of possibility and potential. The mother can be interpreted to be home with a hearth fire to warm and sustain us through food for the body, mind, and spirit. She is the waxing of the moon and all things that help to nourish us. The crone is dark and mysterious. She is the inky obscurity of night and the waning phase of the moon. The crone is the Queen of the Night. She helps us to let go and release that which no longer serves us and teaches us to love the less than savory aspects of ourselves.

Three is a magickal[1] number. It is the first odd numbered prime number in our counting system possessing the power of indivisibility. It forms a trinity with the numbers one and two. In the Bible the number three represents omniscience, omnipresence, and omnipotence. How fascinating that this number was borrowed from our Great Mother Goddess.

---

[1] Magickal spelled with a "ck" is the inexplicable—the supernatural. Magic spelled with the "c" alone is foolery and prestidigitation.

In the deck of Tarot[2] the Roman numeral III is given to the Empress. She is a content ruler happy with her environment, pleased with all she sees. Plump and adorned, she wears a robe decorated with the symbol for the Goddess Venus as she lazes in her garden. There is no sign of her partner on the card and in spite of this she looks fulfilled as she oversees the care of her subjects.

Three is the number of the androgynous planet Mercury who rules the mind and communication. He is swift and possesses great analytical skills. Mercury is the messenger of the gods. He is the mediator between the Sun and the Moon. In many cultures the mercurial qualities are of a trickster and a keeper of the crossroads. In our counting system this is the way the number three gives hope to find stability in the idea of what is to come from the next number in the progression — which is four.

We can find three represented by masculine-oriented deities; however they always have a strong sense of nurturing and a motherly quality or must be appeased prior to getting through to the Goddess herself. In West African mythology this three character is Elegua who opens the gates so that we can speak to the three goddesses Oshun, Yemaya, and Oya.

In the ancient tales of India, Ganesha is the vibration of three. We must get through his guard before we can address and ask for help from any of the aspects of the goddesses. We often find Ganesha seated beside Laxmi, the Goddess of good fortune along with Saraswati the Goddess of spiritual enlightenment.

In Native American stories we learn of Spider Woman who is the progeny of the Sun and Changing Woman. She is a great teacher and provider. In order to address her we must stand up to the tests and chiding of her trickster helper Coyote, an echoing of the vibration of three.

These initial deities are guardians of the front gate to the Great Mother's castle and require obeisance. In all the respective traditions, it is considered a bad idea to ignore them. These creatures have many things in common. They love children and have many childlike characteristics. They love to play jokes on others — therefore they keep us on our toes! They love music and singing. Physically they are shorter than others and have unusual faces. Most importantly — they love to laugh.

When we look at this resonating number three in connection to the Goddess we can translate its vibration to signify communication, information, and our connections. Three can represent siblings even if we have none in our physical

---

[2] Tarot is a deck of 78 cards used for divination. The imagery referenced is from the Rider-Waite tarot deck illustrated by Pamela Colman, Smith.

families as it holds the essence of relationship. Three is the imbalance point when two beings come together and topple into the idea of the third thing — me plus you creates us.

The Great Mother Goddess has many faces that glitter and sparkle like the facets of a jewel-cut gemstone. We can see her honored and worshiped in many ways by the varied cultures of our world. These rituals celebrate her in a variety of her aspects through intricate ceremonies. The personification of her characteristics play out in stories and myths, poetry and song. We can track these back through *her-story* — and why not call it "her story" rather than history?

This can spiral like a chicken and egg paradox leaving us wondering which came first. There is no need for confusion as many cultural stories tell us of a first woman. One of my favorite versions is the Sumerian myth of Lilith, which inspired my first book — a novel by the same title. I see a bit of Lilith in all of us. I am so inspired by this aspect of the Goddess that I use this concept as a point in astrological charts to identify where we get our 'freak on'!

We are ironic as a group of beings and I wonder what led us astray? How did we lose the path of matriarchy? In all truth we are just like babes calling out to be fed, cleaned, and nurtured. This repeats throughout *her-story*. Humanity has cried out for love and support from the Great Mother of us all through rituals, celebrations, and religious ceremonies. We are children looking to her for guidance, spiritual upliftment, and comfort. We want to be held in her arms and fed at her breast. We yearn to be soothed by her for she is our mother. She has thousands of names in many different idioms.

Let us celebrate the Great Goddess either as a singular form or a triple grouping and as the infinite being she is. We can witness that she is a marvelous combination of powerful **Prana** प्रण *praNa* combined with the Goddess power of creation. I call her **Shakti** शक्ति *shakti*, the Divine Mother.

Her voice is the celestial music which vibrates in every quark and particle. She is the fertile ground where all seeds of thought are planted and then manifest in nature by the vibration of sound. It is her energy which combines with the vast nothingness to make everything we perceive to be real and full of substance. She gave birth to all of nature as we know it, and in her enormous heart she understands our quirks and needs.

When she laughs, the rippling pulsations vibrate and sprinkle the Universe with galaxies and stars. When she inflames with rage, we experience her powerfully destructive forces in weather and earth-shifting tremors. When she cries, the gentle rain of her tears washes our souls and clears the air. She gives us gifts of food and shelter and quenches our thirst.

Can we return to her and allow her to lead us with her wisdom? Is it possible to be irresistibly and magnetically pulled to her in polarity? Can we find the unified field and be one with her? I believe that we must honor her beingness in every particle of existence and that not only are we a part of her — but that she is very much a part of us.

May you be inspired to hear her and feel her in your own heartbeat. Let her spark of creation and the flame of love Ignite the flame in the center of the jewel that is resting upon the lotus flower of your heart. Feel her as she sings you into existence and know that you are part of her in the supreme consciousness.

Ambika Devi – United States of America
International award winning author and indie publisher, expert astrologer,
Insightful coach, and dynamic speaker
www.AmbikaDevi.com

CONNECTION

ALLYNE HENESEY

"Claim your inner power and own it without apology."

My hope is that you use my story to reflect on the archetype of the goddess and understand her influence in your own life. I invite you to cast your highest and best goddess self as the leading lady in your life.

TURN THE LIGHTS ON

I sat in the open field where two small creeks met and mingled until they became one larger creek. I loved that spot and everything about it. It was behind my parent's backyard and on the way to my dear friend's house. I loved jumping the creeks, catching crayfish, and cloud watching, unless the *Brady Bunch* was on the television in which case you would find me sitting on the plush evergreen rug of my parents' living room. My childhood was good; I was fed and clothed by two loving parents and teased and tickled by four siblings. I had time to read books like a little Athena goddess, climb trees like Artemis, play mother to my younger sister and baby dolls like Demeter, and daydream like pleasant Persephone.

One might say it was quite an ordinary life. The problem was I soon realized I didn't want to be ordinary.

By the time I hit 13, my inner rebel archetype came for a very long stay to challenge my beliefs, starting on the day that I received a really bad haircut. The style was supposed to look like the Olympic figure skater Dorothy Hamill. Instead my fine straight hair fell lifeless to my earlobes, resembling a young

Prince Charles — a fact my friends teased me about for weeks! I felt ugly and unattractive. It was a devastating blow to my sensitive and still innocent ego. After my friends' incessant but good-natured taunting, I vowed to grow my hair long. With that one thought, my inner Aphrodite was born along with a new love of blue eye shadow. Lucky for me, Charlie's Angels was about to override the popular figure skater's haircut with long 'feathered wings' — a style I quickly adopted and adored!

My teenage years were rather complex, but not because of outside trauma. No, my journey of self-discovery has always been an inside job. It started at age nine with reading every book I could find on extra-sensory perception; then I developed a love for mythology in my early teen years and Jungian psychology as an adult. I grew to learn that each one of us is deeply connected to the collective unconscious — think of it as a cloud-based warehouse where all thoughts and feelings are stored. Within this collective, there are archetypes (thought forms) that live within each one of us. The archetypes are like actors who strut and fret upon the stage of life. There are hundreds of archetypes, including the goddesses. They wear costumes with both light and shadow attributes. The language of archetypes is easier to interpret than you may think. It's evident when we say things such as "She's such a diva," or "He's a bully." It's a subtle language that is right under our noses! Seeing the connection between the archetypes helped me answer questions regarding my life and the cast of characters with whom I share the stage.

The marvelous world of Greek mythology and the idea of gods and goddesses frolicking up high on Mount Olympus has always lifted my imagination. Joining from this symbolic vantage point, I find it easier and less painful to explore my own experiences. My fascination with the ancient Greeks and their myths is more than self-indulgence. Studying their stories helps understand their civilization and their motivations. This is especially important because our western world of democratic capitalism was built on the Athenian city-state model — which was the envy of other Greek cities. Five thousand years later, we live and work in a magnified version of Mount Olympus where the gods' interests are placed above the mere mortals and well-being of Mother Earth. The goddess is still being exploited by power mongers while her vulnerabilities are cast to the tabloid coliseum where the masses take part in a feeding frenzy of dishonoring her power. The courageous voices of mortal heroines and heros sometimes rise above the din but always with great personal sacrifice. The goddess must begin her own hero's journey if she wants to evolve. She needs to ask, "What needs to be healed?" "How can I better serve others?" Understanding our own mythology helps us create connection points to support positive transformation. As Gloria Steinem said, "God may be in the details, but the goddess is in the questions. Once we begin to ask them, there's no turning back."

I've discovered this same process of inquiry applies to personal development as much as it does to business or government affairs. After all, everything in our life relates to power — and what we do with it.

In my teenage years, my inner Athena wanted knowledge to expand the power of my intellect; Aphrodite wanted to look sexy and wear ridiculous three-inch 'Candies' stilettos even though it meant walking a mile to school while wearing them. Artemis wanted freedom and appreciated horseback riding and moonlit adventures. Persephone loved poetry, dreams, and mystical experiences. Armed with these four goddesses, I pushed the boundaries beyond what any teenage girl should do. After Athena finished her homework, Artemis, Aphrodite, and Persephone called the party — all the better if there were boys involved! Dear Athena, goddess of strategy, kept me from getting caught by my father, the Colonel!

The downside with having a super strong Aphrodite and Persephone at a young age is they didn't help me make good choices — I was too immature to understand there are shadow sides to each of the archetypes. My teenage self was dancing in the dark on most days, and this was especially true after experiencing my first broken heart. My acute sensitivity to being rejected sent me whirling to the underworld. I eventually moved on and fell in love again at 18. When that relationship ended, the same Persephone pattern emerged, propelling me into a secret depression that no one saw. To avoid having that experience again, I held my Athena shield over my heart and rationalized that it was better to intellectualize relationships than to truly feel them.

Only that was a lie. It was a lie that I wanted to believe for the next 10 years. But, as with all lies, one can only stay in darkness if the lights are turned off.

My son's birth turned the lights back on. With Amy Grant's *Baby, Baby* playing on the airwaves, my heart swelled with love for my little guy, and Athena laid down her shield. But with her shield gone, another truth entered my heart: staying with my son's father would not be healthy for either one of us. Dreams are hard to let go, I realized, much more challenging than saying good riddance to my fiancé. I was not going to manifest the 'white picket fence' and family life with this man. Staying would be akin to Persephone's experience living with Hades in the dark underworld, devoid of happiness and peace.

Money wasn't exactly growing on trees, but I had the means to raise my infant son as a single mother. Knowing that my son deserved a life filled with love and laughter, I let love Ignite a fire under my feet to create positive change. A deep sense of hope sprung forward when I gazed at my baby with the Goddess Demeter coming forward in an incredibly powerful way. Her attributes helped me take full responsibility with creating a nurturing home for both of us. I had faith that I could raise my son on my own; not in a broken home as some might have said in days gone by, but in a comfortable home that was filled with hugs, kisses, laughter, and the occasional smell of chocolate chip cookies baking in the oven.

My saving grace through the ups and downs in my life has always been my strong sense of independence and an ability to navigate interesting landscapes, qualities that are attributed to Athena and Artemis. In lieu of the 'white picket fence' and hours of yard work, I purchased a townhouse with a magical forest and creek where little feet could run wild with imagination.

While I was enjoying being a mother and doing things my way, I realized I needed to further my education in order to advance my career. A night time dream showed me a Catholic university with statues of saints. And I listened! I decided to enroll at Immaculata University to finish my undergrad in psychology. My mother was really upset with the news; she didn't understand why or how a single working mother could go back to school. I was angry, perceiving her reaction as a lack of support. I didn't talk with her for two weeks — the one and only time we didn't speak. Didn't she know what I was made of? Did she doubt my abilities? The silent treatment ended when my father asked me to call her. After all, when Zeus asks his daughter Athena to do something, the logical thing to do is to comply!

Soon after, my mom offered to watch my son while I attended evening classes. They had wonderful times together: playing games, doing puzzles, and watching *Jeopardy* like two peas in a pod! My father preferred scavenger hunts and entertained my son by hiding coins around the house — a game my son absolutely adored! This continued for six years as I completed my studies one course at a time, with summers off to enjoy the creek and watch the fireflies on lazy evenings. I worked hard to achieve my goals while creating overall balance. My focus to build a better life kept me aligned with what needed to be done.

I learned that life experiences, especially the hard ones, build character and helped me move beyond judgment into a place of discernment and acceptance. My parents' support directly influenced my success. They are no longer here in this realm, but my gratitude and love for them forever dances in the stars.

My relationship with the divine feminine goddess emerged slowly as if an invisible silkworm was secretly weaving an exquisite dress. She came through dance, yoga, meditations, and studies. I must admit it felt strange identifying as a goddess — who am I to make that claim? Then in 2012, I decided to forge a more intimate connection with her because it suddenly dawned on me: she is my higher Self — the one who knows my purpose and guides me to reclaim my spirit whenever I falter. Playing small doesn't help anyone. Like others, I sometimes need a reminder that I am enough just as I am. I am lovable, intelligent, and worthy. My dreams have value and the skills and motivation to make them come true are at my disposal. To amplify that Source energy, I decided to give my goddess a name that represented the positive attributes of all the goddesses I know and love. It was my way of uniting the many Greek goddesses into One Divine Feminine Power, thereby calling back the fractured pieces of my soul. Her name came to me in an instant, as if delivered from a miraculous 'inner net' of wisdom directly to my lips. She is the Emerald Goddess©. Her consciousness connects me to the ancient Hermetic teachings of the Emerald Tablet — an actual emerald tablet rumored to be inscribed with the 'secrets of the universe.'

When I want to connect with the Emerald Goddess, I wear my teardrop necklace, put my hand on my heart, and remember that each and every person, like the emerald under my fingertips, is precious and rare. Emeralds are green which correlate with the heart chakra. When we open our hearts with intention, we are transmuting the desires of the ego by nudging those thoughts and feelings upwards until a spiritual truth is revealed. When the energy hits the pineal gland, spiritual awakenings burst forth like sunlight. Thus, when I call on the Emerald Goddess, I expand my perspective and experience myself and the world with a sense of oneness.

I'll admit it is difficult to articulate a spiritual experience in words because we don't really have the language for these holy awakenings — that's why the great mystics write poetry! However, I'd like to describe an event that was close to my heart. I was gazing out the back door on a beautiful spring day, thinking about taking a chance on love with a new romantic interest. Suddenly, I was transported elsewhere — where I don't exactly know! I felt like Jodi Foster in the ending scene of the movie *Contact*. She's inside a spaceship expecting to have contact with an extraterrestrial being and she has this amazing look on her face as if she just touched IT... the face of God, the Holy Grail, Source Energy, pure, unadulterated Love. And that's exactly what I felt for I don't know how long. It was brilliant, all encompassing, and exquisitely divine. Then my brain got involved and the thought that I might spontaneously combust if I stayed in this other world drifted into my awareness. I'd be happy, but I'd be gone from the earth, gone from my son! My thoughts brought me back instantly. After that experience, I was spiritually high for a week. One of my colleagues saw me walking down the hall a few days later and said I looked like my feet were not touching the ground. And that's how I felt. That extraordinary phenomenon was a gift with a profound message — love truly comes from the divine energy that lives *within* our hearts!

Our world is transforming quickly, and now more than ever we need to call upon the energy of the Divine Feminine to help shape our new world. It doesn't matter your gender and it doesn't matter what you call her. There is *only* One Power, One Source that is omnipresent, omnipotent, and omniscient. Call It whatever makes you feel comfortable. The goddess is the Holy Spirit, the creative life force that moves through your body and experiences life through you. The Divine Feminine Goddess guides you through your choices and helps you discover who you truly are and why you have come here — you are a divine being having a human experience.

We each have a part to play on the grand stage of life. You are part of the whole and what you do matters. Your life exists in one unified collective consciousness, and as such, we are all connected. Each one of us has the power to invite our unique aspects to the stage, to design our own playbill, and cast the best parts of ourselves as the leading actors. Today, more than ever, the world needs us to show up as *empowered* goddesses. We need to have healthy dialogue and ask creative questions that will act as a beckoning light during our darkest days.

I invite you to reflect on the goddess in your own life — what is your story? Give yourself permission to enter the theater of imagination and leave your analytic mind at the door.

Explore the world of the goddesses to learn which ones resonate best with you. Feel the deliciousness of Divine Feminine dance through your body. Meditate, reflect, and play with her essence to learn how she influences your life. What's her name? What are her attributes? How can you promote her to the position of leading lady in your own life? You have permission to claim *your* power and *own it* without apology!

IGNITE ACTION STEPS

Access goddess wisdom through an oracle deck. A fun and easy ritual to tap into your goddess energy is to use a deck of cards. Such as the one I designed called the *Emerald Goddess Oracle Deck©*.

You can pull cards at any time during the day, however, I especially love to do this in the morning before too much activity takes place. Find a quiet place where you will be undisturbed for a few minutes and center yourself. Recognize the sacredness in this space. It is your time to connect with divine wisdom. Trust whatever comes up in your intuitive heart.

Place your hands over your heart and take a few deep breaths until you feel centered.

- Place the deck in your hands for a few more breaths.
- Call on your Goddess Guides by knocking three times on the deck.
- Say a prayer or simply say, "Hello Goddess, what would you like me to know today? Let this be for my highest and greatest good."
- Pull one to three oracle cards.
- Gaze at the chosen card(s) with curious eyes.
- Read the associated message. Think about how this may influence your day. Feel free to ask your Goddess questions. Allow the yumminess of whatever comes up to settle into your heart.
- Take a few deep breaths of appreciation. Thank her and yourself for taking time to connect with Source energy.
- Write the message in your planner to keep the energy close to you as you go about your day or leave the card in a prominent place where you will easily see it.
- At bedtime, spend a few minutes reviewing the connection points between the card and the actual events that unfolded.
- Repeat the next day!

Allyne Henesey – United States of America
Soulcologist & Interfaith Minister
www.AllyneHenesey.com
www.SoulcologyCenter.com

UNDERSTANDING

HANNA MEIRELLES

"You are surrounded by Goddesses, including the one inside yourself."

I wish for you to wake up every day and decide on your desired state of being, then allow yourself to express it through every moment of the day. I want you to access your own divinity, accepting yourself the way you are. Open up the possibility in your heart that you are already divine. Life is about who you are *being* in the precise moment that you are doing whatever you are doing.

THE PATH TO UNDERSTANDING

I was anxious, feeling like I was about to have a panic attack, talking to my friend in her car on the way to our favorite organic market in Brisbane, Australia. I did not have a clue what to do next with my life. She suggested, "I know a massage therapist who not only treats the body but she is also very sensitive to what your heart is aching for. Maybe you want to consult with her." In my desperation to find a solution to the stress I was feeling, I slowly nodded my head in agreement.

I made an appointment the next day. As I stepped off the bus, I saw an ordinary white building that from the outside looked like such a normal place. I walked through the door feeling a little skeptical. Mandalas and mosaics caught my eye and I smelled a gentle incense that instantly made me feel calm. Instrumental music was playing in the background and the entire atmosphere was comfortable. The very energy of the room suggested something completely different from what I was living until that moment.

About six years before, I had been working in male-dominated industries while living in four different countries. One day, while I was working with a mining company in South Africa, my boss said, "I know you are a free bird, but I want you to come to work in our headquarters for two years to experience another side of our organization, and then you can go anywhere you want." She knew me well — that promise of freedom was the only thing that would make me leave my beloved South Africa.

With the promise of great learnings as well as challenges, I left my life in Johannesburg and moved back to Brazil, close to my family, to take up that opportunity. I experienced lots of challenges indeed! For four months, I worked like crazy to produce as much as I could with my team. One day, I encountered my boss in the elevator. She asked me, "How are you?" and tears started dripping from my eyes without any control. We sat down after to talk, and I told her that I could not see the results of my work even though my team and I were working so hard. I felt like we were rowing to nowhere. She pointed out all the outcomes we had achieved and how my contributions were positively perceived by the company, saying I was on the right track, but I was so motivated by results that I could not see or enjoy the beauty in the journey.

Concerned for me, she recommended I should see a coach. Not just any coach, but the one who was supporting lots of executives in our company and knew the reality I was going through. Coaching was something new and uncomfortable to me. Till then, I had never had a therapist, psychologist, or sought any type of emotional or mental help because I thought I was able to deal with and solve my own problems. My parents and grandmother had raised me to be independent and sort my life out without needing anybody's assistance. Little did I know the Universe would present me with the support I required in the form of several wise women who I called Goddesses.

My first Goddess was my coach. Sitting in a chair across the table from her, I had no idea what to expect. She was skilled, gracious, and very nurturing. She guided me through my own history and opened up a portal to my past so I could see who I had been throughout my 27 years. Little by little I was shown new possibilities for how my life could look and feel. I got clarity about what I liked and what I disliked. I felt more confident that I could succeed in a work environment I was still getting used to.

The next months were difficult. The world was changing constantly: global financial crisis, lay-offs, restructurings. But I wasn't changing the way I was doing my job. I worked long hours, pushing harder and harder every day. I was putting myself through very stressful situations that were crushing my spirit and making me extremely emotional. The burnout was manifesting physically in my body as a tendinitis in my right arm, pain in my shoulder, migraines, and constant colds and flus. My body was *tired* and looking for a chance to escape. I kept asking myself, "Is this sustainable? Does everybody in their late twenties in the corporate world go through the same things I am going through?" I remembered looking at other people in similar management positions and seeing that the women especially were suffering the same symptoms in silence, holding the space for the changes to happen.

My two years at headquarters were nearing an end so I approached my new boss to suggest my role for the next year. The company was beginning new projects in Asia and, as I enjoyed being a pioneer and moving to places where others wouldn't naturally go, I saw Malaysia as a great opportunity for me. After hearing my proposal, my boss said, "Well, it is not going to be Malaysia and it is not going to be next year. It's going to be Australia and it is going to be right now."

That was a completely new opportunity that I hadn't seen coming. The company was having massive challenges in its operations in Australia, trying to understand the culture and produce results with different approaches. They needed someone to support the Human Resources processes and they needed them *immediately*, so I relocated from Brazil to Australia.

On one hand, I was super excited about a new country, new perspectives, and new learnings. On the other hand, I was running away from myself, from the truth that made me work so hard, endure stress, ignore my body and my feelings of well-being.

My initial six months in the land down under were priceless. I was back in a male-dominated environment, facing a new reality, discovering new beliefs and habits, making new friends, and appreciating a culture which values nature, sunlight, harmony, and peace. My first impression was one of perfect weather, beautiful coasts, unique animals, and an easygoing, pleasure-driven population. Although all of this was available to me and right there in my backyard, I stuck to my hard working routine: doing, doing, doing. Achieving, achieving, achieving. Stressing, stressing, and stressing a little more. I did try to enjoy my weekends traveling the country and getting to know beaches and trails, but I was so tired and so focused on work that I could not fully enjoy those experiences. In fact, I was getting ill repeatedly and often ending up in the hospital with no diagnosis other than burned out.

Eleven months into my new job, I stepped through the door of that massage therapist practice in Brisbane. Calmly, the therapist, Marieke, introduced herself and invited me to have a cup of herbal tea. We talked for half an hour about what I was feeling and why I was there. Then she began the full-body massage session. It started with me lying down on my stomach and her touch made my body start to melt into the table. When I flipped over and laid down on my back, she started massaging my chest in between my neck and breasts. I could feel my heart thumping trying to find comfort. But I was tense, feeling suffocated. Within a few minutes that sensation wanted desperately to leave my body. Suddenly I burst into tears. I was crying like a baby in the crib, screaming sounds were coming out of me, releasing the pain in my deeply wounded heart. I cried as I have never done before. My soul was screaming for help. I had no idea what would take me out of that state, but I knew there was something wrong with me and I wanted to find what it was.

Marieke was actually a lifestyle and psychosomatic therapist and had a specific program designed for people like me. It would change the way I was living and help me find harmony within me again. She would be the third Goddess to cross my way, highly intuitive and beautifully creative.

Who was the second? She was my dear friend in the car, Jacquie, who recommended me to Marieke. Jacquie has always been a source of light for me whenever I needed. Being in her presence felt as if I was at a campfire in ancient times, surrounded by the wisdom of the elders in the tribe. She has an old spirit and a magical way of expressing herself that captivates everyone around her. She is truly an enlightened soul who brings inspiration to earth, as she has brought it to me on several occasions.

Trusting fully in Jacquie's judgment, I started Marieke's Lifestyle Program. In the first session, Marieke took a picture of my face. She then did a process called Face Split Analysis. She put my picture in the computer and divided my face in the middle. Then she duplicated the right side of my face onto the left. In this way, my new face now had both sides with the characteristics of the right. I looked at that picture and saw myself with pink cheeks and a round face, as if I was eating very well. I looked serious but healthy. My natural bright color was visible. Marieke told me that the right side of our bodies represents the masculine. This is where the mind, the action, the thinking, the analytical, and the drive resides. And that was me in my masculine — firm, colorful, and strong. Seeing that face, immediately I thought, "Well, it looks like it is all good!"

Then she did exactly the same process with my left side and showed me a new picture. I was shocked!

I looked like a rat! I could not recognize myself. The picture showed someone skinny with big dark circles around the eyes and a totally depressed expression. I asked her, "Is this me? Are you sure?" She said, "Yes, this is you; in your feminine."

The idea scared me. I asked her, "What does that mean?" She started to explain. "The feminine is the creative, the nurturing, the receptive, the intuitive. Are you using your intuition in your daily life? Are you nurturing yourself… taking care of yourself… or just taking care of others? Are you open to receive the opportunities for love and affection that show up in your life? Are you creating something new or are you just doing what needs to be done?"

I started to cry. None of those things were happening in my life and I realized I was only using my masculine. I had discarded and even forgotten my feminine. The masculine energy in me was really important for getting things done. But my feminine energy was the one that would guarantee my survival! It would empower me to do things with grace and ease, without stress and burnout. The feminine is the sustainability energy. It's the energy that creates us, as it literally generates lives, nourishes us, and makes us truly human. It is the divine energy that all Goddesses have. And in me, it was missing.

I was totally unbalanced. I was feeling incomplete even with all the luxury in my life in Australia. I wondered why I had been in the hospital six times in less than a year. I wondered why I had many dreams that didn't seem to come true, no matter my efforts.

When I realized that in some ways I had been doing everything wrong… that I had a total lack of awareness of my feminine… I was not even considering my own intuition, my own wisdom… a new awakening bubbled up in me; it blew me away. The heaviness I had been feeling in every part of me was lifted right out of my body — in an instant. I felt such relief that finally I could envision a way forward.

That day was a massive Ignite moment. I understood the importance of having and expressing both energies. My body and spirit were tired of that excessive masculine energy in me. I needed my feminine energy again. I wanted to embrace the feminine power that was hidden inside of me, exactly as I was born. I understood for the first time that I was a Goddess myself, but my emotions were not allowing me to see Her. I had lost touch with Her brilliance, radiance, and power.

I suddenly understood that self-realization could only be achieved by *Being*.

I had been focused on *doing*, not on *being*. *Doing* is one of the qualities of the masculine. Therefore, to reconnect with my feminine, I had to integrate a desired *state of being* in everything. I asked myself many questions at that stage, "Who am I being so far?" "What do I want to be from now on in whatever I am doing?" "Do I want to be patient, loving, courageous, forgiving, graceful, kind, inspiring, confident, and uplifting?" "How do I want to behave around others?" "Do I want to be helpful? Optimistic? Curious? Constructive?" "What is the state of being that will make me access my own divinity — the best version of myself — and fulfill me?"

The purpose of our soul is about who we are *being*, not about what we are *doing*. As Neale Donald Walsch said, "Divinity is a state of being; it is not an action."

I would feel as a Goddess again, KNOWING without doubt how divine I was in my femininity, only when I would decide the way I *wanted* to BE in this world.

Being is a decision; a choice. Only in rescuing my feminine energy would I be able to sustain myself as a person, sustain who I truly was. I wanted to embrace my femininity in its entirety, as well as my masculinity. Gods and Goddesses in my vision are complete entities, with all energies, in all their beauty. And they are inside of us, expressing their power to the outside world through our decisions on how to act.

Finally I was aware of what had been happening throughout my life. Now I understood the motivations behind previous decisions. Now I could be compassionate, kind, and forgiving to myself. Now, I knew the Goddess was not out there — She was inside of me, sleeping the entire time. Now, I could decide on my new *state of being*, embracing all that I really was. I did not need to be only in my masculine anymore. With the understanding of where I was coming from, it cleared up a space for my feminine to re-emerge.

From then on, I started my journey of developing my feminine energy. I engaged in training and studies on this subject, deepening my understanding, but most importantly I discovered and developed who I truly am. I reconnected with myself. From that understanding of who I was, I became much more open to comprehending others.

I had finally found the Goddess within me. The Goddess who is attractive, gracious, compassionate, feminine, and joyfully believes in her own beauty. I learned how to integrate both masculine and feminine energies in my life, which allowed me to achieve with ease and grace everything I always wanted, including manifesting the most incredibly supportive, kind, loving life partner whose deep sense of respect allows the space for me to be who I am and fills my every day with adventure and delight.

Choose a *state of being* daily, so you can BE *that* in whatever you are doing during that day. It is the easiest way to manifest the power of the Goddess within you. I choose *Understanding* as my preferred *state of being* in every interaction I have. Understanding allows me to connect deeper with myself and others. It also lets me see life with lightness and ease. What do *you* need to understand about you?

I almost missed out on my dreams because I shut down and suppressed my feminine. I don't want you to miss out on yours. No matter which dreams those are, you deserve to achieve them. Your dream may be to buy a big new house, or to start a new career, or to be more successful in your business, to have kids, or have more kids, to improve the relationship with your husband. Or your dream is to find a life partner, or maybe you want to change the world but you don't have too much support because our world has been run for too long by masculine energy.

It is time to bring more of the feminine energy to the table. To our lives, to our homes, to the entire planet. And this process starts from inside of you.

IGNITE ACTION STEPS

- **Be open to dive deep** into yourself and to discover who you truly are. Introspection is a great ally in the journey as well as silence and focusing on your own spirituality.

- **Practice yoga, dance,** or any other movement that will bring you flow. It will boost the feminine energy around you and open up your body and new possibilities.

- **Decide to love yourself** everyday. Practice affirmations out loud that emphasize how beautiful you are, how lovable you are, and the amazing qualities you already have.

Hanna Meirelles – Brazil
Global Trainer and Development Facilitator,
Leadership Specialist and Founder of Life Level 10
www.hannameirelles.com

COMMITMENT

SUYOGI GESSNER

"The true power of a woman lies in her heart and soul. The more she is connected to her soul, the more she can tap into her inner joy, bliss, and happiness."

I want to show that there is a real, deep hope inside of each of us. You can truly transform your life *from within* when you witness the spiritual connection and wisdom in the women who live the Goddess essence. Their purity, divinity, and transformative energy can guide each of us to know that our true happiness and love lies within.

STRIVING TOWARD TRUE CONNECTION AND LOVE

I have always felt true joy and curiosity, with a desire to grow and learn rooted deeply inside of me. From a very young age, I felt closely connected to God, comforted by the faith that He would always guide me and love me for who I was. I believed, even as a young child, that whatever happened in my life was for my benefit, that it would help me learn and grow, even if it was difficult at first.

When I was around five years old, my Dad came home with a great gift for me. I loved reading; I was very curious and full of enthusiasm. So when he gave me a huge illustrated book about India, a new world suddenly opened up before my eyes. Colors. People. Women with beautiful saris and red dots on their foreheads. It was a whole new world of adventure and godliness. My mind was filled with pictures of temples, gods and goddesses, new customs, and jewel-filled rites. Things I'd never seen before growing up in Germany. My parents were typical Catholic Germans — they had both grown up in Bavaria, hadn't traveled much, and were focused on raising their family and working hard.

I was fascinated with my new book. I began looking for colorful materials in our own home. I took my Mom's red lipstick and made a red dot on my forehead. I wrapped a red piece of cloth around me, unskillfully but full of joy. Then, I packed a little suitcase and went to show my mom. I was ready to travel — or better even, to move — to India. Mum was shocked. "What an idea!" It was too far, too unknown. I was too young and I should stop making myself so ugly with the clothes around me. "Lipstick was for the lips, not for the forehead," she said. I felt horrible — I had gone from feeling beautiful and ready for adventure to misunderstood and rejected. In that moment, I learned for the first time that it is not always wise to share your dreams too early. It could be that people don't understand your dreams and your motives, and don't share the same thinking and feelings.

A year later, when I was six, my parents moved to a tiny little village, still in Bavaria. My life took a completely different turn. We were the first family to move there that hadn't grown up there and were considered coming from 'outside.' It was a closed community and the kids were very cruel. From the beginning, they didn't accept me. I was out, never in. I didn't belong with them. They were either ignoring me or teasing me with horrible words, forbidding me to play with them and calling me unforgivable names like 'ugly bitch'; 'stupid,' and 'idiot.' It felt like my life had become hell. Every day, Mum had to force me to go to school and every day I came home crying. I introverted and became more quiet. I lived in my own imaginary, beautiful world and dreamed about the colors and magic of India. I never shared my hidden inner world with anyone, out of fear that someone might take it away from me.

After seeing my failure in school and my growing quietness, my parents decided to send me to a Catholic boarding school. At first I was overjoyed. I had so many dreams about my new life, my new adventure, and the new friends who would accept and understand me. I hoped that I would finally be able to connect to my inner world of joy again, and to God. I had so many great fantasies about how my life would change.

Reality hit me hard. The 'black nuns' were not what I had dreamt of. They were very strict, devoid of joy. Routine and discipline were more important than a loving heart and understanding. I had hoped so much that I would find true spiritual role models and a spiritual connection to God and the soul.

We girls were no better than our role models, the nuns. The atmosphere was often full of jealousy, expectations, envy, and negative talk. Rather than a profound spiritual experience, the boarding school became a survival camp. It trained us to believe that in womanhood the strongest and loudest were best. There was nothing at the school that showed us what true womanhood really meant. Disappointed but not without hope, I continued to do what I had done before. I immersed myself in my own inner kaleidoscope of beauty, heroes and heroines, gods and goddesses.

Around this time, my passion for reading was reborn as an escape from reality. In the monastery's library, I found volumes upon volumes of autobiographies written by saints, men and women who were ready to give their lives for their belief in God, their soul, and a higher purpose. I felt my fascination with learning reignite, and I started to dream of one day finding extraordinary people to teach me how to connect with divinity and the pure bliss within.

Of course, many stories of the saints were also scary and extreme. But I admired their dedication, their conviction, their love for God, and their higher purpose. I developed techniques to listen to my heart and soul. I learned that prayers were a great tool for connecting with the higher power. I felt protected and safe in my own small internal world of fantasies, bliss, and happiness.

Before I could fully embrace the free world I had envisioned as reality, I had to pay a high price. Since my grade school years, I had been programmed to think of myself as a loser. The more often I heard that I was a loser, the more I was convinced of it myself. This belief was rooted so deeply inside each and every cell of my being that the outside soon confirmed the inside.

I could not meet the school's grade requirements. When I was fifteen, I had no choice but to leave, feeling ashamed and unworthy. My belief that I was the biggest loser had been confirmed again. I had to leave the boarding school and go to a lower standard school, hiding my true self as I reverted to survival mode.

By this time, I was showing my true nature less and less. In some ways, I was living a double life. Externally, I was anxious and reserved. But inside my heart, when I was alone with myself, there was a whole world of bliss, brightness, cheerfulness, and power. I had never forgotten about the book from India, and I made the vow that one day I would travel there to find my soul.

Years later, when I was 29, after many more sad experiences and struggles, I finally had my breakthrough. I quit my job as a social worker and decided to go on a world traveling tour with my future husband. I wanted to experience the new cultures, new beliefs, and new ideals about my femeine energy and its power. But most importantly, I wanted to get to know India: the birthplace of true spirituality, saints, goddesses, godly incarnations, and infinite wonders.

At that time, there was no Internet. I couldn't just go to 'Dr. Google' and search for ashrams, saints, or spiritual mentors. But I did have one tool: a catalog about Indian holy places and ashrams, which my yoga instructor in Berlin had photocopied for me before I set off for the holy land of spirituality. I eagerly tried to connect to more than 150 ashrams, sending them beautiful, long letters. Surprisingly, not many replied. I wasn't deterred.

When I first arrived in India, my heart and soul immediately fell in love with the energy and the people. They were so wholehearted, kind, and loving. It felt like coming home. We went to many ashrams and met many amazing people and saints. But I had no clue how to find a true master or awaken my sleeping power. We met many people who told us miracles about gurus or enlightened beings. Always open and always curious, we spoke to beautiful spiritual individuals and I was awakened to a whole new world that I had no clue existed outside of my dreams. I didn't know what I was looking for, but the inner conviction from my heart's wisdom told me I had arrived in exactly the right place.

After a year of searching for a guru, we finally arrived in our spiritual home, an ashram in West India, Gujarat. There were many new customs and nothing seemed familiar. It was very confusing. I had to stay in the women's ashram and Manfred, my future husband, stayed in the men's. At first, I found this separation odd and strange — and I was extremely uneasy to be in the company of women after my terrible experience at the monastery.

When I met the women of the ashram, it was like arriving on a foreign planet and exploring a new species of women. I couldn't figure out what was so different. Yes, they were lovely beings, overflowing with joy. Their energy was soft but still powerful, so grounding and full of clarity and stability. I had never met women like them, offering love, yet without the emotional reactivity that I had become accustomed to over my life.

The women were living together inside four walls, with seven of them in one room. I had lived in a similar situation at my boarding school, but here there was a harmony and unity that touched my heart. They didn't expect anything from me. They were so giving and accepting. I felt like a newborn, embraced by their energy. I basked in a deep sense of belonging. It was like

I was floating on an ocean of love — no water, just love. I had never experienced anything like that before.

It took me quite some time to understand this new divine species of women, whose identity was completely different from the women I had met before. They lived from their power *within*. Everything they did was for God, for a higher purpose, and they acted with all their heart. Instead of reacting to the outside circumstances, they were connected to the divine power within. Their beauty and power came from their connection with their soul: their divine goddess energy. There was no need to indulge in the version of beauty seen from the outside. They found no joy in comparing their appearances. Here I saw the most natural beauties I have ever seen.

Divinity makes you glow and shine. True beauty comes from within. This is a sentence I had heard many times before, but at the ashram it had finally manifested its truth.

I wanted to explore and study their divine secrets: surrendering, accepting, giving, and living your life for the service of others while still serving your own soul every day. These beautiful goddesses became my role models. I was fortunate enough to have some of them as my guides, sisters, mothers, mentors, and friends. I had finally found a way to get rid of my old negative beliefs, my fears and my blocked energies so that I could manifest my dreams. This first visit to the ashram in India was divine proof for me: my dream was not just a fantasy, but the deepest reality.

From that moment on, my life took a completely new direction. My professional, personal, and spiritual life was transformed. On this beautiful journey, I began to explore and redefine my feminine identity.

I meet so many women who are torn between the feminine and the masculine. Many are forced to play the masculine role and have lost touch with the qualities of a woman and their femininity. I have learned that the true power of a woman comes when she is connected to the *source* of her being — her heart and her soul. The qualities of women are beautiful when they flourish from the source of their being: kindness, compassion, creativity, and unconditional love. The more a woman develops these qualities, the more she can create a new energy on this planet. This woman is the one who inspires the family, her children, her partner, her community, and all those around her — unconditionally.

After that first visit to the ashram, I began studying the ancient healing secrets of Ayurveda in India. I became a healer and spiritual mentor. I have devoted my life to helping thousands of women all over the world reconnect to their true divine power within.

I learned in my journey to the land of inner Source that, whatever I try to do, I will find the strength from within. I connect to my own inner *shakti* and feel the divine guidance of God and the benevolence of the Universe supporting me. Effort is not needed; all falls into place. Life manifests more richly and more beautifully when we surrender ourselves to the divine. My old idea of fear and disappointment was replaced by my true goddess within. Listening to my inner truth created a new divinity in me.

In my Ayurvedic lineage of Siddha Veda, we believe very much in the *shakti*: the divine creative power of the female, the divine mother. To activate this true femininity, you have to journey within, to the very center of your being: your soul. Only then can you touch, inspire, and move your own heart and the hearts of others. I believe that every woman has the ability to find her true divinity within. The divine power inside every woman is the *shakti* that can transform the world. Embrace that. Love and experience it. Shine and glow in all of her beauty and colors.

Ignite Action Steps

- Have a true spiritual *shakti* woman in your life, a true friend who can guide you spiritually, who has a daily spiritual practice herself. Have an open-hearted relationship with her, love her, trust her and make her your sister, friend, or divine mother. Be inspired by her *shakti*.

- Train your senses daily to hear, speak, see, think, and be loving. Cultivate an awareness about how much the input of your senses impacts your mind, body, and well-being. Nurture your loving, giving, caring, compassionate feelings.

- Create a daily spiritual practice. Give food to your heart and soul daily through prayers, meditation, gratitude exercises, forgiveness, and the selfless service to others.

- Meet like-minded people. Share your spirituality with them.

- Be humble, be connected to your heart and work on reducing your ego.

- Connect daily to the center of your being: your heart and soul.

- Be focused on your female vision identity. Ask yourself powerful questions and answer them honestly. What does it mean for me to be a powerful woman? Which qualities should I develop and cultivate? What makes me glow and shine from within?

- Find a spiritual mentor: someone who authentically and selflessly shows you the way from darkness to light, Igniting a true path within.

Suyogi Gessner – Germany
Ayurvedic Expert of the Siddha Veda Lineage
Spiritual Mentor, Heart Opener
www.theheartswisdom.com
suyogi@theheartswisdom.com
◎ theheartswidsom
🔗 Suyogi Gessner

LOVE

RACHEL T GREENE

*"Radical self-love is essential for the journey to great
physical, mental, and spiritual health."*

Center your thoughts on the Goddess of Love. The kind of powerful self-love that allows your cup to fill up quickly, overflow, and stream out into the world. I pray that you uncover a deep, passionate, RADICAL love for yourself. Grace yourself with the same patience, love, thoughtfulness, and kindness that you generously give to others. When you love yourself so radically and passionately, you glow, shine, and have the strength to uplift the hearts of others.

DEEP DOWN INSIDE BY MY PINKY TOE

I'm a native of Chicago, Illinois. While living in Charlotte, North Carolina, far from family and friends, the unthinkable happened. I was at work walking with my manager from one meeting to the next and laughing while telling a story about my strong, no-nonsense mom. My heels clicked against the floor as we strode through the hallway catching up on each other's personal lives. I entered the room, sat down, and began to speak. My phone buzzed. I glanced at the screen, ignored the call, and kept talking. Again, my phone buzzed. Again, I ignored it. It buzzed a third time and I turned it off. After the meeting, as we were sitting around talking, I pulled out my phone and listened to my voicemail. It was my aunt and she was hysterical. I couldn't make out what she was saying. All I heard was mama, paramedics, three times, and 20 minutes. My stomach dropped. I felt fear and anger at the same time. What the hell was she saying? Was something wrong with my mom? All the color drained from my face. The voicemail ended and I told my coworkers, "I have to go."

That day had started so beautifully and I remember it vividly. The September sun kissed my face as I awakened that warm early-autumn morning. My alarm was playing its usual medley of instrumental music and I smiled at the sound as I do every morning. I jumped out of bed, changed the playlist to my favorite dancing music, and grooved through my morning. After working out in the gym two floors below for an hour, I ran back upstairs and woke up my nine-year-old son. The sounds of his eclectic music intertwined with mine, was a happy example of our two-person rhythm. My activities expanded to include his needs alongside my own. While he showered, I made myself a smoothie and cooked him a breakfast fit for an up-and-coming king. It was a day like any other, filled with small shared moments of love and caring until it came time for us to part as he headed off to school and I to work. And then came that meeting and my aunt's call, and the ease and flow of the day was shattered.

I immediately sprang into action. I ran to my desk to grab my car keys and started making calls on my way out of the building. I called my aunt and she informed me that they had taken my mom to the hospital, unresponsive. My heart stopped beating and the breath wouldn't enter my lungs. It felt like the immutable and unchangeable foundation that had allowed me to fly so high in my life was starting to crumble. I called the airlines and booked two tickets home. True project management style, I was making a checklist in my head and ticking off action items as I completed them.

Driving out of the parking lot, somewhere between action item #5 and action item #10, my phone rang again. It was my aunt calling to inform me that my mom had just died. Everything in my body went limp as the adrenaline-fueled rush of activity I had been doing suddenly became irrelevant. I don't cry, but tears started leaking from my eyes, blinding me. I had to pull over and park. I felt defeated. I felt like someone had just ripped my heart from my chest. Why did she leave me? Why didn't she wait for me? How could I still be breathing without my mama? I kept shaking my head no as hot tears streamed from my eyes. This can't be true. She would never leave me.

After what felt like forever, I shifted the car into drive and started moving forward again. The tears stung my eyes and blurred my vision as I drove. I felt like an abandoned orphan, but I picked up the superwoman cape that my mother had always worn. When I got home, I began packing bags for the journey home. I wiped the tears from my face, tightened the strings of the superwoman cape, and headed to pick my son up from after-school care. With a new painful list of things to do, I called the funeral home to arrange for my mom's body to be collected from the hospital. I called my mom's pastor. I started phoning to inform the rest of the family. I sent a note to my manager. I sent an email to my son's school. The 'git 'er done' cape was flying high.

I shared with my son that his grandma had passed away. He cried as I held him close to me. His head laid on my chest and I tried to breathe for both of us. After a shower and putting him to bed with his favorite story, I reserved a rental car and finished packing. I went to bed, tossed and turned for the two hours I had before our 6 AM flight. I woke up at 2:30 AM, woke up my son, got him dressed, and put him in the car with our bags. That day became known to my soul as the day that my heart broke into a million pieces. I felt lost but kept moving forward with no direction or destination. I felt small and hurt, but kept a strong demeanor for my son. I felt like an abandoned orphan, but I picked up the superwoman cape that my mother had put down and carried on.

By the time the plane landed in Chicago I felt drained but tightened the cape strings and kept putting one foot in front of the other. After we landed, I realized that somewhere between Charlotte and Chicago, I had lost my driver's license and couldn't get a rental car because of it. After running from counter to counter and sapping all of my limited capacity, I started to cry. I was so close to getting to my mom and now I was stuck. I didn't know who to call. Who would help me? I felt depleted and broken.

My son sat down beside me and gave me a hug. I heard him talking on his phone but couldn't concentrate on what he was saying. He hugged me again and said in a soft consoling voice, "My dad is coming to get us." I was grateful and smiled through my tears. "Do you know how I knew to call my dad?" he asked. I shook my head no. He said, "My dad told me that I could call him anytime for anything and he would always be there." I was grateful for my son's father and despite not being with him since my son was five months old, I had encouraged and nurtured their relationship.

Driving the half hour to my mom's house felt surreal. It was as if the world was smaller, my body was closer to the ground, and all of the shapes and colors around me were blending together. Even though I was one step closer to my mom, I was exhausted.

Arriving at mom's house, I felt a complicated rush of relief and pain. It felt unreal. I was walking around with a knot in my stomach that wouldn't go away. Something wasn't right. I was home, in her house, and she was gone. I felt lost without her. I was exhausted, but determined to stay strong, so I tightened the strings of the 'devoted daughter' superwoman cape I had so abruptly inherited and kept pushing forward.

I planned every detail of my mom's homegoing service, filling it with music, laughter, and love. The church was packed to the rafters and I made sure to keep the superwoman cape flying high. I avoided saying good-bye and stuck to what I knew: stuffing my emotions down and doing. After three weeks my son and I returned to North Carolina. My son went back to school and I to work. But nothing would ever be the same. I had the cape on, a knot in my stomach, a broken heart, and I still hadn't taken time to grieve.

I began to take on projects and responsibilities to fill up every second of the day and night, not wanting to deal with my feelings. The guy I was dating started pressuring me to marry him and although there were many red flags, I ignored them, wanting to move forward, longing to replace my mother's unconditional love, support, and belief in me. After agreeing to marry him, I went into full wedding planner mode.

Our wedding day was a beautiful day. All of my friends and family came to Charlotte to celebrate our wonderful love. I hadn't seen them since my mom's funeral almost a year ago. Having them there made me feel reconnected to a foundation. I felt happiness once again. The next day we left for our honeymoon to the Caribbean. We played all day in the sand and water and spent the evenings exploring under the night sky. The time was magical and it felt as if the Goddess of Love had finally come back into my life.

Immediately after returning from the honeymoon, our relationship changed. My husband began to be mentally abusive with me. He started to ignore my calls and not come home at night. Things escalated; the police were involved. The guy I viewed as loving and supportive turned out to be nothing like that. We lived together for eight months and then I moved out.

I spent many days and nights wondering what the hell happened. What did I miss? What had I done to deserve such awful treatment? At the courthouse where our divorce would be made final, I took the elevator up to the second floor, shivering from fear even though it was a hot summer day. I hadn't seen my husband since I left and a protection order was put in place. My high heels made a confident clicking sound as I walked into the courtroom, reminding myself even though I'm scared, I must keep moving forward. My mind may have been saying, "Stop," but my body knew to just do it. The room was sterile. I saw police officers sitting on the right and a judge at the front, the court reporter at his side. I took a deep breath and steadied myself for what was to come, settling my shoulders and lifting my chin as I walked over to sit next to my attorney. She leaned over and whispered that I should show no reaction to anything being said, so I didn't. I listened as lie after lie was told. I stared at the wall; I couldn't bear to look at the face of the man I had married.

When my attorney called me to testify, I rose to my feet and slowly walked to the stand. As I crossed the floor and climbed the few steps to the witness box, the familiar comforting click of my heels was a reminder that I was still me and that I would be okay. There, I raised my right hand and swore to tell the truth and nothing but the truth, so help me God. *Help me God.* How many times had I prayed those words over the last year? *Help me God.* Sitting on the closet floor crying. *Help me God.* In the parking lot at work. *Help me God.* On the side street after dropping my son off at school. *Help me God.* What's the right path forward?

And sure as shit — God showed up! He showed up in the form of a question that changed my soul and allowed me to start rebuilding my crumbled foundation.

My attorney proceeded to ask me questions about the events in our relationship that had led to us being there that day. She asked about a concert, a winery, and the nights he hadn't come home. She asked about good moments and bad ones, things that were intimate and things that had been witnessed by others. With every question, I sat on the edge of the seat, my body tense, focusing on a point on the wall across from me as I recited the facts of the truth I knew. My testimony was backed up by those police officers who had been there for some of the most awful events and their calm recitation was validating.

And then my attorney asked it — that one question that clearly came straight from God. The pinnacle question that flipped a switch in my brain and turned my outward focus internally. She asked me, "And how did that make you feel?"

How did that make me feel? I had no idea! My eyes moved from the wall to her face and the breath left my lungs in a rush. I opened my mouth, but nothing came out. I had stopped *feeling* the day I listened to my aunt's voicemail with screaming and crying in it. The day my mother died, I put on her superwoman cape and wrapped myself so tightly in it that I almost squeezed all of the life out of me. How my husband made me feel was outside of my restricted viewpoint. I hadn't thought about my needs or made room for my feelings in years.

"Rachel. How did that make you feel?" she repeated. My eyes stayed locked with hers. I searched my heart for the answer to the question, and it was there. *The* answer. *My* answer. Buried underneath the broken pieces, underneath the hurt of deceit and loss, underneath the pain of feeling abandoned, I unearthed it.

"I felt like I was nothing. Like I was worthless. I felt like a piece of garbage that had been tossed away." As soon as I said those words, it pulled the scab off my pain. My attorney had no further questions, but I had plenty. I had tons more questions. How did I get here? Who's going to love me? What if I fall? What do I want? Where do I want to be?

After that day, I asked myself these hard questions and searched my soul, digging deep down inside to the end of my pinky toe. The answer always came back the same: *Me! I* had to love me. Take care of me. Provide for me, and give myself what I wanted. *Me.* I had to determine what I loved and didn't love, who to allow or disallow in my life, and ensure I thrived for my son. *Me.* All these questions made me realize I had to make some radical changes so that *Me* would be up for the task.

I started by dancing Friday nights. Dancing out every emotion a human can feel until I was dripping wet with sweat and my body hurt. It was free and liberating. It felt like I was excreting all the toxic people and experiences from my body and my world.

I began taking candlelight baths, soaking until my fingers wrinkled with deep ridges, immersed in salts and oils to heal my body and soul. I played music with heavy drums that resonated in my chest and I began to take deep breaths in time with the beats. I would place my hand on my heart while I walked on the greenway and say out loud, "I am still here. I am alive. I was created not only to survive but to thrive. I am a thrival." My voice was soft, yet strong, and comforting. It sounded a lot like my mom's. My heart would beat a little stronger with each repetition and my superhero cape was mending.

I eliminated things and people from my life that I didn't enjoy. If I didn't LOVE an item of clothing, then I gave it to charity, feeling lighter with each thing I released. I resigned from all of the non-profit boards I served on. I literally and figuratively put *my* oxygen mask on first. I vowed that when I was whole again, when I had more than I needed, then I would start to give from my overflow, not my brokenness. For now, radical self love was all I could muster, and it was enough.

I burned sage to clear any negative energies from my home. I went to the gym to make my body temple strong and flexible. I took a class to uncover my beliefs about life, replacing the bad ones with good ones to create a beautiful vision for my future. I went through all of my mom's belongings that had been collecting dust in my storage unit. Box by box, memory by memory, tear by tear, I moved through the pain, hurt, and heartbreak of losing my mom and my marriage. I picked up new hobbies. Golfing and running provided a way for me to ground myself. The fresh air and beautiful scenery made me feel like I could fly again. The same love, thoughtfulness, kindness, and grace I had spent so much time giving to others, I gave to myself. My beautiful wonderful self!

I traveled to Athens, Greece. As I walked through the ruins, next to the Temple of Athena, I remember thinking that I was just like those broken stones: discarded, trampled on, yet beautiful. Her Goddess energy permeated the air with strength and love. I embraced the true Goddess in me and felt the beauty that abides both in brokenness and wholeness. My superhero cape was flying freely.

Awaken your inner Goddess of Love. Uncover a deep, passionate, RADICAL love for yourself that allows your cup to fill up quickly, overflow, and stream out into the world. It's the love that you give yourself during times of great pain. Bless yourself with the same grace, patience, love, thoughtfulness, and kindness that you generously give to others so that you can thrive. Goddess… put on your superhero cape.

IGNITE ACTION STEPS

Dance often to music that penetrates your soul. Sage your environment to clear out negative energy. Soak in salt baths until your fingers are wrinkly. Meditate. Burn your favorite candles — don't save them until a special day. Diffuse essential oils and inhale the goodness. Exercise. Leave the country — broaden your perspective and get a feeling of connectedness across the world. Turn off your alarm and sleep until your body is fully rested and ready to move. Say out loud, *"I am still here. I am alive. I was created not only to survive but to thrive. I am a thrival."*

Rachel T Greene – United States of America
Senior IT Program Manager / Radical Lover of Self
@enjoylifewinning

BRAVERY

Tara Heinzen

"You can't rush your healing; you are exactly on time for you."

If my story inspires courage in just one who struggles to break past conditionings, it is enough. We hold so many beliefs around feminine beauty, value, and identity, struggling to love ourselves through deep wounds and fears while facing unknown storms. Our outer image oftentimes is a mask, hiding the inner disconnect with our authentic truths of self. Trust, YOU are a gift. My heart sees you, Sister. Keep going.

Reconstructing the Goddess

What labels and images sum up our identity and how we view ourselves?

Eight years ago, if I had a 'Hello, my name is…' sticker on my chest, it might say: single mother of three, artist, survivor, college student, competitive athlete, activist... My identity was wrapped up in being a supermom speeding one hundred miles a minute, struggling to juggle all the balls in the air while simultaneously running a marathon.

In the spring of 2012, that sticker was ripped off my chest. I started experiencing some concerning symptoms in my breasts that were not entirely unknown to me. As a teenager I watched my mother fight for her life through Stage 3 Inflammatory Breast Cancer after the same symptoms surfaced in her breasts. I proactively chose to immediately have a double mastectomy, not wanting to slow down my active life.

I was healing from the Mormon culture I was raised in and married into. Still immersed in a superficial society, searching for my own spiritual path… an authentic identity separate from the image and ideals of the woman I felt conditioned to believe I needed to be. My outer image represented a healthy, artistic, and optimistically strong single mother who had a hectic life, yet kept things fairly together. As much as I felt the fear of putting my children through the trauma of a mother facing cancer... I didn't want to admit it; I also feared facing a severely disfigured body. I said goodbye to my natural breasts, the socially idolized center of femininity, and opted for breast reconstruction.

My breasts were replaced with silicone implants and I moved into a new life with more attention-drawing feminine curves than my sagging post-baby breasts had before. My clothes fit differently and I reveled in the attention. Shortly after that initial surgery, I attended my first transformational festival which sparked a new and longed for soul journey, while I dove back into my supermom life. However, this was not the temporary speed bump I expected. What followed was beyond anything I could imagine…

A transformative journey began to unfold. At first, just a small complication with the implants requiring reparative surgery, that led to another surgery, and another. Each surgery had a two-month recovery. An infection resulted in six months of bed rest. Months would go by and, thinking I was fine, I would restart with hope and motivation, trying to catch up from being down, promising my children the surgeries were over. Continuing to explore every path as my heart searched for deeper self-discovery and healing, my goal was to become empowered, financially independent, and emotionally healthy. Facing repeated disappointments and difficult surgeries, navigating soul-expanding highs and discouraging lows, it was a 'yo-yo' of internal chaos.

After a few years, unsure of an end, I realized I had to surrender. I couldn't promise my children when it would be over, and I couldn't plan for my future. As the illusion of control faded, my goals and dreams began to shift and change. With what felt like a choice of survival, I set my intentions to the simplicity of flowing with what life presented, using my art to express this rising belief, and living as fully and vibrantly as I could between the medical stop lights. In this space of surrender, my soul began to open.

My reconstructed breasts had become a source of physical pain and limitations. My surgeon kept saying he/she could fix whatever was wrong or I just needed different implants. I felt I was aging many times faster than I should, experiencing growing debilitating and unexplainable whole body symptoms that would often land me in the hospital. No battery of tests or specialists could explain the causes.

Determined to feel better, I tried numerous lifestyle and health alternatives, attended workshops and transformational events, trying to heal both my body and soul. I was falling further behind in life, the anxiety of trying to catch up was intense. Efforts to heal from previous traumas felt buried under a growing mountain of new traumas. I didn't feel like the 'brave strong woman' I continued to be seen as and praised for. The search to uncover my identity was still in motion.

Six years after my mastectomy, I had a powerful life shift, attending an event that awakened something deep and ancient inside of me: concepts of the sacred feminine and masculine within, my innate Goddess rising, launching me onto an unconventional spiritual path, helping me find connections and answers within my inner self. I could find divinity in everyday living, drawing on the powerful feminine energies that anchored my core, the beautiful Goddess within me. I felt deeply that there was an answer on this new path for how to fully embrace my scarred and disfigured body. I struggled to see myself as whole and heal completely.

Ready to move on with my life as an awakening Goddess, regardless of 'fake' breasts, I embraced them as my own and loved my body as it was. Believing I was finally coming out of the darkness, I dove deeper into spiritual growth and experiences, working particularly on my own shame and personal forgiveness. I learned new ways to communicate and build intimacy, discovering and using my voice, vocalizing my truth and what I desired in life. Living authentically, orgasmically, and connected, my soul felt more alive in my truth. I loved who I was becoming and the evolving process. Unaware I was just skimming the surface...

My compounding physical symptoms seemed to slow all my efforts and attempts at living a full and healthy life. It became the norm for me to bury the fears around my physical body. I would share my story, receive praise and accolades for being 'a brave example to women,' for making a difficult choice, facing so many surgeries, and embracing my scarred disfigured body. No one ever suggested that, for me, my implants and all these surgeries might not be necessary.

As weary as I was, I continued moving forward. A girlfriend who knew my health struggles connected me with a Facebook group for Breast Implant Illness. I had no idea what that was, the name alone revealing. I read story after story of women who were sick with the same issues I had, the shared frustration and heartache, and these women's stories brought me to tears. I saw myself in them.

I immediately made an appointment with an explant surgeon in San Francisco. While I waited for the consultation, so many emotions surfaced that I didn't know how to process. My youngest child only knew a mother who'd been sick for the past seven years. I felt the guilt of all the mornings that my young children woke to a quiet house... got themselves ready and off to school alone while I was sick in bed. My older children carried the responsibility of running the house because I was too ill to be a mom. I thought about how my health affected my relationship attempts and dating life, my mental health, my ability to work and care for my family. I asked myself many hard questions... What if toxic implants were the problem the whole time? Years wasted for deep insecurities? Was it all for nothing? I thought I had found my inner Goddess, my self love and acceptance! I thought I was finally living my authentic life... hadn't my spirit truly opened up? Was any of the growth real, when something so shallow as an attachment to breasts led my painful path? I felt so much fear and grief for all the lost years.

I had to dig even deeper and surrender to the unknown. I didn't want another surgery, I was exhausted. Feelings of deep shame arose from an unexpected truth I had not wanted to face before — I didn't want to lose my breasts. I had just accepted them as they were. I had curves, even if they were scarred and disfigured, and I loved them. If it truly were the implants making me sick, and I had them removed, I would be so drastically disfigured and concave that it scared me. Could I really do this, if this was what was necessary after all I had been through? Each surgery left me weaker, sicker, affecting my mental health and memory. It had been years since I was able to lay on my stomach or flat on my back without pain. My body internally was a mess with numerous debilitating symptoms, without any answers for how to heal, simply trying to live with the way my body was now.

This new form of confusion was overwhelming. My whole self-image felt shattered; I wasn't a strong warrior mother making a brave choice to remove my breasts. I rejected everyone who told me I was. I was still feeding into the cultural image and pressure of the 'ideal feminine body,' not truly accepting my own.

My world turned upside down and fractured into pieces the day I had my consultation with the explant surgeon. He was kind, empathetic, and assuring. Knowing what I had been through, he looked at me with such compassion and said, "It will be over soon." The tears began to flow in his office, and although I didn't want to have another surgery, I knew I needed to. Leaving the medical center, I had a two-hour drive home but the tears were so intense, I could barely see. All the pain, guilt, and fear I had suffered was because of my decision to have reconstruction after mastectomy. I was afraid to be without breasts completely, afraid to lose the curves. Who would I be without them? Would I still be feminine? The thought had never occurred to me to take them out as my surgeons kept telling me they could fix whatever was wrong, and I believed them.

It was like a dam broke right there on the side of a busy San Francisco street. I reached out to a dear soul brother who lived nearby. As soon as I walked into his apartment, he put his arms around me, I fell into him, sobbing fiercely and uncontrollably. His strong arms guided me to the floor where I sobbed and screamed into the space he held for me. I let myself feel without judgment or shame. The anger flowed at past lovers who told me they would get me a 'boob job' if they could, at every comment I heard suggesting women with large breasts were more attractive than those with small, at the men and women who suggested my sagging nursing breasts needed a 'lift.' Anger at the media that pushes the focus, sexualizaiton, and idolization of a curvy chest. Anger at the male doctors who cut me open over and over to 'fix' my breasts.

Mostly, I was angry at myself, for not realizing how strong, beautiful, sexy, radiant, and powerful I am without something toxic in my body, regardless of the outer image. I felt shame that I wasn't 'brave' enough to go flat from the beginning like other women I knew. Years of buried emotions rushed out with more force than I could have imagined was in me. My rage and anguish crashed like fierce ocean waves against the solid granite mountain of my soul brother's presence... until my inner storm ran its course.

I couldn't have asked for a more perfect space to process the deep emotions I carried from all those years. Held safely in a place of support, my emotions slowly subsided and released to make way for truth to rise up. What I thought were truths in my life had to die. We talked and shared, and as I spoke about my journey, I saw the amazing process of death and rebirth, realizing it was all part of my path. None of it was wrong, it was all necessary. Every experience was a needed part of my journey. It brought me to this point, recognizing that I had to let go on multiple levels, to live my truth. I began to pick up the fractured pieces, only the ones I needed to reconstruct a new life. It wasn't just about breasts. My breasts were mere symbols. Throughout the years, I had been taking baby steps in breaking chains from the society and culture I had been raised in, unwinding all that society feeds us from infancy — a process that takes some painful cuts. I had this last part to let go of. I wasn't ready to release it before but I was now.

I realized bravery is not being fearless. Strength is not measured in how much we have endured. I was scared... terrified actually... weak and exhausted after seven long years of fear. But I began preparing for another surgery with a new hope for healing. Leaning into my emotions this time, without shame or suppression. After all I have learned and experienced through the soul work I sought after, I knew I needed to embrace this next leg of my journey, surrender to all that was ahead of me in spite of the fear. The most important thing I came to value, and what I wanted to share with and model for my daughter and two sons, could not be seen with the physical eye.

As the autumn leaves began to fall in 2019, I finally let go of what no longer served me. I woke up from my explant surgery with immediate relief from the anxiety that had been plaguing me for years. Processing the loss of my breasts permanently this time felt like the mastectomy all over again. It took days before I could unwrap my chest and see what was left. Emotions still tender, I allowed them all to flow, and simply trusted the process. I handled recovery differently, reaching out for support, letting myself rest while letting go of prior expectations, taking cues from the season we were in. My then 22-year-old daughter came home to help with my recovery; my three children and I together brought this journey to an end.

It was a new emotional journey, to see a concave and severely scarred chest. I sometimes wondered if I would ever be desirable; would I ever feel whole? As I slowly regained mobility, the seeds of soul work from the prior years proved to be a priceless gift. Each week, my BII (breast implant illness) symptoms lessened and lessened. Emotional and mental clarity rose through the highs and lows of it all. Amidst the challenging days where I would fall back and question my choices and purpose, I looked for ways to honor the Goddess I had come to know inside, and to continue on healing. Trusting the path, I surrendered to the unknown, and slowly began to love my body for all it had endured, without judgment or blame. Emerging with new vibrancy, I felt my most beautiful and powerful Goddess looking back at me in the mirror. Letting go of needing to fit an image or idea, embracing the wild and fantastic feminine energy that was my deep truth. It didn't take long for new connections to flow into my life, reflecting what I felt sparkling inside, regardless of my non-trending figure. My sensuality and beauty was not tied to the traditional icons of womanhood or related to an image. It was in my whole being and could not be altered with a scalpel.

Going into 2020, I am still healing. My symptoms have reduced from over 50 to a handful. I feel a new form of closure, release, awakening, and healing like never before. The labels I used to wear on my chest now feel so distant. My strength is known to me now, not in how fast I run, how much I can lift, or even in my survival stories. It is my ability to keep walking through chaos, to rise when I fall, and to surrender to the unknown. My resiliency lies in the gentleness and grace I offer myself, in my ability to embrace death and rebirth. My beauty is not in the size I wear, my curves, or a smooth physique. My beauty lies within, in my ability to consciously mirror, radiating self-love, sharing it authentically. It's in my ability to connect vulnerably and deeply. In the absence of something I didn't realize I was holding onto for identity, I found the truth where my strength, bravery, beauty, and self are sourced — deep inside. In letting go of a primary aspect of my physical female body, I felt my inner Goddess rise authentically without restrictions. No barriers over my heart, no barriers between another being and I, no barriers from living fully and heart forward. I am a liberated reconstructed Goddess, mother, artist of life. I am whole.

Bravely ask yourself the hard questions; you are stronger than you realize. Take time to sit with your heart and ask, "What is blocking me from rising into my full potential of healing and strength?" Sometimes there is so much unknown, we just have to ask what is the next step, and trust our strength. You are so beautiful, inside and out, traditionally or non-traditionally. From our own inner self-love we find connection to the true Goddess. Everyone has a unique body, magnificent in so many ways. Find that passionate spark in you, about yourself, and light that up. Shine that. Be that, and you will see the greatest beauty imaginable, in your own reflection .

IGNITE ACTION STEPS

Honor yourself with the gift of time, sit in front of a mirror and hold the parts of you that you struggle to love and accept. It may take time, but try to speak gratefully to those parts every day. Thank those parts of you for what they have brought to your life, maybe it's a soft wrinkled stomach from giving birth, or full thighs that carried you many places but are not the size you want. It may be how emotionally you react, or intense fear you feel you have not overcome. Take deep breaths and feel into how those parts have served you, kept you alive, protected, or pushed you. Hold them and speak love; give thanks for what they have brought to your life. If it's something you need to let go of, an idea or fear, know you have the strength inside you to release. Little by little, your truth will rise, embracing all that you are will come.

Tara Heinzen – United States of America
Ceramic Artist, Women's Art Circles,
Facilitator of Communication and Intimacy
heinzen.studio@gmail.com
f heinzen.studio
heinzen.studio

COMPASSION

CHARLENE RAY

"Embrace Your Magic, Your Powerful Gifts Are Needed In The World!"

It is my dream that you embrace who you are; step into your powerful gifts and goddess ways. The world needs the divine feminine in all her fierceness and strength. I hope this story inspires you to break through your barriers, step out of doubt, and be your most amazing Goddess self!

SOARING OWL ON THE PRIESTESS PATH

The owl was dying. Right there amidst the gravel and dust of the laneway, its spirit was leaving its body. As I stood there watching the creature's life force ebb away, it felt like I was living out something from a fairy tale, one of the dark and scary ones that my parents always warned me not to read right before bed. The trees loomed overhead, casting their shadows in the early morning light, and the stony road crunched under my footsteps as I approached the majestic creature lying, wings spread, amid the rocky detritus that was the driveway to our cabin. I had no idea this moment was about to completely reawaken my life's path.

When I was a small child, I was obsessed with mythology and reading stories about goddesses and gods. I was a daydreamer. I would often find myself imagining stories of the goddess, seeing myself as Athena with her owls, strong and powerful. Claiming to be a goddess always seemed a bit 'too much' for me. It was easier for me to deny my intuitive gifts and make myself small. I grew up feeling it was best to be invisible and not take up too much space. Later in life, I realized that MY version of the goddess was one of inner strength, deep love, fierce compassion, and powerful spiritual connection.

When I moved to the misty green forests of Whidbey Island, Washington from the angular, busy, and big city of Chicago, I began looking for a way to connect to my authentic spirituality. I had read a couple of books on shamanism but had not met anyone who practiced it before. When a friend of mine introduced me to a shamanic teacher, it was like every cell in my body came alive. It was the path I had been waiting for my whole life. Shamanism includes journeying, often with a drum, to reach altered states of consciousness in order to connect with the spirit world and channel information, images, and energy into this world. I resonated with the deep connection to the divine in all things and seeing all beings in nature as having a spirit. I realized that I had been practicing this spiritual way of being all my life, although for many years it was hidden. Fascinated, I began to study with a shamanic teacher, reading every book and taking every workshop I could find on the topic. I wanted to know *everything* about it.

Working with the shamanic teacher was an exploration of wonder and light, but a decade later, I found myself stuck and unhappy. My marriage was suffering, my work was not challenging enough, and I was tired all the time. My connection with myself and Spirit took a backseat to the day-to-day busyness of life. My skin felt tight and restless and if I could have jumped out of it, I would have. I did not make time to be in nature or connect with my inner self. Instead, I found myself going through the motions of life, all the while knowing something needed to change. It was unclear as to how and when that could happen. I focused my energy happily on my son who was five at the time. He was a bright spot in an otherwise gray world.

One morning I was busily getting my things ready to head to work at the nearby alternative school where I was a counselor. My mom had arrived early that day to spend time with my son, which gave me a little 'me' time before heading out for the day. I walked outside heading toward the garage when something on the driveway caught my eye.

We lived in a log cabin on five acres tucked away in the woods. The land there was almost primordial, this old mossy, misty primeval forest full of mystery and stillness. Our driveway was a quarter-mile gravel path surrounded by cedar, Douglas fir, and alder trees filled with many creatures large and small going about their lives alongside us.

As I moved closer to whatever was happening on the driveway, I quickly realized that it was a barred owl lying there. It was fairly young, only about 18 inches tall but fully adult in its brown and white striped feathers. Its rounded head was face down as it lay there on the ground. A surge of anxiety sparked through my body, electrifying me. I approached slowly and the owl turned its head to look up at me. It was still alive, but I recognized it was unable to move. Immediately I thought it must have a broken wing.

I ran back to the house and called the local vet who had helped me with injured birds in the past. While explaining to him what I saw, a voice in my head screamed, "Get off the phone, get back outside!" The vet, unable to hear my mental scream, kept talking, saying I could try to bring the owl in and he would have a look. He started to say more, but I could no longer hear him; all I could hear was the voice in my head say loudly and firmly, "Go outside now!"

I ran back to the driveway, my feet noisy on the gravel lane. My heart was pounding as I raced toward the owl. A feeling came over me then, sudden and strong, stilling my breath in my chest. I could feel a threshold before me. It felt like a doorway to a church. The next step I made was going to take me into a sacred place, a ceremonial space. Slowly, intentionally, I inhaled deeply and stepped forward across that undefined threshold, knowing something monumental was about to happen. This time, as I drew closer to the owl on the ground, I knew in my heart that the owl was dying. And I needed to be with it as it died.

Once I was close enough to the owl, about 20 feet, but not *too* close, sensing the owl's anxiety, I stopped and stood very still. I was calm and present, rooted into the earth and part of its energy. As I softly gazed at the owl, it turned its head and, in a moment that I will never forget, we locked eyes. A blessing for the owl spontaneously began to emerge from within me. We looked at one another for what seemed like many minutes but was most likely only seconds. Suddenly, I felt an energy move away from the owl and move across space between us. It entered at the top of my head and flowed into my heart. My body began to shiver and tremble from head to toe. I can still feel it as I write this.

I knew at that moment that this was what my shamanic teacher would call a *giveaway*. The owl gave its spirit as an ally to me, as my supporter, my guide, my companion. Sitting on the ground across from the owl's motionless body, I sat and wept.

I desperately wanted to save the owl, but the owl was here to save me.

After a short time, I went back to the house to get a box, a towel, and my now-curious son. We went to where the owl was lying on the driveway and I explained what had happened. Carefully we wrapped the feathery creature in the towel and placed it in the box. My son helped, a quiet observer with gentle little hands. We would decide later how to bury it.

Excitedly, I called my shamanic teacher to tell her what happened. She listened and affirmed what I already knew; this *was* a giveaway. Immediately we scheduled a time to meet and explore the message of this *life-changing* moment. Owl medicine. Powerful medicine — *my* medicine. Those words went through my head like a mantra.

My heart was still pounding, resonating with the power of the experience, and I was unable to focus that day. I went to the sacred space in the forest where my teacher and I often met. She was there waiting, a calm and grounded presence with a white owl feather with her. She gave it to me and said she knew this day would come. We spent three hours in deep shamanic work that is incredibly hard to describe in words. We worked with the four directions: east, south, west and north, invoking our allies in prayer and meditation. It became clear to us both that I could no longer deny my work with death, rebirth, and transformation. I was given my spirit name, Soaring Owl, that day. Already a grief and spiritual counselor, I now experienced a call to go deeper.

That Ignite moment brought me to the threshold of my priestess path. My love of ritual and ceremony was newly infused with magic. I followed my interest in vision quest work and rites of passage for the youth that I worked with. I embarked on my own rites of passage and the journey of becoming a priestess. The deep transformative experience with my sacred winged-friend echoed strongly within me.

Back at my home after my session with my teacher, I went outside into the woods on my property to reflect and sit in silence. I could hear other owls calling in the trees. I could feel the earth's energy humming beneath me. I felt different. I knew I was changed even though I did not know what it meant at the time.

That evening at twilight, my son and I dug a hole in the woods overlooking the pond. I opened the box and gently caressed the owl. My son placed flower petals from the garden on the owl and an obsidian crystal in the grave. He said it was for the owl's journey home. At five, he was wise with the ways of nature and a natural ceremonialist. Together we buried the barred owl. We placed a large log on top of the grave to deter the coyotes from digging. We sang songs and danced around the grave in the woods. We stretched our arms out like wings and pretended to fly, singing:

"Wearing my long-winged feathers as I fly,
Wearing my long-winged feathers as I fly,
I circle around, I circle around,
The boundaries of the earth."

So many things changed after that Ignite moment as I began to embrace my Owl medicine. I began following my truth and connecting with my inner wisdom. I allowed my intuition to guide me as I took a stand for what I believed in. My marriage came to an end and I separated from my husband. I moved to a sweet little rental cottage about 15 minutes from the log cabin where we had all lived as a family. My son started his journey of living between our two houses and I felt my spirit soar.

The following year, I traveled to Ireland and discovered my soul's home. I connected with the Celtic Goddess Brigid and reconnected with lifetimes of wisdom. I knew that part of my priestess path was to honor my intuitive gifts and immerse myself in connecting with the spirits of the land and to bring groups of people to experience the magic of that beautiful country. One of the places where I felt the energy of the goddess was at the ancient holy wells, especially the wells that were covered in moss in overgrown forests. These stony wells infused my heart with clarity and love for Ireland, for myself, and for the path I was now following. The ancient water holes are places of ritual and reflection for me and they call to me every time I visit Ireland.

Life continued to change. A few years after visiting Ireland, my mother was diagnosed with ovarian cancer. I was by her side when she died, and my son and I created a ceremony on the beach to celebrate her life. We spread her ashes in a rose petal heart by the sea, watching her spirit awaken and be free.

Just before her passing, I went on my first vision quest — a 10-day journey in Death Valley to experience being alone with myself, fasting, seeking and doing deep inner work. I was anxious about leaving my mother and about being alone in the desert. My stomach was queasy. I was restless and uncomfortable in my own skin. The anticipation was the most difficult part, yet once I got there I eased into the experience. Under the glowing moon, I felt the presence of my owl, at my side, each night as I got closer and closer to becoming more of a priestess.

Returning home, I then created a similar program for the youth at the high school and saw the same sort of growth in them. I also began leading programs for adults on living and dying. My grief counseling practice became my focus and my purpose. I was reconnected with the power of magic and wonder in healing. And owls were visiting me more, in my new backyard, and in my dreams.

After a while I found myself returning to my old dream of becoming a pastor. It was a dream I had when I was 14 that I put aside when I grew disenchanted with organized religion. I also knew that the title of pastor did not suit me. After some research, I realized that I could attend an Interfaith seminary; the thought of this path resonated with my soul. Once I found One Spirit Interfaith Seminary in New York, the call to the priestess path took on a life of its own. The two-year experience challenged me to claim my beliefs and stand strong in them. I was eager to learn about the different religions and study the works of prominent spiritual teachers. The classes inspired me to step into my power as a ceremonialist and ritualist. My deans gave me tasks that shed light on my blind spots and stretched me, heightening my devotion to seminary teachings.

On the day of my ordination, I was standing at the front of the chapel with the hands of the three interfaith ministers on me when the white owl appeared in spirit and enveloped me with a light that I felt all the way to my bones. I was surrounded by a feeling of sacred transformation just as I had been that day in my driveway, the day I experienced the giveaway from the barred owl.

My vow at ordination was, "I vow to be the presence of love and compassion, to be kind to myself and others, to say yes to where I am called and serve with a grateful heart."

As I said these words, a vision of Kuan Yin, the Goddess of Compassion, appeared and said, "Embody me!" Kuan Yin is a highly respected bodhisattva goddess in Asian culture and Buddhism. Her name means 'she who hears the cries of the world.' Embodying Kuan Yin meant embracing and nourishing my feminine energy and no longer denying my gifts and strengths. It was a call to bring myself out into the world, to step into my role as a priestess. She reawakened in me the need for self-compassion and kindness and the desire to share those gifts with others. I repeat that vow every day as a reminder of the path I have said yes to.

It has taken me a lifetime to embody the goddess. When I was younger and put myself in the myths that I read and imagined, I thought I wanted to be like Athena. With an owl as a companion she was one of the wisest and most courageous goddesses. After I became Soaring Owl, it was Isis who called to me with her power to love and heal. She is pure Magic! At ordination, Kuan Yin called me to deepen my work with grief and death, bringing me to a place of pure compassion on the priestess path.

Now I live my life embodying the priestess. It is not a ceremony in a church of four walls; it's a cathedral of trees where I worship. It's also my office where I sit with clients and help them connect with their inner wisdom. My path brings me to nature to heal grief and guide my clients to move into their purpose and potential. I walk my priestess path when I teach workshops or give talks at the local library. I invoke the power of Kuan Yin as I sit with people who have lost their way, are in a transition, or need self-compassion and self-love to heal.

It is an honor and a privilege to recognize all priestesses with love and compassion. I encourage you to claim your Goddess nature knowing it is not 'too much', in fact, it is just what the world needs.

IGNITE ACTION STEPS

There are many ways to embody the goddess or priestess. Here are some steps that you may find helpful as you discover more about your unique walk with the goddess!

- Do you have feminine wisdom and gifts that you long to share with the world? Does doubt or fear get in the way of you walking this path? What are the gifts you long to share? What is one step you could take today to bring your gifts to the world?

- Is there a particular Goddess that calls to you? What are her gifts and teachings? Take a walk in nature and listen for the wisdom of the goddess there. Use all your senses to take in the beauty and wonder. Listen for the lessons she wants to teach you.

- If you were to step fully on the path of the goddess, what would you have to leave behind? What would you need to embrace? Use writing, art, or dance to express your answers.

Charlene Ray – United States of America
Heart-centered counselor, happiness strategist, teacher, and interfaith minister.
www.charleneray.com

GRATITUDE

JB OWEN

"Let Grace Reign"

My intention is simple... first to make you think, then to make you feel. I want to inspire you to establish a profound connection between your mind and your heart that then awakens your soul. There is great reverence when we step into the wholeness of our 'entire being' and bask in its grace. A divinity blossoms that allows all things to become possible and lets an absolute knowing reign. I wish wholeheartedly for that glorious feeling of wholeness to be bestowed delightfully upon you.

THE LOST CHILD GODDESS

It is hard for me to write a story about being a goddess when I don't feel like a goddess, when my head and heart feel severed by a connection that was never fully made. It is difficult for me to rejoice in the beauty and reverence of the goddess when I only feel an emptiness echoing in a barren wasteland as tumbleweeds travel across my inner landscape. My goddess feels out of reach. She is there but not there. It is like she is hiding behind a big tree in a forest teaming with spirits and angels yet camouflaged from my view. I search for her there and try to feel her, but the echo of her gentle laughter tells me she is miles away and I have far to go to find her. I am not used to this feeling of not knowing; of something outside my grasp. I command her to appear, but she plays games, running from me and insisting I embark on a journey to find her.

Her cheeky inavailability confuses me. I've been successful at many things in my life. I have made the money, driven the cars, and lived in the houses with the seven-digit price tags. People have seen me on stage, on TV, and on the cover of books. I continually smile at them through their social media screens. I have won the awards and received the accolades. From the observer's point of view, I've reached success in a number of ways.

None of that means much to my Goddess. Laughingly, tauntingly, she demands I seek a different path to find her. She insists I pull back a hidden curtain and step into my most honest truth. What she wants me to share is that the outside world hasn't seen the inner mechanics of my thoughts and feelings. They know nothing of the swirling contrast that makes up my self-identification. They see only the artfully painted and carefully curated dolled-up outward manifestation of the image I portray. There is a vast crevasse between the woman I am and the woman I aspire to be. Yes, I am a mother, a daughter, a wife, and I stand tall for the critical issues of women; their plight and injustices against them. Yet in the deepest, darkest corners of the curves and edges that make me a feminine goddess, I am lost like a blindfolded child in a room full of taunting tricksters and deep sinkholes to fall into.

Like most things, this disconnected feeling travels back to my childhood where I somehow abandoned my way and grasped aimlessly at feeling happy or proud that I was a girl. Instead of loving my femininity, I felt a niggling sense of shame combined with vacant ambivalence toward my gender. I wasn't aware of women's rights and female advocacy when I was young. Our family was not political and my mother was not a feminist by any means. She was, on the other hand, a magnificent provider, powerful businesswoman, and ground-breaking changemaker in her own way. I witnessed countless examples of her intelligence in the homes she built, the business she grew, and the way all the 'important' people in town knew who she was. She was a relentless 'doer' who never took 'no' for an answer and was masterful at finding ways to make things happen when others deemed them impossible, citing a problematic economy, a small-town mentality, or a systemic climate not ready for a woman to step out and lead.

Sadly, I didn't fully admire my mom for these qualities. In my childhood mind, I wanted her to be more like my friends' mothers who stayed home and baked cookies, helped with homework, read bedtime stories, and showed up at cheerleading practice. I was the only one of my friends who had a mother who worked. She was the only mother who was the owner of *her own* business; where bankers, lawyers, accountants, and city council meetings were the reasons she was seldom home. She did her best to support not just our family but also her mother, and much younger brother and sister as she felt it was part of her responsibilities.

Looking back, it is hard to fathom how uncommon her fiercely dedicated work ethic was among women in that generation. Nowadays, that level of responsibility is normal for both myself and most of my female friends. Many of us are working moms making hard choices and missing our kids' special events, completely unable to carve out one-on-one quality time. Baking cookies is a rare event and few of us have time to stand waiting, arms wide, smiling calmly when our kids arrive home from school. Our own domestic goddesses are challenged to the core and the tendrils of apron strings and ponytails are a glint of a memory from a forgotten era.

Yet, as a child sprouting up in the seventies, that tranquil domestic goddess who devoted her days and nights to my wellbeing is what I wanted. The mom who spoke softly, listened intently, and wore a cute string of pearls around her neck. Instead, I had a mother who worked with tradesmen building homes and apartment buildings. A mom who ran a business with employees and customers to please. She spoke directly and decisively, never slow or soft. She was adamant, determined, and devoted, not to domestic life but to work life. To me, she was a hard-working powerhouse and someone more to revere than lounge freely with in her splendor.

I will admit that it was due to the amazing accomplishments of my mother that I found my own grit and personal pride. She never put any limitations upon the women in my family. Both my older sister and I had an endless array of opportunities and possibilities available to us. In my mother's mind, we could do *anything* and none of it hinged on our gender. My world, in fact, was neutral when it came to being a girl. It was a place where the cute giggles and silly squeals were tempered. My hair was never braided. My closet lacked frilly lace and charming dresses. I had a lot of things, traveled on frequent family holidays, and was more privileged than most, but I didn't bask in the glory of being feminine nor fabulous because of it. Instead, we accentuated our male energy; working hard, accomplishing more, and doing what was necessary to achieve what we wanted.

It seems the old adage of 'what you don't have, you covet more' applied doubly for me. I dove deep into dance classes, sparkly costumes, and edgy fashions. By the time I was nine, I was doodling pictures of dresses, watching beauty pageants, and 'bejeweling' my outfits from head to toe. As I made my way into my teens, I followed Madonna and Cyndi Lauper, pushing the envelope of punk, rebel, and beauty icon all stir-sticked into one. Even though I tried to dress like a modern goddess, her presence was missing. Her essence of grace and tranquility were nowhere for me to see. After graduation, I went on to excel in designing costumes, clothing, homes, graphics, and products. I became adamant, determined, and devoted to work, exactly like my mother had shown me to be. I lived in the throngs of artists filled with wild and wonderful feminine creativity, yet stood rigid like a soldier at boot camp; unsure of how to be.

Then came the opportunity to write a story in this book, the modern goddess compilation. It was a chance to reflect and share what I knew about my goddess and the energy that *she* had given to me. I floundered, lost in the murky waters of what my head thought a goddess was and what my body felt vacant of possessing. I couldn't pinpoint my goddess essence and as much as I tried to *feel* her, I only felt hollow and disconnected from her. My shyness emerged, my discomfort grew, and I felt safer nestling into my mascline energy as my 'go to' emotion of comfort.

Feeling this obvious vacancy prompted an inner exploration to look deeper into why, how, and where I had lost touch with my inner goddess. Had I failed somehow and not heard her whispers feathering their way in light-footed meanders through my existence? I had to ask myself, did she somehow bypass me? Was I overlooked when she was handing out fragility and femininity? Was there a reason her flirtatious nature and sensual proclivities eluded my behavior ?

Years back, I sought the guidance of a successful self-love coach. On a devoted pilgrimage to find *myself,* I traveled to France to spend 10 days in the countryside uncovering and discovering how I wanted to emerge as a new butterfly. I read books, learned new techniques, and watched intently as I was shown the ways of the woman and hand-held down a path to self-love and devotion. The training was superb and I left feeling invigorated and inspired, destined to be the woman I wanted to be. And I became her: joyful, radiant, and happy. Yet, I found through the process of creating this book that the passion of my goddess still seemed unclear. She is a lost melody floating on a tranquil breeze. She beckons me to know her despite my limited reference; and once again, I am back where I started, wondering where my goddess is.

Admitting to her void, her untouchable presence, was the staff that struck the ground, that rumbled the earth and cracked open the shell of my 'non-existent' Ignite moment. I faltered in the feeling of not having a single clear Ignite experience regarding the goddess in me, but not able to feel her, not capable of summoning her to me was the spark that lit the flame to find exactly *where* she is and *why* she has been hiding.

Forced to go deeper, I sought to look back over the threads of my life. I wanted to retrace my steps down the trail that led me to why my goddess was missing and what had caused her to never show up. I ventured into my soul, seeking to understand and review the contract I agreed to live in this lifetime. Here, I saw the woman that I choose to be my mother. The young 23-year-old girl holding the hand of a man just two years older; strong, tall, and full. She loved him deeply, adoring his street-smart, rough-around-the-edges, get-it-done attitude. She knew he would protect her, be bigger and stronger should her step-father ever try to find her. Much of her young life had been riddled with horrifying sexual abuse from her replacement of a father. His abuse was the worst possible and my mother escaped his terror in her teens; running away, reinventing herself, and eventually marrying a man she felt would always keep her safe.

Her first daughter arrived soon after. A few years later, I agreed to join the family, pushing the 'approval' button and saying yes to the life she would give me. And it was a good life to the standards and expectations of what society pressures young families to achieve. Both my parents worked insanely hard to move from our small bungalow to a bigger house, then bigger again. Eventually they built a house and built another until we arrived in my mother's dream home; her childhood aspiration driven by her vow to never have her kids live as she did, in a shack, with a dirt floor and an outhouse in the backyard. Instead, my childhood was spent frolicking in our backyard swimming pool, sleeping in a huge room of my own, and playing hide-n-seek in my mother's walk-in closet. She gave me all the 'things' I wanted and worked insatiably hard to provide in every way.

Yet among all the privileges I had, I realized I missed receiving the gifts of my goddess. I began to unravel the ball of yarn that represented the beautiful parts of my childhood. Beneath the many layers, I discovered the gnarly knots and complex tangles that caused the blemishes and holes in my tapestry of life. I briefly recall my mother's sideways glances, her firm hand and her non-negotiable discussions. The clues were there, but so subtle I couldn't understand them at the time. It required a microscopic level of investigation to tune into what was going on in my seemingly picture-perfect childhood. The underlying current was so low and infinitesimal that I didn't see it then. I only see it now, desperate to uncover how and why I grew up feeling as I did, and with my goddess beckoning to me in the background to unravel more.

An odd recollection had percolated to the surface in a tiny thought a few years ago when I saw my 12-year-old stepdaughter sitting on the lap of my new husband as we sat around a picnic table. It was a completely foreign scene to me. A man, a dad, in such close proximity to his female child. Seeing them together showing normal affection left me wide-eyed and critical. I felt uncomfortable seeing them so connected. I had never sat on my father's lap. My dad never held me. He never tickled me, never played with me, never tucked me into bed. In fact, unravelling more, I don't ever recall my father hugging me, kissing me good night, or being there to help me out of the bath, tie my shoes, or comb my hair. When I was growing up, dads didn't do that. Or so I thought.

Transcending even further into the unique dynamic of our family, I never remember being alone with my father. He didn't watch my sister and I when my mom was gone — we had a neighbor lady do that, and eventually a housekeeper. He wasn't a part of my life in the areas of grooming, playing, sleeping, or just lounging around. He kept his distance, something I blamed myself for. In my eyes, he didn't really love me. He didn't care about my needs. He was so absent from my life and yet he wasn't. He was always existing on the fringe; there but not there. Not allowed to be too close. Not able to enjoy the fun times, the spontaneous girly stuff.

Sitting here today, my heart breaks for my father. I feel that he might have been kept at a distance from his daughters by a wife terrified that sexual abuse would rear its ugly head in her own family. Never overt, always covertly, I felt I was kept away from my father for fear that my budding breasts or short, frilly dresses would in some way entice him. Somewhere, someone feared helping me from the tub or laying together watching TV would trigger his desire. Consciously or subconsciously, my femininity was kept harnessed. My goddess was sequestered out of sight for fear of what she might unleash.

Sexual abuse affects one in four women. It is an unspeakable act of violation and changes the very fiber of a person forever. As a child of a sexual abuse survivor, I understand that I live with my mother's trauma in my DNA. My neural pathways are precoded with her fear and terror. I own the markers of what happened to her in the genetic makeup of my mind. In the recesses of my knowing, her anguish lives in me and when I consider her story, my goddess screams like a banshee for the pain she must have endured. I cannot comprehend the violation and anguish she feels from her years of abuse. I only know she must have immensely struggled to comprehend the atrocity of what was inflicted upon her. Her goddess was loved in all the wrong ways by a person who was supposed to hold her in the highest regard. Her stepfather's awful behavior and criminal acts marred her feminine nature in an irreparable way.

I know her unconscious protective measures were not done to hurt me or my father. I can see my mother's precautions through the eyes of having my own two daughters; how diligent and careful a mother must be to safeguard their innocence. I have seen both my girls stepping into their new bodies filled with curves and beauty, hormones blooming. They too are exposed to those who may see their goddess as something worth possessing. I can relate to the need to protect them and ward off any potential harm. I see how my mother's past influenced my childhood and why she kept my goddess at bay, leading me to embrace strong and confident characteristics. My mascline was encouraged because to my mother, that would keep me safe.

Never developing my sensuality nor delving into my femininity was exactly what happened and my goddess was left waiting, unnurtured until now. Writing in this book has done exactly what it was designed to do: awakened, activated, and enlivened the goddess in me. It has knocked on the door of my divine feminine energy and given me the strength now, although almost 50 years old, to unleash her and set her free. I am not sure what mischief, greatness, or gloriousness she will bring to me, but I can say for the first time in my life that I am thoroughly excited to meet her.

IGNITE ACTION STEPS

Time travel in your mind, back to when you were a girl. See all the messages you got and all the impressions you made of your divine self and who she *should* be. With the eyes and knowing of who you are today, tell her who she will grow up to be. Paint the picture for her of who you have become. Nurture her with your knowing of what you will endure and love her for every facet that she is. Love that little girl more than anyone has ever loved her and describe to her the Goddess she will one day grow to be.

JB Owen – Canada
Speaker, Author, Publisher and newly found Goddess
www.thepinkbillionaire.com
www.igniteyou.life
www.lotusliners.com
@ThePinkBillionaire
Ignitewithjb
thepinkbillionaire

CREATIVITY

ELIŠKA VAEA

"I stopped waiting to be discovered and I found myself."

By sharing my story I hope to support women on *their* path to *their* heart and *their* true Divine Feminine Flow. I want them to understand and truly feel the pulse of magic, the sparkle of joy, and the ecstasy of their body as they make love to everything they touch and create. I want every woman to *trust* her *creative* power and the guidance of her yoni ~ womb ~ heart that is completely self sourced, independent of any outside influence. I am calling all women to RAISE THEIR VOICE, TRUST THEIR VOICE, and share it unapologetically.

I'M THE VOICE OF THE EARTH

I see the little skeleton-skinny girl with her ears sticking out looking like a fairy and wanting to reveal her inner world of mermaids and unicorns. She wants to share it with her classmates and does, only to be made fun of. The girl who wanted to dance, play in the wind, and sing twirls up to her teachers only to be sat down and told to sit quietly in the corner of the classroom. I see all the moments she has been determined to stand up, speak out, and lead, only to face-plant on the cold hard ground of her thin-ice layer of self-worth. She would put herself in dance classes for years, following the routines of others, never unlocking her own wild inner dance. She would lift her voice in song alongside her mom, an amazing self-made guitar player and singer, only to be told often how her singing doesn't match the tune. She would be the presenter in middle school with everything she needed to say scribbled on small pieces of paper, knees trembling, standing at the podium, all shades of red flowing through her face, and her voice shaking as she speaks. The tiny papers start to crumble as her shyness takes over. Sweat trickles around her eyes and somehow, in the depth of her soul, she knew this is the place for her. She is learning to overcome her insecurity and find her own inner strength as she leans in and trusts in a greater guidance. What that is, she is yet to discover.

She is me.

I was only sixteen when I was diagnosed with pelvic floor dysfunction (PFD). I was a high school professional athlete and I ran a long run from Venice in Czechia to Venice in Italy. And on one of the steep hills over the Austrian Mountains, I peed myself while running. Yes. I peed myself. I would pee myself jumping on trampolines or even sneezing. I had no idea what was going on. I wasn't a grandma nor had I experienced childbirth. I was a very healthy thriving medal-winning athlete. I trained a lot. I pushed myself a lot. I was so hard on myself! Back then, I didn't know the importance of being held, helped, or supported, nor what it felt like to receive. This transferred into my sexuality as well… or was it the other way around? I forced my way through almost everything, even taking my own virginity being on top of my then dear high school sweetheart. I hadn't allowed myself to receive anything for years. I strived and strived. I had to work my ass off for every trophy and medal. I also had to earn the permission to be worthy.

Peeing myself in front of the whole athletic team did not conform with the image of the successful cool sporty girl I saw myself as. I now know it was one of the big kicks from the Goddess. I was offered a few options to treat the PFD: pharmaceuticals, Kegel exercises, and if they don't work, a surgery. The pills didn't work. Kegels didn't either. And having a pelvic floor surgery at 16? No thank you. "There is another way", she whispered into my ear, her tiny little voice within guiding me. I felt the truth of her words piercing through my own illusion like a golden arrow released straight into my heart, "You are meant for more… there is more for you… follow me." And I followed her, chasing that whisper, going on an adventure around the world as I worked to heal. Over 70 countries, countless womb healers, medicine mamas, shamans, western practitioners, books, articles, trainings, before landing a few years later on the island of Gods; Mama Bali, they call her. This island bursts with powerful feminine mother energy and is covered in a haze of smoke of incense carrying sacred prayers from the Balinese in each waking moment. It's New Year's Eve and I'm holding hands in a big circle of people, a lot of them I haven't met before. 10... 9... 8... I feel so at home here, thousands of kilometers away from the tiny village in the Czech countryside where I grew up. A warm tropical breeze is touching my skin and announcing the arrival of a new beginning. I open my mouth and inhale. Little did I know that it wasn't only a new year on a calendar, but also the start of my upgraded version of me as a woman. 7... 6... 5... the wind carries a question from her: "What is your intention Eliška? What do you choose?" 4... 3... My body shivers, the people blur in the background, and I hear myself ask with every cell of my body invested in the response, "I want to know and feel everything I possibly can about being a woman. I want to lead myself, and every woman I meet, home." 2... 1... People, of many cultures start hugging, wishing each other well, and celebrating together... a chosen family for just a short moment before I head home.

In the middle of the night I wake up shaking, shivering, and at the same time feeling orgasmic. My whole body is awake and I'm there riding a wave of bliss that permeates through my entire being. I'm *awake*! My womb is *pulsing* with creation. There is so much pleasure; can I even feel that much pleasure? It is so intense. After all these years of 'searching and learning,' I'm *now* receiving the gifts from nature, from her. The ecstasy of nature is pulsing through me. Aaaah. I'm beyond my body. This is the real feeling of being receptive to life. These are the gifts for me because I chose to stop forcing life. I chose to 'unnumb' myself. This is HER gifting me with feeling it all, pain and pleasure. I grab one of my obsidian crystal healing wands (a healing, self-pleasure tool) and I wait for my yoni, my sacred temple to say YES, and open up. At that moment I'm rewriting my first experience of making love. I'm rewriting the story of my wounded masculine. The part of me that has always wanted to force, push, and control. With a little moan and a deep full body exhale, my cells remember what it feels like to deeply receive. Suddenly I start coughing. I feel the energy rising up my spine. My belly dances like a jellyfish. My awareness keeps moving all the way from my cervix to my throat. My jaw rolls and I scream like a wild wolf for all the anger stored in my vagina and womb for decades. I cry, my heart grieving all the moments I have controlled my divine wild powerful feminine within.

My body stops shuttering, my heart is grieving for all the moments the feminine was controlled in this world.

I feel sadness for not allowing or knowing the divine feminine earlier, for all the moments I have been hurt, separate, and longing. She is taking over now. She is showing me what's next. I drift through the gate of my womb into the *yoniverse*, where I hear her speaking through me:

My voice is cracked open, that voice that comes from her through me. My creative energy moves from deep within, wild and free and untamed. I start writing poems, the words rushing out from my heart. I start singing songs, spontaneous and loud, my voice echoing off the stars, the sky and the Universe. I dance under the moonlight, her silver caress leaving a trail of bliss over my skin. She is now part of me and over the years she hasn't stopped showing me the truth to understand my/her pleasure and pain.

> *what are you searching?*
> *the depths of your soul?*
> *what are you searching*
> *up on the surface*
> *do you look below?*
> *there are many locks and I have the key*
> *come, follow me*
> *without force we let the energy flow*
> *up from deep inside, you already know*
> *you will laugh, moan, scream, and shake*
> *within you that's where the boundaries break*
> *you are breaking open and what you might see*
> *it's the truth, the feeling, the light, the love*
> *I'm you and you are me.*

Embodying my goddess and embracing her, the time passes. I'm sitting on the ground, the rough canvas of the tent fluttering behind me, moving through a forgiveness ceremony where the masculine meets the feminine. The charge and polarity is palpable all around me as all the men are gathered on one side of the room and the women on the opposite. My whole body is charged. Some women are moaning. Some crying, some burping, some screaming. So much energy is being transmuted in the space. In my very first experience of energy work, it felt like someone just teleported me to the middle of a Native American tribal gathering gazillions of years ago. I have been through the deep body opening to nature so many times before. I know this scene well.

One by one, each woman stands up as a representation of the feminine in the world, throws away her clothes, and shares her pain out loud. She is in the center of the space, speaking directly into the eyes of the men in front of her. With each woman standing, my body connects to the pain of all the wombs of all the women in the world. All the wombans. I'm sitting put. Is it my turn yet? Here we go again… as I stand facing my next podium, I'm scared. The train of moments of all the times I have stood up, courageous, rolls in. "I faced that before; I don't have to now," I hear myself say.

"Bullshit," the Goddess within replies.

But somehow I cannot move. I'm locked as an observer of myself. I sit for three hours listening… feeling the pain of all these people letting go, not being able to stand up myself and share. Again I'm being shown the biggest wound I carry, revealing the pain and hurt that has been done to the Earth, to the goddess. I remain locked within. From the outside, it looked like I was part of it. I was moving my body, mostly breathing, making sounds; but inside, there were places completely shut, scared to move, to speak, to be seen. I yearned to move and I couldn't. I yearned to speak. I couldn't. I yearned to express my anger, my rage, my roar, myself… and I couldn't. Even after all these years of expressing nature through me, I was locked within the deepest pain of the earth of the goddess with no way out. Three times I felt an S-like shape as if I was taken by a snake moving through my body, activating me… and still I didn't go. That was SHE showing me. SHE whispered into my ears. I wanted to be seen. I wanted those around me to see how I was trapped, powerless, in that locked down cage that the masculine had created for me. Deep inside there is a storm raging, rattling the bars with all its strength. Opening my mouth, I make a sound without noise, without words. I was afraid of my expansion, of the strength of my light and dark. My soul takes a deep breath in and out.

The space holder asked twice at the end of the ceremony that was pressing way over time for anyone else to stand up now and share. My body was pinned to the ground, my heart racing, and… *nothing*. I couldn't move. And just like that, the ceremony was complete. But not for me.

I needed to unlock the deepest expressions in me. I reached down for my medicine drum, swept it up in my arms, and ran out into the wilderness. Pounding it under the stars with the greatest force, I screamed in complete frustration and disappointment. Eliška, you have done this before… Why was this time so challenging for you? I dove deeper. I sang the voice of the truth being witnessed by the stars, being held by nature, cuddled by sand, and sang up by the wind. "In your own precious time you will bloom," I heard. "In your own precious time...Be gentle with yourself, soften… you don't have to push yourself. Release all the stories, energies, places, and connections where you learned that fear means LOVE. You carry the wisdom of the ancients. You are the VOICE of the EARTH."

Throughout all of this, I have unlocked her within me: creative energy, ecstatically pulsing in my body. I have recorded vocals and meditations, and have led thousands of women home. I have softened into sharing my truth in paintings, songs, and prayers. I stopped waiting to be discovered and I found myself. And it's just the beginning…

You too are meant to find the path to your heart and your real divine feminine flow, your *Goddess Within*. RAISE your VOICE, trust your voice, and share it unapologetically. Feel the pulse of magic and the ecstasy of your body. Your yoni is the key, your womb is the gateway, and your heart is your truth. When they all connect, they kiss each other in a deeply feminine and unshakeable belief, a mystic wisdom. You *are* the voice of the earth. RECEIVE.

Ignite Action Steps

Most women spend their lives walking around with a totally numb vagina. No wonder the orgasms are almost non-existent or that they feel stuck in life. There are so many little muscles, nerve endings, and magic ready to bloom within you. I invite you to take it slow and rewire your body to deeply feel and receive. Your TURN ON and ability to FEEL PLEASURE is directly connected to your daily experience and what shows up for you in your life. Commit to a SACRED self-pleasure session every day from 10 minutes to an hour. Remember, your YONI and your body are sacred. Show up for your own experience with PRESENCE and RECEIVE the many gifts of the goddess.

The following is a glimpse of an 8-day practice I use and share with other women through BEARTH™ and Amazonian Academy™. If this practice resonates with you and you would like to continue beyond the guidance presented here, look in the Resources at the end of this book for the link to a recorded guided 'I LOVE MY BODY' meditation you can download and start your day with an 8-day slow sex magic ritual. I promise this practice can bring loads of MAGIC into your own life and body that you had no idea existed.

First set your space to create a sense of sacredness, ritual. As you wake up, light a candle or incense stick, use essential oils, and put your favorite soft sensual music on.

To start the practice nothing is more important than BREATH. You can set an alarm if you have limited time, otherwise flow in your own rhythm. I recommend 10 minutes each day as you wake up for visible results. Open your mouth, relax your jaw, and breathe deeply through your mouth.

With each inhale, move within the body and scan your inner landscape with your inner kind eye.

- Take an inhale into the front of your **heart**. Exhale.
- Take an inhale into the back of your heart where it is close to the spine. Exhale.
- Take an inhale into the sides of your heart. Exhale.
- Take an inhale into your **belly**. Exhale.
- Take an inhale into your **womb**. Exhale. Deep soft sight with the mouth open: Haaa.
- Take an inhale into your **yoni**. Exhale.
- Take an inhale into your **tailbone**. Exhale.

Now, come back to your yoni and connect to the little tiny muscles there. With each inhale relax and soften, and with each exhale activate and move.

1. clitoris (tiny muscles around the clitoris) Continue for as long as you feel and then move on
2. muscles around the entrance to your urethra (pee hole)
3. opening to your yoni
4. perineum (between yoni/anus)
5. anus
6. back to entrance of the yoni
7. left side of your vaginal canal
8. right side of your vaginal canal
9. middle of your vaginal canal
10. little muscles around your cervix

For most women it takes about three months to start feeling the movement. Visualize your muscles moving, connect to them, and keep practicing. To finish your practice, put one hand onto your womb and one hand onto your heart. Give yourself permission to feel it all. Take it easy, be SLOW & GENTLE, and see where your body takes you.

Eliška Vaea – Czechia
Freedom Catalyst, Soul Mentor
www.eliskavaea.com

UNITY

ANNE-MARIE CHAREST, PH.D.

"The sacred journey home starts with a single step of reverence."

**In our society that favors 'doing' over 'being', competitiveness over collabo-
ration, ambition over compassion, and forcefulness over patience, reverence
for the divine feminine has been predominantly lost. As a woman, I invite
you to feel your unique wisdom, embrace the beauty of your being, and
navigate your own inner realms and ancestral heritage. Tapping into your
inner worlds will allow you to gain access to your divine. Inspire yourself
to re-awaken, Ignite, and ground yourself into the deeper truth of who
you are: your sacred goddess within.**

SANNA: THE GODDESS OF THE SEA

Laying on her warm belly, an earthy iron smell grounded every cell of my
body into another reality. As a sense of calm settled in, the call of baboons
intensified in the distance and a gentle winter breeze caressed my naked skin.
Luminous rays made their way down the African canopies, reawakening a
sense of hope as I was birthing like a caterpillar into a butterfly. Tha-thump,
tha-thump, tha-thump… my heart beat echoed in unison with Mother Earth
like a newborn resting on its mother's bosom. Connected through my senses,
I felt held by her nurturing warmth. Tears of gratitude washed over me as I
basked in her abundant love. A sense of aliveness emerged from my bones as

rippling waves of ecstatic joy jolted me back to life. For the first time in years, I felt at home again.

The spell of the sensuous had re-awakened me from a deep unconscious trance that had left me lifeless. In awe of my newfound essence, I wondered how I had lost my way and neglected the subtle yet potent lifegiving force that invigorated me. More importantly, I wondered how I could cultivate this radiating vitality moving forward.

Despite this renewed force now flowing through my body, an anxious nervous system kept tugging relentlessly in the distance. Years of climbing the illusionary corporate ladder, staring at life-sucking blue screens of high-tech environments, and dealing with the predominantly male attitudes rampant in aerospace and telecom industries, left me depleted and empty as a woman. My shriveled spirit was anaesthetized by the callousness of technology; the robotic, repetitive, fast-paced existence of modern living and the illusion of achievement. For years, society had painted the canvas that masculine values were honored and preferred over those of feminine ones. This paradigm also manifested itself within my family.

As a child, I remember hearing the subtle rage of the women who resented the inequality they experienced in our family business. Men were offered positions of power through decision making, lucrative opportunities, and executive roles denied to the women. As a result, a palpable yet subtle tension between genders rippled through the air at family gatherings. A discrete clenching of the jaw represented all the unspoken dissatisfaction of this status quo. Back then, my French Canadian culture kept women quiet, engaged in repetitive and clerical tasks while men climbed the ladder of success.

The media, the church, and society at large also painted a similar reality with the denial of women's presence in various institutions. I remember asking myself why there are no women priests in the Roman Catholic church and few women judges in Canada. Over the years, I witnessed women of my community fight for their rights, as little value was placed on the inherent contributions they brought to society while men took center stage. I also remember that I rarely heard my father compliment my mother nor heard the men in my extended family express their reverence for women. The truth was, women were kept in a box of strict gender role identification while men roamed free. I longed for this freedom.

In my teens, I was determined to embody the qualities of a man: assertive, powerful, independent, and able to conquer all, do it all. I was fierce in wanting to show the world that women, too, could do what men do — and, for that matter, do it well. To launch my determined path, I followed my dad's footsteps in sports. Whatever sports he engaged in, I was set to play them too and prove that I could succeed at them as a woman. From competitive sailing, downhill skiing, soccer, tennis, water skiing, kayaking, triathlons, there was no stopping me. My drive to be just like my father in the hope to be seen, loved, and recognized led me to even attend the same private college as he. Subconscious imprints left me longing for validation, as a deeper void kept me in search for something, but what?

Despite a degree in the healing arts, life had propelled me to work in the same telecommunications and aerospace industries as my father. As a marketing manager, my business suits cried out for power. I was determined to make it in a male-dominant environment and prove to society that women could succeed there also. Despite this inner fire, every day at work was a continual reminder of the gender inequality that prevailed. Once married with two beautiful boys, life kept me out of breath, drained, and stressed as I attempted to climb the 'ladder of success.' Long hours competing in a male-dominant environment was not easy. Boardroom power battles had to be won and excellence was required to dominate the competitive landscape. With determination, I presented myself as strong and unbreakable, yet my inner landscape cried out in an ancient and distant voice, "You are not good enough." Over time, this voice accentuated itself as the desire to pierce the shield of the old boys club of high-tech industries became inevitably unachievable without tremendous loss of well-being. Torn in all directions for over 15 years and exhausted in pursuing a man's world, I began witnessing the patterns that plagued my unconscious and realized that this was no longer working for me.

Lost in a storm of chaos at the age of 38, I found myself questioning *WHO AM I?* A void had amplified itself as all futile attempts to fill it yielded no results. Something had to change and the only direction unexplored was a part of me that I had successfully pushed away for years: my *Goddess Within.* I was called to return to the cradle of humanity, Africa, and to face the unknown that laid dormant inside of me.

A musky veil of incense ascending into the darkness amidst the lushness of the African wildlife. At the center, an old Sangoma (South Africa shaman) performed his ceremonial dance as women drummed him into trance. My body shook into movement with each drumbeat as the Sangoma's dark piercing eyes stared at something unfamiliar and hidden to me. Stunned, I wondered what he was seeing. As drums continued to echo forcefully in the background, a low, deep voice asserted, "You are a Sangoma, a shaman, a healer." I felt confusion rippling through my skin, leaving me questioning, "What is a shaman and what does this all mean?"

I left Africa and returned home to the United States with a greater reverence for the divine feminine spirit and a palpable connection to Mother Earth that left me grounded, but the relentless tension of my high-technology environment continued to burden my inner world. The strain grew like a pressure cooker, out of control, as no one had taught me the skills to tame the dragons of anxiety, stress, and anger that lived inside. I knew it was time to quit my job as the director of marketing, stop my competitive sports, and truly begin my journey of claiming my inner goddess. Having surrendered to the unknown, I was led by a friend to attend a 10-day silent meditation retreat in the mountains of Northern California. Not knowing what I was getting into, I simply knew that I was exactly where I needed to *BE*.

The silence was deafening and the stillness unsettling as my body longed to *DO*. Hour after hour, I was asked to sit quietly, yet my body hollered another reality. Inner fidgety chaos kept knocking at my door. My body ached and shouted, "I want to move!" My thoughts raced through my head, memories surfaced unexpectedly, uncomfortable sensations revealed themselves throughout my senses, and emotions fired relentlessly from within. It felt intolerable. Yet, with each day of silence, restlessness transformed into peacefulness, peacefulness transformed into nothingness, nothingness transformed into fullness, and fullness transformed into Love.

Breath by breath, sensation by sensation, instant by instant, I learned the art of being *present* and to listen to a quieter place inside that seemed to point to a deeper *Truth*. The path of embodiment opened me to new dimensions of reality, of inner peace, and of experiences that grounded me into the bedrock, solidifying my existence. Paradoxically, I also grew to embrace and welcome impermanence as moments of consciousness evaporated. It is in the stillness of *Being* that a new magical place began to reveal itself.

As time crawled to an abrupt stop, each inhale and exhale reminded me that, in this sacred vehicle, my body, *I was home.*

On the sixth day of meditating 11 hours a day, my body began to dissolve itself, molecule by molecule, as waves of unconditional love flooded my existence. The world as I knew it had vanished. No longer able to distinguish myself from a reality separate from me, a sense of oneness emerged. In that moment, I understood I was one with all of creation. Pain had transformed into love, boundaries evaporated into unity, separateness evanesced into connectedness, and chaos calmed into peace, leaving me experiencing quantum levels of joy and bliss. In that awakening, I knew I was the Goddess, the creator, life itself, and capable of infinite unconditional love, which permeated life's deeper truth. This *LOVE* was deeper than the deepest oceans, vaster than the greatest galaxies, and entirely unconditional in nature. My new experience engulfed me in the immense Love that lived in me and through me.

Returning to society with this new understanding was not easy. Attempts to share the unshareable were pointless despite a fierce voice that wanted to howl this reality to the world. My inner goddess continued to emerge as a new understanding of love paved the road ahead of me. A gentler, more compassionate self emerged. Competitiveness made way to movement and dance; sports converted to long, contemplative walks in nature; and linear thinking transmuted itself into colorful and playful creativity. I felt alive. Despite this revival, the Sangoma's words, "You are a shaman," kept ringing in the distance.

On a crisp fall night, standing on a street corner, I saw a flyer calling members of my community to join in circle to Melt the Ice in the Heart of Man. It was then that I met Angaangaq Angakkorsuaq, shaman from Kalaallit Nunaat, Greenland. In that circle, a circle that has no beginning and no end in which we all belong, I began learning the teachings of the far North. As words of wisdom were shared, my heart opened wider. By the second day of the gathering, my body could barely contain the love, an experience I knew well. With gratitude and with love racing through my veins again, I decided to make my way to Costco to purchase fruit as an offering to my new group of friends. As I walked through the aisles, something mysterious began to happen. Every person within a 30-foot radius of me would stop, turn around, and offer one of the most genuine and loving smiles. At first, I rationalized this occurrence as coincidence, yet it became clear this strange phenomena was not random. Something else was happening.

Uncomfortable, I immediately began looking at my body in an attempt to explain the mysterious behavior . "Were my breasts sticking out of my shirt? Did I have a trail of toilet paper hanging from my pants?" I asked myself. It was at that moment that lights lit up and I understood that people could feel and experience the immense love that radiated from me. With this new information, I also understood that the one thing I could do to make this world a better place was to live from the place of the heart. I began seeing the rippling effects of love throughout the world. This was a pivotal moment for me. I experienced firsthand how conscious love and 'out of form', manifests 'in form' and in present reality. I could see the effects of cultivating that love in my body and taking it out into the world.

Research has demonstrated that the first organ to emit and receive information from the outer world is the heart through its electromagnetic field. By cultivating our heart coherence, we consciously choose to love, in turn transforming our inner and outer worlds.

For the next 10 years, I began the journey of melting the ice in my own heart as I learned to go deep within. At my first wisdom keeper gathering, my reality was once again shaken as Angaangaq looked into my eyes and firmly stated, "You are Sanna, she who lives at the deepest places of our oceans. You are Sanna, the Goddess of the Sea." Once again stunned, I wondered who was Sanna? According to Inuit and Greenlandic legend, Sanna is known as the Goddess of the Sea. She is a beautiful mortal woman who became the ruler of the underworld after her father threw her out of his kayak in his attempt to survive. Her fingers were cut off by her father as she clasped the kayak before she sank to the depths of the ocean. It is said that as she sank, her fingers became the animals of the sea. When this story was first shared with me, my body trembled at the resemblance of my own relationship with the betrayal of the masculine. The years that followed opened portals of suffering as I began diving in to melt away the painful layers of ice hidden in my DNA, in my family system, and in my heart. As I slowly descended into the depths, shamans from around the world came to place their hands on my aching heart and share their medicine, wisdom, and love.

With each layer of ice melting away, I began transmuting the trauma of my ancestors and the pain of my lineage that I unconsciously carried for them. Tears carpeted the floor as I witnessed my female ancestors being burnt at the stake and hung for carrying the wisdom of the hidden realms, for their intuition, and their capacity to know without knowing. Nowhere to hide amidst this vast ocean, I raged at men for their atrocities, grieved the inequality of genders over centuries, and released the perceived injustices in my own family. I wailed at the destruction that men had left behind and the loss of precious life and resources on earth. This grieving made way for forgiving, as I too was part of this reality keeping my silence.

These years taught me to forgive those before me who lived in the shadow of their unconsciousness. ~ I learned to embrace my own humanity. ~ I learned to face pain, mine and that of others, and to no longer run away from it, but rather be with it. ~ I learned to navigate the many inner realms of my inner sea helping me reveal the complex web of existence. ~ I learned to honor my body and that of Mother Earth, by weaving together body, mind, and spirit like strands of sweetgrass. ~ I learned to honor my ancestors, the mineral world, the plant world, the animal world, and the two-legged world for their gifts. ~ I learned to listen, respect, and celebrate life in ceremony by dancing under the full moon and to the sounds of the heartbeat. ~ I learned to stand tall and powerfully as I am meant to be for times and times to come. ~ I learned to come home to myself, in heart and love for the goddess within. ~ I learned to love Sanna, the Goddess of the Sea.

I invite you to fully embrace the qualities of the feminine: transforming 'doing' to 'being', competitiveness to collaboration, ambition to compassion, and forcefulness to patience. Revere the divine feminine within you. Feel your unique wisdom, embrace the beauty of your being, and navigate your own inner realms. Be inspired to re-awaken, Ignite, and ground yourself in the deeper truth of who you are, unifying you and your sacred goddess within.

IGNITE ACTION STEPS

If you find yourself pulled into chaos by modern living, feeling lost within, trapped, and stressed in thinking you need to do more, rest assured there is another way: the Way of the Goddess. The following are nurturing steps to re-Ignite your Goddess Within.

- **Let nature nurture**. Allow your mind, body, and spirit to be nurtured by the delicate touch of nature. Let your senses bring you to life as you wander into the magic of the wild.
- **Be Still.** When chaos prevails, take a pause and dive into the quiet space within. Listen. There you will find what you are looking for: the solutions and the dreams.
- **Cultivate Love from Within**. Nurture its essence daily by watering it with acceptance, kindness, and self-love.
- **Stand Tall and Powerful**. In the midst of fear and pain, be the gentle strand of sweetgrass that stands tall and powerful as it's meant to be.
- **Be the Sacred Mirror**. Ignite the sacred Goddess in each woman you meet by reflecting her innate beauty with words of appreciation and gratitude.

Anne-Marie Charest, Ph.D. – United States of America
Licensed Marriage & Family Therapist, Mindfulness & Wellness Facilitator
www.heartfullyU.com

KNOWINGNESS

JOANN LYSIAK

"Follow your heart in love and passion; it will always guide you on your magnificent goddess journey."

It is my intention to empower you to awaken your modern goddess within and to embrace your feminine energy — the creative, intuitive, love-centered energy. I support you to live your divine purpose by sharing your unique gifts and talents with the world.

AWAKEN THE GODDESS WITHIN

Experiences and events in our lives impact us in ways beyond our initial comprehension. They shape and influence what we believe, who we become, and how we live our lives, often more than we are aware. Whether challenging or rewarding in the moment, they are the gifts that allow us to rediscover who we truly are as we awaken our goddess within.

There I was. Paul, the V. P. of Sales, was offering me an opportunity that most people would never refuse. I was on my way in corporate America to achieving what I believed was my dream career. As I wondered whether I was willing to leave this comfortable business world in which I had been so successful, to enter a world that spoke to something deeper within my soul, fear suddenly took hold. I managed to thank him graciously and let him know I would consider the offer and get back to him. I reflected on my skills and all the work that I had been quietly doing to launch my new business. Guided by my lifelong dream to create beauty, I summed up my courage and followed my heart in love and passion. I turned down the promotion, so I could move closer to where I knew I was called to be, as I continued to uncover my divine purpose on my goddess journey.

I have always been drawn to various forms of arts and crafts. In high school, I was actively painting, sewing my own clothing, and taking on every art project before me. This was my happy place, an escape that allowed me to enjoy my solitude and create art as an expression of my true self. In this quiet space, ideas flowed from and to me, including answers to questions that I was constantly asking myself. Even then, it felt as if I was being guided toward something within, although I did not know it at the time.

Despite my passion for art, my very practical father had an ingrained belief that being in corporate America was my only ticket to success and that my passion for art would lead only to starvation. I also had my own doubts about my ability to succeed considering other people's talents, and I wondered if I was 'good enough.' In the end, I felt I wasn't, so I opted not to pursue art as my major in college, but focused on a degree in marketing instead.

By the time I graduated from college, I was sold on finding my place in the world of marketing, largely because it appealed to my creative spirit. During that period, I dreamed about working for the number one cosmetic company in the world, and I consistently envisioned myself there.

Soon, I was offered an opportunity to interview for my 'dream job.' Although the interview was a success and I received a job offer, the vibe was all wrong. That little voice that had always guided me, which I now recognize as my feminine gift of intuition, told me to decline because a better opportunity in the same company would be forthcoming. Even though my headhunter disagreed, I had the knowingness that it would happen… and it did, just three months later, exactly as I had envisioned it!

I thought, how surreal is it that I'm working for the #1 cosmetic company in my dream job that I have been visualizing for a full one year? To say that I was overjoyed to work for a prestigious FASHION company was putting it mildly. After all, I would be receiving every perk I could ever desire. What else could an up-and-coming young woman ask for? I dove right in and used my creative and interrelational talents to great success. I loved working on the displays and building relationships with buyers. I was ecstatic.

On the flipside, I had entered a fast-paced fashion business that came with all the standard stresses of aggressive sales goals. I jumped in and gave it 150% on my road to corporate success. Because my sales division was a bit of a boy's club, I found that I had to prove myself at every turn as the token woman. I became more competitive, driven, and stressed out.

One night, on my drive home from an extremely chaotic day at work, I could feel my tension rising. I was beyond stressed, running behind and over anxious. With no time for lunch, I had downed a 'super nutritious' hot pretzel and a soda. When I arrived home, my heart was racing and my legs were shaking, and my head was spinning. My whole chest was pounding as I started to panic. I thought, "I must get to the Emergency Room!" I thought I was having a heart attack at 26 years young. In the ER, after being diagnosed with an anxiety attack, I realized I had experienced my first WAKE UP call. I was spending too much time operating in my driven, male energy: analytical, fast-paced world with no time for self-care and no space for a personal life. It was clear to me that it was time to get back in balance, care for myself, and slow down my pace. My heart had spoken to me, encouraging me to refocus on what mattered most to me by embracing my divine, feminine energy.

Although working at that company had been a wonderful adventure filled with many accomplishments, it was time for me to move toward a more meaningful path. I was grateful that I had fulfilled my dream and achieved immense growth that had magically opened another door to a different corporate experience, one which would begin to awaken my goddess within.

The Universe had provided me with a perfect opportunity to pursue an attractive career path with a more balanced lifestyle in a newly-created sales management position with a top hair care company. The culture was a perfect fit for me. I felt more connected, collaborative, and creative as part of a cohesive team fulfilling a vision. One opportunity after another became available to me, as I moved quickly up the corporate ladder in a few short years. My final position as Sales Training Manager was where I excelled; it was where I discovered my uniqueness, my talents, and my goddess gifts. This was where the seeds for me to empower others as a coach and to create training programs that inspire transformation were planted and germinated.

In retrospect, I realize that I was so much more aligned to the vibration of this company, and I felt free to be creative, to step out of the box, and to own my feminine power. That company was a people-centered culture, one that was open-minded about embracing change and growth, allowing me to flourish and share my gifts and talents.

During this time, my artistic side was calling me to nourish my soul by creating beauty. I found a unique gallery that offered various classes. The one I was immediately drawn to was a metalsmith class. Right from the start, my goddess took off in bliss, as I created my designs during a series of classes over two years. When wearing my designs, I was inundated with compliments from other professional artists who encouraged me to make jewelry as a business. While I was overjoyed at their enthusiasm, I found myself reverting to my old subconscious high school beliefs that I wasn't good enough as an artist to succeed. Fortunately, this time, I had unleashed my inner goddess through my role in the hair care company, allowing me to feel confident and comfortable and own my talents. Thus, I chose to listen to my heart and to follow my dream, for I knew I was more than good enough to create distinctive jewelry.

My practical side guided me to attend classes for aspiring entrepreneurs through the Small Business Association, where I began to create business, marketing, and product development plans. Finally, with strategies in place, I was ready to take the plunge. What had begun as a creative hobby had morphed into what I knew was meant to be my next passion. I allowed myself to fulfill my high school dream to be a fashion designer. I didn't know when or how this would happen; I just knew that it would.

My story returns to Paul's office, where he had laid out the entire plan for my next promotion. Even though it had every perk and creature comfort I could ask for, it clearly wasn't **MY** desired path within the company nor did it allow me to use the talents I loved most. Following my heart, I knew I couldn't accept it and I intuitively knew this was the perfect time to continue my goddess journey creating what I love... and so Joann Lysiak Designs was born.

To gain valuable knowledge and expertise in the jewelry industry, I began to ask questions, discern information, and jump in by showing my designs to others. My passion in doing what I loved Ignited me to partner with retail stores and galleries where my designs became established, and, steadily, my business grew.

I was in my happy place, once again, creating stunning jewelry and following my intuition in selecting specific gemstone combinations for my collections. I dreamed about my aspirations constantly, which were manifesting at an impressive rate of speed. Soon, my collection was featured in major films and on television, as well as in magazines and on fashion websites. I was in awe of how my dreams were coming true! I had just returned from a New York fashion show with a folder full of orders when the tragedy of September 11th happened. That caused a devastating domino effect of order cancelations and shipments put on hold, just as I had expanded my business and moved into my new loft space.

To grow from a thriving business to losing half of my wholesale volume in a few months was one of the greatest business challenges I had ever faced and I needed to find an out-of-the-box solution — pronto. The answer that intuitively came to me was to develop my retail sales by designing a showroom within my studio for my personal clients. I created a beautiful oasis to connect with my customers, discover more about their desires, and construct unique designs that were energetically perfect for them as I embraced my goddess energy. It was through our deep interaction that I became aware of which gemstones they were attracted to, and, even more importantly, I received feedback on how the stones activated their energy. Soon I found myself sharing the energy properties and intuitively selecting gemstones best suited for my clients' needs. In hearing their stories, it was clear to me that my jewelry was helping them to gain confidence, uplift their energy, and allow them to manifest their desires. Women were drawn to the mesmerizing gemstones on a level far deeper than they were aware. My retail sales exploded, as my clients referred their friends to my goddess oasis for a day of female bonding and fun playing in the energy of gemstones.

Three years after the crash, and my business was, once again, booming! It was the holiday season and my calendar was booked with a multitude of shows. To prepare, I camped out in my studio until late into the night and found myself running on empty. The next thing I knew, a serious infection developed in my body after a medical procedure, and due to a misdiagnosed treatment, my health began to decline, impacting my daily activities. I soldiered on in my business and, at the same time, focused on my health. As traditional medicine had failed me, I found myself open to going down the rabbit hole of finding alternative healing modalities.

As I was discovering and using these unique modalities and remedies, my body began to heal. By applying and watching the results firsthand, I became more intrigued and passionate about natural health. At the same time, the business climate began to shift significantly, as more jewelry became mass produced, moving away from my high quality, hand-crafted designs. I realized that if I could no longer fulfill my original vision as an artist, it was time for me to move on to my new-found passion: I felt called to serve people on a deeper level in wellness.

I harnessed the creativity, intuition, and hard-working ethic that had served me so far and channeled them into my new passion. As I gained education and skills to serve people through natural health modalities, it became apparent to me that there was more to being healthy than the standard protocols. To my surprise, I further expanded my usage of energy from my jewelry days by learning how to test energy, balance energy, and release energy blockages in the body. This new world of working with energy and developing my intuitive abilities in the healing arts resonated with my goddess within.

Through my own personal journey, I realized that for me to heal, I had to change my response to stress, live in alignment, and master my mindset. In my understanding of mindset, I knew that it was the key to unlock the door not only to health but also to everything in life. I knew that to help my clients achieve long-lasting results, I needed to help them master their mindset first and foremost which led me to complete my certification as a Master Life Coach.

My personal journey of wellness, energy, lifestyle, and mindset came together when I realized that my success in achieving health, wealth, love, and spirituality was connected to the integration of body, mind, and spirit. This connection is through energy and my application of the various forms of energy work. This cognition caused the shift in how I interacted with clients in helping them to integrate the connection of body, mind, and spirit into their lives through various energy modalities.

In addition, I gained a new understanding of who I needed to become to live this integration. First, I had to come out of the spiritual closet in openly expressing my spirituality and my intuitive abilities. Second, I had to be authentically ME by allowing others to see my unique gifts. Third, I had to fully embrace my feminine energy to unleash my goddess capabilities out in the open.

Once my energy began to shift, my life began to shift in every way imaginable. During this time came one of the most surprising epiphanies yet. It was a message from the Divine telling me to return to creating powerful jewelry, once again using my intuitive and energy abilities on a deeper, spiritual level. With the intuitive and conscious application of energy testing, feeling and reading energy, I would use gemstones both in my designs and as individual pieces to help people shift their energy, raise their vibration, and manifest their desires. Not long after this realization, I had a clear vision of a past life in which I was a high priestess putting jewelry that I had created on other women. As I placed the jewelry on them, I became aware that I was also activating their energy centers. This led me to be certified to access Akashic records, which has allowed me to help clients on an even deeper level as I clear their energy blockages, align their energy with gemstones, and coach them to live their divine purpose.

As I look back on my life thus far, I can see how everything in my goddess journey has been there for a purpose in a very deliberate and timely fashion, from my early love of fashion and art to my corporate adventures and my work with jewelry and mindset. What I learned along the way was that I have always been deeply connected to the goddess within myself as a creator and an intuitive coach. This has allowed me to follow my dreams, even when the pathway was not entirely clear or seemingly logical. I have also learned to embrace my feminine energy — the creative, spiritual, and compassionate energy of Gaia — and connect more fully with nature.

My mission now is to empower women to activate their energy centers and to use that energy to uncover and share their gifts and talents as they live their Divine purpose. To unleash the goddess in women, I have recently created a retreat in Sedona, inviting women to gather together in Nature to connect with and embrace their feminine power. Working with their heart-centered energy, they can rediscover their creative passion and compassion which are both powerful and necessary in the world.

My desire is that my story will inspire you to listen to your intuition and to follow your heart as you fully embrace your uniqueness and immerse yourself in the beauty of your feminine light. Ultimately, it is time for you to step into your power of love and to lead the world as the magnificent goddess that you already are!

IGNITE ACTION STEPS

- Find your beautiful spot in nature where you can connect to the loving energy of Gaia, Mother Earth.
- To connect fully to Gaia, take your shoes and socks off. Stand, evenly balancing your weight in your hips and legs. As you feel Gaia's pulse, allow her feminine energy in.
- Visually take in the sights of nature before you; listen to the sounds and feel the energy.
- Place your hands over your heart, close your eyes, and breathe in deeply as you allow yourself to connect to the feminine energy flowing through your body.
- Be grateful and appreciative that you are one with the loving, Divine energy of Gaia.

Joann Lysiak – United States of America
Nutritionist, Mind~Body~Spirit Coach,
Akashic & Energy Specialist, Jewelry Designer
www.JoannLysiakGems.com
www.EmpowerCoachingNetwork.com

WISDOM

YENDRE SHEN

"Own Your Power"

My intention of sharing this story with you, the reader, is that the parts of us we try to disown and discard make us whole and complete when we finally acknowledge, understand, accept, and value the gifts they represent within us. This is your power...

I WANTED TO BE A BOY

My journey of embracing my inner Goddess began from the moment I was born. I come from a culture that values boys over girls. When my mother gave birth to me, my family had hoped I would be a son. Imagine their disappointment when they discovered I was not — instead I turned out to be the third daughter. My mother, failing to bear a male child, would have likely had harsh disapproving glances cast upon her. This was how I came into the world, not being valued for who I am.

For the longest time as a child I wanted to be a boy. I wanted to be the male child they had wanted me to be — especially, when at 18 months old, my mother died from a head concussion after falling from a ladder. My father was the only son in his family. There was now no chance of a male heir unless he remarried. So I tried to be a boy. I did things that boys did, like climbing trees. I wanted to be good at things that boys were good at, like sports, and smart like boys were in math and science. I became a tomboy and was proud of it. I looked upon things that were girly as a waste of time and useless. I began to devalue a part of myself without even knowing it.

It didn't help matters that my two sisters, who are seven and 13 years older, were the image of femininity and beauty in my eyes. When I compared myself to them at four or five years old, I noticed their bodies looked so different from mine. They were curvier, more filled out in places than my tiny, scrawny, and angular frame. I felt like an ugly duckling whenever I stood beside them. I remember not wanting to be in pictures with them because I felt my presence would ruin the photographs.

I have a flat face and a flat nose, gap teeth, and lips that move rather funny when I talk. As a child, I had knobby knees that always had scrapes and bruises, with thick elephant skin from kneeling when I played. My hair was always cut short to be manageable. The carelessness of my appearance and disregard for my body were signs of being a motherless child, but also highlighted the absence of knowing how to be caring and loving toward myself.

At 11 years old, I started to develop acne on my forehead. This marked the beginning of my depressive mood patterns that I struggled with most of my life as I had to deal with acne throughout my adulthood. The acne which started as tiny pimples grew more severe and even became cystic. Having breakouts still in my forties seemed like a cruel joke that I can only laugh at now. They would pop up anywhere on my face, nose, and chin. Blemishes make their appearance at the most inopportune times, like before important photos or meetings with people I wanted to make a good impression on.

At puberty, I became aware of boys. I remember, as early as 10, I wanted the love of a boy. I became more conscious of my appearance and noticed the conflicting feelings of wanting and avoiding the attention of boys. Suddenly boys meant something different — before they had been something I could emulate. In my simple 'child's' mind, I had thought trying to be like a boy would make me one. Puberty made me realize that was not possible — I was different from them.

The increasing awareness of my body and appearance was a confusing time as it created a sense of frustration and feeling that I just couldn't be 'the girl.' The stereotypical girl that people wanted was just not me. My muscular arms and legs didn't fit well in sleeveless shirts and short skirts. I was mad at myself for not being the image of what the world wanted me to be or how to look.

I couldn't figure out how to put myself together to accentuate my feminine qualities and when I tried I ended up looking like a 'Puffalo', which is a cross between a puffin and a buffalo — as I couldn't decide which one to be. When I dressed myself, one half may have resembled a cowgirl and the other half a ballerina. My oldest sister would give me disapproving looks whenever she saw me. "Why can't you make yourself look more attractive? You have such a great athletic, fit body, it'd be easy for you to look good." My lack of flair for looking 'feminine,' felt like an impediment I couldn't fix and I gave up the effort of claiming my feminine allure.

As a teenager, the awkwardness seemed to never end. I would have secret crushes on boys, which made me more self-conscious around them. If any of those feelings were reciprocated, I was oblivious. However, in high school, I caught the eye of a boy on the badminton team. His interest in me was uncomfortable and I did my best to avoid crossing paths with him. The experience made me scared to get the attention of someone I wasn't fond of and it made me dread attracting unwanted attention from men, even as I got older. This need to be hidden and not be seen had a strong instinctive and protective nature — as if I had no choice in the matter if a man liked or wanted me. I decided it was best not to be the shiny eye-catching object people desired.

In my 20s I fell in love with a man. I didn't realize I was in love until the relationship ended. We first met eyes while I was up in a tree. He was looking up at me smiling, curious, probably wondering what's this crazy woman doing up in a tree. Our encounter happened at a conference for martial artists that came from the Kung Fu style lineage Bruce Lee was originally taught. When I was little, I loved watching martial arts films and idolized Bruce Lee, Jacky Chan, and Jet Li. During my 20s, martial arts was a big part of my life.

My Sifu teacher had driven me to the conference that day. We got there early. While we were waiting in the parking lot, I noticed a magnificent grand pine tree with outstretched branches, like arms, reaching out inviting me to come and climb it. The branches literally looked like steps. It felt free and exhilarating to scale up and up so easily. When the conference ended my teacher had to stay behind and couldn't drive me back. Coincidentally, the man who locked eyes with me was asked to drive me home.

He was introduced to me earlier by my Sifu, after I came down from my tree adventure, as an esteemed fellow martial artist. The way he held my eyes when we shook hands, I sensed his intrigue with me. There was a nervous excitement in the air when we got into his car for him to drive me home. I could tell he was enamoured by the way I spoke. The drive back went quickly as we talked non-stop about our favorite topic, martial arts. I felt he didn't want our time together to end, as he asked what else I wanted to do before we reached my place. We stopped by a park to walk around. It was late spring; I pointed out the fresh new growth on the evergreen trees to him that looked like candle sticks. There was a magnetic energy charge between us. However, I didn't know he was engaged.

Within a week of us meeting, he broke up with his fiancée to date me. I secretly judged him for how swiftly he terminated his engagement, so I didn't take the relationship seriously. I couldn't understand how someone who had made a promise and bought a house with his fiancée could so quickly break up with that person. I questioned his character from his choice of actions. Despite how much fun I was having and how happy I was feeling, I didn't indicate I wanted more.

When it was over, I felt the worst pain I had experienced in my life to that point. I didn't know heartbreak was that painful because my first boyfriend before him loved me more than I could love him. Even though I told him that, he said it was okay because he didn't want to lose me. There was a huge ache, like an empty hole in my chest, from missing 'the object' I desired to direct my love toward. Eventually, an insight came to me that I could direct that love toward myself, and I realized all relationships are simply love affairs with myself. As the pain eased, it helped me appreciate and understand the purpose of pain and what a teacher it can be for us. That realization made me somewhat fearless knowing I could never *really* get hurt from love.

I began to see myself through the eyes of men who loved me. When we were babies, if we were fortunate, we would have had the adoring gaze of our mother, father, grandparents, family, and caregivers. I did not get all that as a child. It was in the presence of someone's love, the love of a man in a relationship, that I blossomed. When I experienced myself as being the source of someone's joy and delight, it gave me the excitement to dress up and dress well for their admiration and pleasure. I bloomed like a flower under the attention of someone I wanted and desired. In the safe environment of someone who loved and cared about me, being lusted after and worshipped by another, wasn't so scary. It was liberating and intoxicating at the same time. I became aware of my sexual energy and how it's a power I could use if I wished. I discovered that Goddesses emerge out of being loved and worshipped. In owning the power given by love's gaze, I became capable of transforming my boyish athletic body into its physical feminine appeal whenever I desired.

However, not all relationships help us bloom when we're in them — some teach us to grow from out of darkness. My last relationship lacked the doting and adoration I experienced in previous ones. At the beginning, I enjoyed the freedom that someone was not possessive or wanting to own me. Over time, the deprivation of attention became more like neglect. From the lack of love and attention, my spirit began to die and, along with it, the relationship began to wither. I continued to love and remained hopeful, as we had two children together. But feeling alone in the relationship was much worse than being alone on my own. I had to end it to preserve my spirit and integrity.

I was once rigid and extremely judgmental of people who committed infidelity. But now, I can comprehend why people would have affairs or end their engagement. The lack of intimacy, touch, connection, and attention from your partner, the person who's to be your source of soul food, can leave you feeling malnourished. Being love starved by neglect creates a hunger, that the urge to indulge and binge, like on junk food, just to fill the void, is something I can understand. Whether unfaithfulness is perpetrated by the body, mind, or heart, it's to escape the unfulfillment and impoverishment of the spirit from the absence of passion, love, and affection.

Sorting through the aftermath of the breakup, I began to piece together how I was responsible for my reality. It was an awakening to realize my first experience of neglect occurred in childhood. The feelings resembled how I felt with my father, that he hadn't taken care of me. So I became strong and independent. I evolved into a woman who didn't need anyone. I couldn't be vulnerable. I wanted to be loved, but I also decided I didn't need someone to take care of me, even though deep down inside I craved it.

I was able to give, but not receive. Love is attention and care. I didn't allow men the pleasure to take care of me, nor give them the opportunity for their purpose to be the giver, the provider. I made men feel unneeded. My strengths were now my weaknesses. I was lopsided. Like in a child's mind, I saw things as black and white, that *only* one thing is good; that *only* boys are good and worthy; that *only* independence is good and worthy. I was unaware of the alchemy within the duality of polar opposites. I didn't understand the balance of feminine and masculine qualities. That neither is good nor bad, nature doesn't cast such evaluations, they are just the visible parts of the whole. It's holding the two polarities without judgment that the right balance can be found.

My life began to make sense as I revisited the past. I was fascinated to see that things didn't happen by chance. The awkwardness I felt in trying to own and understand my femininity came from not knowing what I possessed. My feminine power was a double-edged sword for me; it held a power I sensed but at the same time was afraid to wield. Embracing the Goddess within is acknowledging I'm worthy of attention, of being loved, and worshipped. Loving and worshiping myself allows others to have the opportunity to love and worship me. As I continue to worship myself, others are invited to do so, helping to build the ripple effect of expansion felt within myself.

As for the love of a boy I wanted, I have that today, my son, who continues to teach me to love and be loved. Plus I have the love of a girl, my daughter. I understand they are different, neither one is good nor bad, or better. Preferring a male child over a female child is an oversight in not grasping the immense power and miracle of the woman's body to create life and give birth. We unknowingly devalue one thing over another out of ignorance and misunderstand their true, unique individual worth and gift. Our judgments, in favoring one thing over another, deprive us from seeing the secrets within the dualistic nature of all things. When we claim all the parts we are, we make ourselves whole, the way we're meant to be and experience the fullness of ourselves.

Embracing your inner Goddess is about owning your power. You give away your power by needing the approval and validation of others. Resist being made into the image of what others want you to be. When you accept and love yourself, you teach people how to accept and love you. Be worthy of attention. Allow yourself to be seen and heard. For someone to have power over you, you have to give it to them. Power is given, not taken. You have power; start granting it to yourself. Know that you are naturally gifted with treasures. Claim all the things you want to be yours. You're whole and complete as you are. Allow yourself to shine!

IGNITE ACTION STEPS

Being a Goddess is about having unwavering, unconditional love and acceptance of yourself. You are in an eternal love affair, a love story with you. Start by being kind and good to *yourself*. Do whatever it takes to have that kind of relationship with *you*. Develop compassion. It begins with forgiveness, forgiving all the transgressions and mistreatments you directed at yourself for comparing and judging who you are. Observe the way you judge or criticize others; it's a clue to becoming conscious of how you may be inflicting judgment and criticism upon yourself. Aim to understand the whole picture.

Self Love:

Mirror work: hold yourself in love's gaze. Look at yourself lovingly in the mirror and say all the things you want someone who loves you to say to you. Learn to adore yourself, pleasure yourself, make yourself look beautiful to please you, you don't have to look good only for others. You have to be the first one to love who you are, otherwise you'll be at the mercy of what others' capabilities are to love you.

Self Acceptance:

We are all beautifully flawed. See your beauty. Beauty doesn't have to come from the outside. Don't compare yourself to anyone else; there's only one of you. Accept all your imperfections, especially the physical parts — love the unlovable. There's a power in seeing beauty in the ugliness we once thought. We're all a work in progress. We're always expanding, discovering, and defining ourselves.

Embrace Duality:

The secrets of the Universe will unfold before you when you allow the presence of duality to linger within your awareness. This just means to resist jumping to conclusions, biases, and absolutes in your thinking. Seeing only one aspect of the whole is shortsighted. There's natural duality in all things and a spectrum that spans between the two polar opposites. This gives us variety and balance. Learn to be still and not make judgments. You'll come to see your wholeness already exists within you when you do.

Own it:

Being a woman is a magical gift, like possessing the subtle resiliency of water. Be fierce and courageous in owning this power. Learn to understand it. Be patient. You embody the dichotomy of all forms; be playful and claim them as you like them to be yours. They can be your innocence and wisdom, your strengths and vulnerabilities, your toughness and softness. Be flexible, yet firm and versatile. This ability of holding different energies together will let you into the secrets and power of being a woman and a Goddess.

Yendre Shen – Canada
Naturopathic Doctor, Inner Guidance Mentor
www.InnerGuidance.ca

BELIEVE

MAYSSAM MOUNIR, MD

"Build your Queendom and name yourself The Queen."

Repeat after me, *"Take me Goddess, throw your wisdom upon me. Allow me to learn from you how to trust and let go. How to surrender to YOUR flow."* Here's my wish for you: Rest well assured, you're on a magical journey to Heaven! Believe that, live that, and stop entertaining your worries. My hope for you, sister, is *ease, joy,* and *flow.* Take a deep breath in, and follow me.

ASK, BELIEVE, RECEIVE.

I woke up shocked, the echo of the words were replaying in my head: *To align with the Goddess, you have to align with everything she is.*

She's the lionesses of the wild, fierce and strong. Yet she's the most loving expression that could ever be. She chooses herself and chooses everyone else at the same time — some call it multitasking. Others call it mother's love. The kind of love that gives everyone an equal share. She's the warmth of the womb. The safety and the support. She's the teacher and the way. She's the flow of the river, and she's the beauty of nature — everything alive and flourishing. She's as light as a breeze and as powerful as a volcano that's known to build up new grounds. She's the daughter, the son, the mother, the father, the sister, the brother, the lover, and the friend. She's a Goddess with so many faces but only one essence: Love and Evolution. She is ferocious, savage, and untamed. A fiery hug of a loving expression.

I wrote down those words right away. Then I prayed, "Take my hand as I clear space, purify and detox. Minimize and let go of what's not important so other important things *grow*. Help me focus where it is needed. Cut off my cords of attachment. Be my aid as I make space for you, my Goddess. Help me stand rooted and tall beyond riches, power, and fame. Liberated from all forms and beyond what is manifested." I was twenty-two years young, longing to have the Goddess actualized in all ways possible, but I didn't know how!

I looked back to my journey and recalled; I grew up with strength, faith, and lots of love. I was raised by two super women! My grandma, Fatima, was a scholar and a fighter in an age where women were not socially welcomed in schools and definitely not in higher education. Still, my grandma was one of the first females who graduated from university in Damascus, Syria. Even when protestors were throwing acid on her clothes as she entered the campus, hoping to hit her skin as a way to stop her from attending classes. Fatima held her ground and ended up with not only one but three university degrees. She spent her life living independently, traveling the region, visiting countries and schools to teach teachers and support them in providing education to children. That woman, as majestic as a mountain, was my babysitter. The one who sang me to sleep at night and empowered me every day. She told me over and over again, "You can do whatever you want and be whomever you choose. A real woman always chooses herself and creates life on her terms." I was very young to understand her powerful teachings of resilience and grit. But Fatima, my great teacher, repeated her praise and showed her love enough times to have that planted to flourish later in my life.

My other grandma was a wild woman of nature; the one who had herbs, teas, and the garden. Her name was Wared, which translates to 'roses'. She was the one connected to angels and saints. They never turned her down and always were there to support her in whatever she asked. One morning while we were collecting parsley from the garden to make tabbouleh, a traditional Lebanese salad, she shared, "It's all about faith. Trust and ask for what you want. Learn to become quiet, connect to your heart, and seek help in what-ever you need, from within. This is like planting your desires as seeds in the fertile ground of the creative consciousness; water them with trust and loving attention. If you plant good seeds in good soil, and take care of them with love and support, the seeds will always grow in the right timing. You will never be disappointed."

I worried that I might not have enough patience to wait for those seeds to grow — like all kids, I wanted everything now. "I can't wait," I objected, and asked her if I could speed up the process. She affirmed that 'natural unfolding' needs to take place. "You can't rush a seed to grow, but rest assured, it will in the right time and space." I felt like she might not really understand how it all worked, and there must be a shortcut. Like my other grandmother's teachings, it took many years for her wisdom to bloom within me.

Fatima and Wared were of different religions, countries, habits, and backgrounds, but both celebrated *all* beings from *all* walks of life. Love was the ground we all stood on, welcoming and gathering everyone — no separation. *I flourished in their unity.*

When I was 12 years old and going to school in Damascus, I realized for the first time how strong my belief systems were. It started with my school principal asking me to determine and define my religious beliefs and clarify the system I followed. "What? Why!?" I wondered. Teen blood raced into my head leaving my skin cold and pale as I stood in her gray painted, badly lit, small office. I was puzzled — trying to search my brain for an answer that would satisfy her curiosity. This felt beyond my capabilities. She stressed, "What does your family celebrate?" I responded, "Everything!" She waited impatiently for me to articulate an answer that would please her; however, I couldn't really understand what this answer should sound or look like. Why would I have to choose? I believed in unity and love. I focused on the essence, the oneness of the teachings. What I cared about was the practice, regardless which religion the message came from. I discovered that my strong mind refused the pressure that was being applied by the principal. I understood in a new way how deeply rooted I was to myself and to my family.

I sat in my room that afternoon, reflecting on what had happened. Shiny beams of sunlight touched my face and wrapped my body in warmth and ease. I closed my eyes and dissolved in the light allowing the presence of God, Life, and Energy to shower me with loving support. I felt myself merge with the light, the breeze, and the sounds of people having a conversation in the street underneath my window. A burst of loud laughter brought me back into my body. I was holding onto my pen as my diary was still open. I wrote down, "I feel like a boat in the middle of an ocean; wherever I look there's only water around. Which way should I go?" Grounded in my faith, I affirmed, "Wherever I go, God is my destination and everything is aligning to lead me there. I am never lost and can never go astray. I'm on a magical way to heaven. I don't need to be boxed or labeled. No matter what, as long as love is in my heart,

I'm always free." That was when my heart spoke the loudest... it has been my guide ever since.

I felt both powerful and spiritually supported. I knew that I could break away from any norm and let go of any idea that didn't nurture my evolution, even if the whole world didn't agree. I committed to allowing people the freedom to be who they choose to be, and gave myself permission to freely be who I want to be. While falling asleep that night, I felt the Goddess's fires burning bright, inviting me to throw in everything! *"Surrender your life. You're loved and guided!"*

Years passed and right before I graduated from medical school, life aligned so I learned and practiced energy medicine. This opened the door into the non-physical part of existence — everything is energy first; that's our true nature. We are plugged into a stream of vital life force energy that we can activate and receive. No need for aids or mediums here. It's a powerful, direct connection.

During this same time, my teacher gave me a book entitled *Conversations with God.* The book supported the idea of this direct flow and connection. Reading through the first pages, I was inspired! An idea popped up, a desire to get my own downloads and have my own conversation with God. Clear and direct! I knew to do so I had to let go of everything I knew. I had to open up and experience the *Unknown.* Following the steps of Mikao Usui, the master who gave birth to Reiki Energy Healing, I embarked on a twenty-one-day silent retreat hoping like him to have my 'Satori' — awakening — by the end of the journey.

This was in the days before meditation became mainstream and retreats popped up everywhere. I had no idea what a silent retreat would be, but I had one focus: to be receptive and listening so I could hear the messages. I didn't know what messages were awaiting me; I just knew that knowledge was there and I wanted to make myself open to receive guidance. To fulfill my vision clearly, I couldn't be occupied and busy with mental chatter or outside knowledge even from the best books. Those books were someone else's download and I had become inspired to receive my own.

I left my books, laptop, phone, and other means of input and knowledge at home as I moved out of Damascus into a monastery that was recommended by a friend. The place was located in nature near the city of Homs, far away from busy urban life. The prayer hall was designed carefully as a sacred geometrical octagon with a huge dome in the middle. Windows with colored glass were on every wall allowing light beams of different colors to magically dance in the space. The place was intentionally created to welcome people from any religion under the name 'The Earth.'

Like the Buddha under the tree in Bodhgaya, I simply sat in silent contemplation. Patiently observing and meditating on my Being, my Body, my Mind, and my Chakras (the energy centers and the conjunction points between the physical body and the spiritual/energy world). I had no agenda or frame of work. I simply trusted. I knew that the quieter I was, the better I could hear.

And that is what I did.

My vision was realized. While connected to the 'Akash', the collective mind and life's energy, I felt awakened and alive. I've realized that wisdom in every moment is cognized by the connection to the True Self. Wayne Dyer teaches that, "We are spiritual beings having a human experience," (wise words first uttered by Pierre Teilhard de Chardin). Yet this recognition becomes lost when the mind is busy and distracted with the perceptions of life. False beliefs take up space. I now understood that before my meditation retreat I had been struggling and pushing instead of flowing with life's wisdom. Many times, falling under the effect of the 'fight and flight' trap. Burning up in reactivity, instead, of responsiveness. Wasting my time and energy.

When I returned home after 21 days of meditation and solitude, I observed my home, with new eyes, then noticed the things that were there. Things that reflected my life and the times I had fallen into the illusion of the need to accumulate — whether it was material possessions, knowledge, or personal connections. I had disconnected from the truth that everything I really need is right here and now, preserved in my Being, forgetting my Grandma's teaching: *Ask, Believe, Receive.* I had run through life searching for meaning, trying to understand, what *is* my purpose? I had forgotten that my Being is intact and my purpose is actualizing in every breath, as my heart beats, my hair and nails grow. I am not trying to Be. I *am.* Always have been.

On that day, I promised myself that I will always choose joy, fulfillment, and love. Anything less in vibration has to go. I decided that I will always tune into love as I trust my abundance and my journey. Life is given to me and I will appreciate it by nurturing it and giving back. I called upon her once again, the Goddess of form and transform, the womb of creation and the dance of the cosmos. I asked her to help me keep rising into higher frequencies of love. To tune everything in my life into passion and contentment. To help me serve and ignite.

I put my life under the magnifying lens, corner by corner, drawer by drawer, item by item, and habit by habit. I realized every moment counts, and each action counts. I organized, decluttered, and cleared out my space. I detoxed my body and built a healthy nurturing and energetic lifestyle. I asked through clear intentions for what I wanted. Dreamed big. Committed to take conscious actions. Give back. Never taking a moment for granted. Always trusting the journey.

During my decluttering, while reflecting, it hit me, all my desires and intentions had been realized! Over the years I had the habit of writing down to-do lists and desires. That day, I read everything. I couldn't believe my eyes. My tears ran down in gratitude as I realized how every wish was fulfilled. Many of these had been forgotten as some were very subtle, while others had time and stories taking place between the moment of intention and the moment of fulfillment.

While sitting on the red carpet in my bedroom, with piles of papers and many notebooks scattered around, the world was still. I was no longer aware of the music playing in the background, or the teapot boiling in the kitchen. There was no more desire or anticipation. At that moment I was free of attachment, with no fear or illusions. I had learned to believe in mySelf 'with the capital S' to fuel my own light; and trust in the journey *and* my destination. I surrender only to love, allowing everything to be done with love. I was at peace. The Goddess in me was recognized. We had merged.

Since then, day in and day out, I tend to the fire of my Soul. I fuel it with passion, inspiration, power, creativity, love. I practice active gratitude and cherish my life. I'm always grateful to be alive and attentive to my life. I tend to my body and nourish it with love. I practice healing touch and self-massage with lots of oils for grounding and support. I eat well, I sleep well, and I drink lots of water. I keep my space clean, clear, and tidy. I love simplicity and minimalism. I take care of accumulated stuff and keep my space organized. My space is a reflection of my state of mind. I meditate daily and keep my mind strong, sharp, and focused. To create life on my terms, I write my intentions; I support that with action, then trust that my life is unfolding perfectly.

This has allowed me a life beyond my wildest dreams. Regardless of what's going on around me, I am connected to the eternal peace within. This connection is giving me joy and happiness, no matter what. I have unfathomable trust in my journey. I am assured and supported every step on the path. I am always aligned, grateful, and invite more of these experiences, as it is given.

The Goddess energy is provided for us in every single moment. It is given to charge and uplift your life. In this energy, there are the secrets of Being. Focus on this minute. Are you in a peaceful mindset? How can you make your life full? Go back to the basics of the body and align with the physiology of your natural joyful state. Take care of yourself, have courage to follow your dreams and be at your best. Life will take care of you.

IGNITE ACTION STEPS

The knowledge and wisdom of the Universe are accessible to the quiet mind. To step out of reactivity and tune in, you need to focus on the basics: *Ask, Believe, Receive.*

- Start by taking a deeper, longer, slower breath in. This will activate the parasympathetic nervous system, which will promote you with feelings of peace.
- Tune your mind to gratitude. Count your blessings and write them down. Receive the gift of being alive; it is a miracle we take for granted daily.
- Connect with natural rhythms, essence of nature. Look up and contemplate the sky.
- Massage your body and contemplate its wisdom. Shower your Goddess with Love. Look in the mirror and appreciate your creation.
- Never entertain your worries, trust in the bigger plan. Focus on what is working.
- Have the courage to create life on your terms and believe in yourSelf.
- Acknowledge your desires and intentions.
- Eat energetically-charged food, full of Pranic energy 'life force.'
- Sleep well, meditate on a daily basis. Seek your higher Self and ask for guidance. Merge with your light.

Trust that your life is going perfectly according to your intentions. Focus on what you are doing and embrace your decisions. When you plant desires with care and nourish, they will flourish.

Love,
Mayssam

Mayssam Mounir – Lebanon
Medical Doctor, Ayurvedic LifeStyle Expert, Yoga & Meditation Instructor,
Energy Master Healer
www.doctormiso.com/awaken-your-goddess-challenge

VIRTUE

Activating the Goddess
SHARING FROM AN EXPERT

Rev. Priestess Anandha Ray, MA, DTR

"Within each person is the Goddess energy that can propel us into the richness and totality of living life fully."

'Activating the Goddess within' might sound like a fanciful idea, or it might sound absolutely enticing depending on your previous experiences. No matter where you begin your journey in relation to the Goddess, almost everyone has an understanding that there is a source of divinity within. You may feel disconnected from it or it may be the lifesource of your daily decision-making. This essence is readily available in the quiet moments, when the mind stills and you become open to the tapestry that is the fullness of your true self.

Regaining that connection is a process of choice. You have to let go of your ego attachment. There's this block between you and your inner self — the block is created by the experiences, traumas, and belief systems that have been imposed on you. You can cut through those belief systems and your attachment to what is 'right' in order to find what is true and what is real for you. You *choose*, in that moment, to become connected to the energy deep within you. It's always a choice.

With the busyness of life, we often unconsciously choose to disconnect from the truth of who we are. We get caught up in the traffic and noise of day-to-day life and lose track of the sacred inner energies that can inspire us. Activating this inner source of sacred awareness is a pathway to reconnect to the *being* that was born pure in this world, the most pure expression of you. *This* is the Goddess within. She is the purest sense of your feminine self. And when you connect with 'Her,' it becomes progressively easier to recognize how the miniscule choices you make each day, how you speak and act, creates You. This idea of connecting with the Goddess is one way of framing a journey to become the best version of who you were born to be. Visualizing and giving voice to the feminine energies within you can remove the veils that separate you from yourself. Such inner work allows you to recognize and reprogram faulty subconscious beliefs that sabotage you. It can guide you, from within, to make choices and live your life from the energy of the Goddess.

I invite you to take a moment to take a journey out of your conscious reality and into the space where the Goddess lives. This is a place without words. Step into your prehistoric self from a time before language. This is a place of images and feelings. Sit comfortably. Twist and stretch any areas of the body that feel tense or uncomfortable to find an inner knowing. Get really quiet. Stop... the... thinking... mind. Let go of any thoughts that are words. Sink your awareness deep within. Allow your body to feel any physical sensations that are present. Welcome any images that come into your awareness. See them without naming them. Notice what sensations wash over you and through you. Separate from the thinking mind and enter into this place of 'Silent Knowing.'

Is there perhaps a spinning feeling? Maybe something heavy or light. Maybe there is pain or comfort that stirs. Follow that feeling — deepen your understanding of the feelings and images that have arisen. Now look deeper again. What is in the middle of these feelings? Can you sense a space inside the body where these feelings begin? This space is a place of *centeredness*; it is the middle place of all the feelings that are present. This is where the Goddess lives. From here, you can awaken Her. It takes practice to tune in and find Her, but She is always there. This centeredness falls beyond our ego. Ego is not you. Ego can be a driving force and can serve you well, but it is not you. Nor are your thoughts. There are many thoughts in your mind at any given moment and you can choose which ones to focus upon. You are separate from your thoughts. You are the one who is thinking those thoughts. Your thoughts are not immutable. You were not born with them. They change constantly. So, too, does your personality. Your personality is continually shifting. By changing your thoughts you can change your actions and words and refine your personality.

In this space where the energy of the Goddess resides, there is a great empowerment and opportunity to become a more full expression of the truth of *You*. It is a collaborative space. One where your most deeply held beliefs communicate with Universal energies and inspire you to have an entirely new conversation with your most fragile and powerful self. I speak of this space as if it is conscious, as if the Goddess Herself speaks back to us. I truly believe She does. This space exists in a physical realm. The emptiness between the cells of the human body mirrors the vastness of the void found between all the stars of the Universe. In these spaces, it is thought consciousness might hail. Scientists are not yet sure where in the body our consciousness is grounded. Some, those of the panpsychism school of research, believe that the space between the stars holds a consciousness of its own, as do all living creatures, including ourselves. These spaces within, between our own cells, this inner mirror of the Universe, is the place of Universal energy. This is the Goddess energy.

Activating the Goddess Within is a homecoming to your personal, unfettered connection to source your own divinity. It is the pure expression of balance between your feminine and masculine power. The universal Goddess energy is just waiting to be called into action. While some people refer to manifestations of specific Goddesses when they activate the Goddess within, one can also activate this "Goddess energy," rather than a particular Goddess. The 'She' that is the Goddess is the energy of the ALL, a Universal force that is alive within each of us. It is "She" who guides your awareness as you deepen an understanding of the ambiguities of life.

Embracing the goddess within is slightly different than dedicating your service to *a particular* goddess. Historically, gods and goddesses were deities that some believed were living gods who walked the Earth. Others believe they were perhaps aliens who visited the planet in ancient times, their advanced technology appearing to be super powers to the humans then. Still others believe gods and goddesses were humans of exemplary character who stood out among their peers and, over countless retellings, became the character of a god in the verbal passing of the stories. Whether you believe they are real or merely a symbolic representation, they are meant to inspire.

Connecting to your goddess energy has a quality of awakening your own potential, and utilizing this energy to overcome your personal challenges allows you to become the best version of yourself. To dedicate yourself to a particular Goddess can be a means of stepping outside of the ego and into the guidance of a preconceived energy that you wish to foster.

When you are connected with the goddess energy, you are walking in grace even in your most ungraceful moments. You understand how to suffer the wounds of our humanness without suffering. You celebrate every joyful moment of life without boastfulness or pride. Many engage this goddess energy to find a living grace that permits them to embrace the fullness of life's ups and downs while remaining at peace. They use it to engage and value both the shadows and the light. Developing the tools to remain connected to the spirit of resplendent grace no matter what life presents is a process that takes time and practice. It is the hallowed awareness that *you are enough.*

There are many paths to activating the Goddess. The paths are as various as the personalities and needs of every reader who picks up this book. For me the path of the goddess was first present through a lifetime of dance as an expression of the embodiment of being human. Upon retirement from that career, my connection to the goddess became much more literal as it deepened into a life of service as an ordained Reverend Priestess of the Goddess Isis. I developed a year-long initiation journey in which initiates walk a path to shed the illusions that have been endlessly programmed into their belief systems. As these illusions unwind to the core, they deepen their connection with their own values, beliefs, passions, and ethics — reconnecting with who they were born to become. What is important is that you find YOUR path. Disengage from the thinking mind. When you begin to understand that whatever you know, you know nothing, then you are on the path of activation.

For most humans on the planet, our connection to the Goddess has been veiled. As we grow up in society, community, and family, we are influenced by the beliefs, values, morals, concerns, issues, and demands of those around us. We form an expression of who we will become based on the environment in which we live. This can hinder the full expression of 'you' or it can expand who you become. The first creates dissatisfaction with life. If your inner voice is not in alignment with the beliefs you were raised within, you will forever feel disconnected. This path of remembering returns you to who you were born to become and this 'becoming' allows you to remove that veil of illusion.

The path of the goddess embraces no dogma as a source of truth; rather, awakening the Goddess is something that my temple, the Temple of the Goddess Isis, refers to as a catma; it is a process of finding your own path in the world. Your service. Your values. Your connection to the divine grace of Life.

To activate the Modern Goddess is a powerful process of choosing the pathway that allows you to become the best version of yourself. It requires practice and daily commitment. It requires discernment to choose the expression of this pathway that best suits you.

It is critical to become aware of the thinking mind and to unlock the programming that keeps us separated from a consciousness of the bigger picture of life. When you have a close call with death, for example, you might naturally find yourself aware of the vastness of being. Thereafter, you become less attached to the thoughts, issues, and busyness of the mind. When you let go of the ego, you live bigger.

There's more to life than we can perceive when we are thinking in a limited way and the whole point is to let go of the limitations of thought… a balanced and peaceful way to live in your full empowerment.

Notice what it is that your mind focuses upon. Observe the inner working of your thoughts as though someone else is thinking them. Which thoughts require more of your energy? Which thoughts evoke heightened states of emotion? Which make you feel off balance and which make you feel centered? Life reveals itself more fully when you linger on the positive.

When you witness your thoughts without being attached to what they are, you can become more objective in how you respond to situations, making conscious choices about how you wish to behave rather than reacting, guided by emotions not in your control. Some people will say, "It's just my personality to be _____ (jealous, pessimistic, whatever); I can't help it." But that is never true. Our personality, our way of being, is something that we are constantly choosing. Once we realize this, we can make the choice to choose differently. Being mindful is the first step.

That balanced place of observing the world and responding with your full capacity of emotional reaction in the ways that your centered mind chooses *is* the Goddess energy. The more you practice noticing your thoughts, the more your thinking will expand to be aware of other facets of life that your previous biased interpretations caused to be invisible. That expansive covenant with Life will create greater satisfaction, deeper relationships, and immense creative flow in your life.

You will each find your own way to activate the Goddess within, and then find your own rituals, ceremonies, and methods to stay connected on a daily basis. In my awakening, I use a set of tools to help me remember to keep my mind and heart open. My goal is to detach from the illusions of the thinking mind, to remain open for a wide variety of perceptions, thus creating greater opportunities for living life well and in fullness. This is a tool that allows us all to become a pure vessel, able to remain connected to that Universal energy of truth, the energy of the Goddess. A tool to live life fully in the way of the Goddess, as the best version of our Self.

I invite you to shift your covenant with your true Spirit. To connect with your Modern Goddess. Below is a practical activation you can try right now. It is a tool to quiet the thinking mind and allow the voice of the Goddess to be heard.

The tool of THANK YOU.

Some interpret this as an attitude of gratitude… this is *not* that.

This 'Thank You' tool activates the 'Goddess super power' of clear thinking. It delays triggers that might cause internal dissonance, an imbalanced emotional reaction based on biased interpretations and judgments. Simultaneously, it calls forth a deep sense of ease even in difficult situations. It is the embodiment of balanced thinking, allowing you to remain objective and respond from a personification of your best self. And it engages the energy of the Modern Goddess.

For example, when someone gives you unwanted advice or when they bring to you an awareness that is difficult to hear, pause before you reply. Let's say your spouse reminds you not to talk with your mouth full. Your face heats with a flood of embarrassment and annoyance and your instinctive response may not be kind. Pause. Notice the triggers that are present. Take a breath to calm the voice. Then, in the calm, you can respond, "Thank you."

It might seem counterintuitive, but it is really important to thank someone when you find yourself triggered by them. Be mindful of your tone of voice. Let sarcasm and anger give way to compassionate response and genuine connection. The moment you are flooded by emotion and feel you are triggered, THIS is a moment for the tool of 'Thank you.'

Next, offer compassion. Notice if this was something that might have been difficult for them to tell you, "That must have taken courage to bring to my attention." Or, offer a benefit-of-the-doubt moment. Notice a positive intention behind the words that triggered you and speak to it, "I appreciate that you are trying to help me."

These two actions, *Thank you* and *Compassion*, will change the course of your relationships. You may find that through focusing on the perception that allows you to say thank you and offer compassion, the compelling and seductive force of your negative emotions dissipates altogether. In staying balanced and calm in a situation that might have otherwise gone awry, you wield the force of goddess energy in the discernment of your words and the focus of your energy. Even if at first it was just 'planned word tools' that you used to deactivate the triggering moment, you may be able to tune into genuine appreciation and activate the Goddess energy, filling your response with the grace of a life well lived.

Activating the Goddess within isn't something you do once. Nor is it something you do sometimes. It is a state of being… a way of making choices as you navigate every aspect of life. As you create and enhance your practice of living with the activated state of goddess energy, may you remember your 'unnamed self' as you shed the mind illusions that have fractured the prism of your lens of the world and that no longer serve you. May you find balance in the nature of Life. May you be at peace in the shadows and in the light. May you find the calm fierceness of birthing the fullness of who you were meant to become.

We are all on a path of emerging, unfolding, becoming. The stories in this book serve as a bridge that might assist you to discover paths to reconnect to your divinity, your purpose, your authentic totality of being. Within this book there are examples of many tools to align more closely to the truth of your 'becoming.' May the stories presented within Ignite your path and create a feeling of support to activate the Goddess energy in your life, on your terms, and in your way.

Rev. Priestess Anandha Ray, MA, MA DTR – United States of America
Master Teacher, Choreographer, Cultural Ambassador
www.anandharay.com

RESILIENCE

Katarina Amadora

"Stepping into the biggest version of you sometimes means walking through fire; may you do so fearlessly."

It is my intention that all who read these words will understand that they have the power to tune into their own inner guidance. Sometimes things in your world may feel like they are spiraling out of control, yet there is a Divine presence watching over you. Trust in the guidance of your Higher Self and you will find sure footing once again.

Walking Through Fire

October 8, 2017. I will always remember the night I was ordained as a Priestess of Isis. I was the first among my *sisters* to be called to the stage. I stepped up in my long white flowing Melodia robes and found myself standing in front of the High Priestess. Behind her was the altar of Isis, the ancient Egyptian Mother Goddess, who rules over life and magic, protector of women and children, healer of the sick. In my hands, I held my Book of Shadows, my Athame and my crown. I handed them to the priestesses standing on either side.

The High Priestess raised her right hand and placed it on top of my head. *"In the name of Isis, Goddess of Ten Thousand names, Patroness of this Temple, Mother of All, Great Goddess, bring your light and your love into this beautiful Priestess, for she is your Priestess. Let it be,"* she intoned as my mentor and two other priestesses looked on. She continued… *"The current that is within you, the current that joins us all heart to heart, the current that infuses every priest and priestess that serves in the name of Isis.*" I felt a charge pulsing up through my spine as I breathed in her blessing. She turned around and picked up a bottle of sacred oil from the altar, then asked me which deities I had chosen to serve. "*Isis, Sekhmet, and Wadjet*," I replied.

She dipped her finger in the sacred oil and brought her hand to my forehead. "*In the name of Isis, Sekhmet, and Wadjet, I anoint thy brow,*" she proclaimed. "*May you receive the gift of true vision.*" She dipped her finger in the oil again and anointed my heart. My mentor Anandha's gaze was proud and radiant. "*In the name of Isis, Sekhmet, and Wadjet, I consecrate thy heart.*" Finally, she finished the ritual by applying the oil to my hands. "*In the name of Isis, Sekhmet, and Wadjet, I anoint thy hands.*" She took a silver necklace from the altar and placed it around my neck. "With this Sacred Collar, I hallow thy heart." She turned to accept a headpiece from the priestess on her right. "*With this crown, I dignify thy head.*" Then she took the Athame from the priestess on her left and handed it to me. "*With this wand, I strengthen thy will.*" With that, I was ordained a Priestess of Isis at Isis Oasis in Geyserville, north of San Francisco, on one of the strangest and most powerful nights of my life. "*Your first public act as a Priestess is to bestow a blessing on all those assembled,*" the High Priestess conveyed as she concluded the ordination ceremony.

Nervously, I turned around to face the full hall at the Temple of Isis. "*May each of you walk along your path*," I began after a few moments of silence. "*Feeling all the way down into your toes. Totally in your body. And be present in every moment, enjoying the beauty, the joy, the sorrow — all of the emotions, as you go upon your way. Bless you all.*"

At the moment I spoke those words, none of us had any idea how much my blessings and those of the other dozen priestesses who were ordained that night were needed. Little did any of us know that during the ceremony, dozens of wildfires had been sparked and were just beginning to rage out of control in Northern California. At that moment, we were blissfully unaware of what was beginning to unfold all around us.

That night came to be known as the Northern California Firestorm. For me, it followed a week-long Shamanic Retreat where my sisters and I had been delving deeply into what it meant to be in service to the Temple as a Priestess of Isis. Together, we had walked this path of deep inquiry for a year and a day, since declaring our intention the previous October. Together we had studied, danced, faced challenges, learned about ourselves and each other, and grown as sisters. We had created a sacred container where all emotions and experiences were welcomed, but where we were also held to a higher standard of conduct. It mattered whether I showed up in Integrity, ready to do the work. Each of us had a vital role in creating this container and in supporting each other. Through our months of training... we learned to walk in the world in a different way. Time and again, we came up against resistance and learned to move past it. We created amazing art and we dove deeply into explorations of our individual and collective subconscious through ceremony and movement.

I remember getting dressed that night in our Priestess whites as we always did for Ceremony. We each did our makeup, helping each other to create the dramatic Egyptian eyes and the white line of Quimera down the center of each face. This line symbolized stepping into the path of non-duality. This principle had been important, not only in my path as a Priestess, but also in my Tantric path.

I was excited that I had two friends who were driving up from the Bay Area to witness my Ordination. It felt good that people who I cared about were willing to drive over an hour to be with me and to witness this moment. I was so grateful to be there with my sacred sisters who had shared this journey — the five other women who had accepted me for who I was with all my flaws. Together, we had seen each other through many challenges as we faced our shadows and our fears. I felt so grateful for Eden, a Senior Priestess who had assisted in our training, as well as the new friends who were just stepping up to walk the path of initiation and others still in their year of training.

As we gathered in the Temple that night, the glow of candles on the altar illuminated the figure of Isis in the center. A bust of Sekhmet with her dish of wine sat in front of the altar. Many other Deities were represented in sculptures throughout the Temple. Nervous energy ran through me as people gathered for this rite of passage. I had butterflies in my stomach as I waited and watched for my friends to arrive. A sense of relief and gratitude washed over me when I saw them across the room. It felt so good to hug them, knowing they were here for me.

As everyone settled into their chairs and the High Priestess began the Ceremony, I reflected upon the blessing that I was to offer to the assembled Community... my first act as an Ordained Priestess. I felt a tingle of excitement, wondering if the right words would come to me. So many months of preparation and anticipation were finally coming to an end, but this was really just the beginning of a much deeper and more meaningful path, as we each stepped into our own as full Priestesses of Isis.

The ceremony began as any other, until the mystical Rain Graves stood to speak. Rain is a High Priestess who had been a powerful influence during our training. She channelled Deities who held important messages for each of us. As she invoked the name of the Goddess Sekhmet, there was a sudden noise as two windows blew open and a loud wind filled the Temple. I suddenly felt the presence of Sekhmet, a powerful Egyptian deity who is half lion and half human and who embodies fierce compassion in the fires of transformation. Sekhmet's powerful presence had been felt by us many times in our year of training which is why I pledged to her.

After the Ceremony, we went down to the dining hall for a celebration. My friend Michael wanted to get back home and he left shortly after the ceremony. My other friend Kelly stayed to celebrate with us and left about 45 minutes later. When I checked my phone, I discovered a series of messages from Michael, "Holy shit! There's fire near Healdsburg. There's grass burning on both sides of the highway!" Then another, "You should see Santa Rosa, there is fire everywhere, it looks like the apocalypse!"

I immediately called Kelly and he reported the same thing — but what he described sounded even more horrific. Because Michael left early, he was able to get through and make it home safely to San Francisco. Based on their descriptions, I knew in my gut that Kelly would not get through. I urged him to turn back. They roused everyone from sleep, calling all to gather in the dining hall. Many were trying to get word from loved ones, to know whether they were safe. The air was thick with smoke and we could see the flames of what came to be called the Pocket Fire only eight miles away.

One of the other Priestesses who had been ordained with me was panicking. Her partner had been unable to come to the ordination and was in Santa Rosa, which we already knew had been hit badly. Most everyone had lost cell signal and she was ready to hop into her car to drive into the maelstrom to find him. I was one of the only persons with a working phone line. I was able to get her partner on the phone and he reassured her that he had already loaded the car and he was about to leave. As they talked, he suddenly said, "I've got to go babe. The house across the street just exploded!"

He was able to make it out of the area to a place of safety. He left his car and rode his bike back into the neighborhood, as houses burned all around him. He made it to their house, got down on his hands and knees, and prayed for their house to be spared. Somehow, he managed to make it out alive again. When he returned to their house the following day, it was the only structure within at least a mile radius that had not burned to the ground. It was no longer habitable, as it had been cut off from all utilities; however, they were able to salvage their possessions and even their cat survived.

If that is not a powerful Testament to prayer and to having a relationship with the Goddess, I don't know what is. It was a long, fearful night and I was grateful to have the support of my friend. He and Anandha both kept clear heads and they were sources of comfort and stabilizing presence as others were panicking. The following day, a few of the other priestesses managed to make it back to the Bay Area, but it took them over seven hours to make the 90-mile drive. Their GPS kept sending them down roads that ended in a wall of fire. Time after time, they had to turn back and find a different route.

We found out later that on that night, numerous fires had sparked simultaneously across Northern California... as transformers exploded and power lines were blown down by Diablo Winds which gusted up to 70 mph. Over 250 separate wildfires were ignited... 21 of which grew into major wildfires which burned over 250,000 acres throughout Napa, Sonoma, Butte, Mendocino, and Solano counties. The Tubbs Fire destroyed large regions of Santa Rosa and claimed at least 20 lives. The Pocket Fire started only 8 miles from where our Ordination took place, and we could see and smell the smoke growing stronger each day as it crept closer and closer. In all, 44 lives were lost and 10,000 firefighters were called in to battle the fires which were the most costly in California history.

I had to remain in Geyserville for three extra days because my electric car could not reliably make the trip with so many roads closed. Isis Oasis took in refugees from the fire and prepared for possible evacuation of the exotic animals and birds housed there. We could taste the acrid smoke in the air as we watched the nearby Pocket Fire come closer and closer, eventually only three to four miles away. There was a river between us and the fire, and we prayed that the fire would not jump to the other side. I am grateful for the miracles that kept my friends and me safe even as so much death and destruction raged all around us. Many were not so lucky. I believe that Sekhmet was warning us of the fires that night in the Temple... the disturbance came at virtually the same moment the fires first started, way too early for anyone to know what was coming.

One woman named Jamie lost everything except a few clothes and the collection of crystals that she was able to throw in her bag as she fled. She took up residence in the storage room behind the Temple and in the following year, she was moved to walk the Path of an Initiate as she navigated her own healing. She was Ordained exactly one year later with my sister Priestess Initiates. I will never forget when she spoke that night. Even now, recalling it, I am moved to tears. That evening, as she shared her harrowing escape, I felt such a reactivation of all the feelings that I had felt the year before. She spoke of how she had felt so broken, and how walking the path of an Initiate this year had allowed her to heal and to find gratitude in the face of it all. There was not a dry eye in the house as we viscerally relived what we had experienced the year before.

Sometimes I have been hesitant to introduce myself as a Priestess of Isis because I know that many do not understand what that means, and some have judged me for being too new-agey, too weird. I don't mention it to everyone because without the felt experience of the connection that I have to the mystical, most will not understand. And that is okay. I don't have to be liked by everyone and what others think of me is none of my business. I know that the path of growth I have been on has been long and convoluted, but every bit of that journey has been powerful and worthwhile. I am grateful for my sisters in Quimera and for our mentor, Anandha Ray. Although my healing path has taken me in new directions, I am grateful that it has brought me to where I am now.

I am eternally thankful for the training that has allowed me to walk in service to others and to see the broader perspective of what it means to live a life of service. We often get caught up in our own cares and concerns and we lose sight of the bigger picture. This can lead us off of our path as we get lost in our own fears and worries. We can lose sight of our purpose and why we are here. These Rites of Passage serve as important gateways in our lives, orienting us to what is important, and guiding us back to our path when we get lost. It is important to be seen, to be witnessed by our Tribe, and to be held accountable. This is something which has often been lacking in Western Society, and I think that it is important to recognize these Rites of Passage when they happen in your life or in the lives of others.

May you find your own healing path, no matter where it leads you. Say *yes* when your soul leads you to a teacher who can help you to be a better version of you. Learn to tune into your *Soul's Calling*. It will communicate with you in subtle and not-so-subtle ways. If you ignore its messages, it will get louder. The messages will become more insistent until they become a wake-up call. Listen carefully, let go of judgment, and say *Yes* to You. You are worth it. Even if the journey becomes uncomfortable, when you get to the other side, you will see that every step served a greater purpose and brought you closer to your true self.

Ignite Action Steps

Practice each day staying in your heart. Start with meditation, drop into that space, feel your connection with all that is. Ground deeply into your being, knowing that you are enough and you've got this. If you are looking for inspiration on a deep chakra meditation that can help you connect more deeply with your heart, I offer one on my website which you can download for free.

Once you are in your heart, focus on that still quiet space, knowing that the Universe is there to support you. Think about a decision and visualize how you would feel in the reality that would result from each choice. Let go of *how* you would get there and focus on what it would feel like to live in that reality. How does it feel in your body? Do you feel expansive, or is there contraction? Next, imagine what you would feel if you chose a different path, fully visualizing and feeling how this alternate reality would feel. Repeat this process for each option. How does each feel in your body? If one feels expansive, and the others cause contraction, you know that your soul is guiding you to choose that path. If all the options cause contraction, this means that you have not considered the correct choice. Ask yourself, "Am I thinking big enough?" "Is this choice in alignment with my higher purpose?" "What is my Why?"

Do not choose an option that causes contraction because this is a sign that you are not in alignment with your Soul's purpose. Your mind is a powerful servant but a poor master. Don't allow yourself to be deterred from your Soul's path because your monkey mind is telling you that you can't do it or that it is too hard. The Universe is here to support you. Tune into your heart and make the decision that feels aligned with it.

Katarina Amadora – United States of America
Holistic Health and Intimacy Coach
www.AmadoraTranformations.com
Medicine of Movement Podcast

VULNERABILITY

NOUR FAYAD

"The heart afraid of breaking will never have the courage to love."

My genuine wish for you is to have the courage to be yourself. To use desire as a compass for a fulfilled life. I wish for you to nurture your inner goddess, the part of yourself who loves you unconditionally and supports everything you are with love. Your goddess inspires you to dream, explore, go after what you want without fear. She guides you toward your best self without ever judging you and creates a safety net for you to explore anything you feel like exploring.

VULNERABILITY: MY ENEMY TURNED BEST FRIEND

My sobs are loud and so interrupted I can barely catch my breath. I'm sitting on the bathroom floor, my back leaning on the bathtub, hunched over and hugging my knees. The marble is cold and sends shivers up my spine. I have a genuine feeling my heart is about to shatter in my chest. I can feel the blood rush to my frontal lobe like thunder. Painfully powerful. Powerfully painful. I'm crying so hard and so loud I'm sure I sound like a wounded animal. And I am. I am filled with anger, sadness, and frustration. It's directed mostly at myself.

This is unlike me. I'm not an agitated person. I very rarely, if ever, get this upset. Actually, my friends and family would all describe me as 'zen' and 'colorful', but there and then on the bathroom floor of my ex-boyfriend's house in London following a huge fight between us, I couldn't recognize myself; I was drained of my colors.

I wasn't comfortable with how out of control the situation had become. The fight was just the tip of the iceberg for what was otherwise a mass of frustration piled up over the years.

I try to stand up, but my legs don't hear the order and a voice in my head makes me freeze. It's a voice I'd forgotten about, a voice all too familiar for it always brought up exciting possibilities… but at the same time lots of FEAR. And the voice keeps asking me, "So? How much more of this are you going to take? Have you not had enough?" I know too damn well this voice is my guts. It had been such a long time since I last heard it; I'd forgotten its tonality: firm, steady, confident.

The voice and all its confidence brought out the fear in me back to the surface. I had put myself in 'numb' mode for so long but now reality was catching up to me. And it hurt.

It is said that pain will only go away once it has taught you what you need to learn. It will come at you stronger every time until you face it, process it, go through it, and come out the other side victorious. So I wondered, was this the scenario that was playing out here? While I cut off the oxygen to my gut, how far away from myself had I gone? How far in the other direction had I wandered? Had my inner goddess abandoned me all this time? And more importantly, why?

I'm 29 years old, living in a city that doesn't feel like mine, with a man who is clearly not right for me. Nothing alarming, except this loop has been repeating itself for about 15 years. My life has mainly revolved around family, boyfriends, and jobs that felt safe. The choices that originally seemed like my own were made out of my need for safety. In fact, I had never put the time or effort to focus on anything that required courage and commitment, such as a career, choosing the right partner, or even investing in my health and self development. I was passive.

To understand how I came to the end of my rope, I probably have to take you back a few years and layers to when I was 14 and my dad passed away from lung cancer. Losing someone that is as much a part of your growth as a vital organ forces you to adapt. Each human being responds differently, but the main goal is to survive. Think of it like a train that suddenly loses its conductor, derails off the tracks, but keeps moving. All you are trying to do is not crash. In trying to stay on my own rails and retain some sort of sanity, I became numb. I fully embraced numbness.

Numbness kept me safe. It didn't require much effort or engagement from my end. It didn't take me on emotional rides. It didn't make my heart beat that loud and it certainly didn't require much effort or planning. It was easy.

Brenee Brown says, "Vulnerability is not winning or losing; it's having the courage to show up and be seen when we have no control over the outcome. Vulnerability is not weakness; it's our greatest measure of courage." I'm convinced now that when I was 14 years old, consciously or unconsciously, I decided to stop being vulnerable and as a consequence: courageous.

I believed for a long while that this lack of passion, this lack of emotion, freed me. I felt like a grain of dust going with the wind, not minding its direction. Having this freedom was exhilarating. But as time went by, deep in my loins, this 'freedom' started feeling aimless, flavorless, and anchorless, like that train with no direction that could crash at any point or like living your life with your entire being outside of your body. Unembodied. Disassociated from what is around you; from what is real.

But now, sitting on the bathroom floor with all this pain in my chest and a sudden rush of emotions, I'm introspecting: Perhaps numbing my heart was in fact a slow death killing me bit by bit rather than protecting me? Maybe all I ever wanted was to feel? As I write this, I want to shout it from the top of my lungs, "YES, FEEL!!!!" I know my inner goddess is cheering me on, eager for this internal revolution.

Your inner goddess is that part of yourself that loves you unconditionally and with zero judgment. She is the one who nudges you when you need to fly and catches you when you need to fall. She is the one who encourages you to try, to fail, to stand up again, and most importantly, to feel. Feelings! How liberating! How vital! How necessary!!! Feelings are so resourceful. I believe they lead the way to the answers we are looking for in life. They're the 'GPS to our soul,' as Oprah would say.

I've always liked feelings. They're the ones that make us shiver, imagine, dream! They're the triggers that make us dance, laugh, and cry! They're the emotions that bring us close to people who become friends and then family! Feelings are life, colors, and taste. They're what makes us humane, interesting, intriguing. Feelings are the extra sprinkle of magic, the zest. True, they can be overwhelming, but to judge, shut them down, and cut them off is a premature death, one that I had self-inflicted.

At this very thought, I snap out of my head and back into my painful reality. A wave of cold passes through me and in an epiphanic moment I realize: The reason why I'm on the floor crying is because I'd shut the door on my feelings for years; I'd silenced their voice and cut them off cold. I'd come against my own feelings, against myself.

Then suddenly, in the most unexpected, unusual way, perhaps like a caterpillar giving its last breath and effort to get out of the cocoon and turn into a butterfly, a rush of life and strength invades my lungs. I stand up and look at myself in the mirror. Ever so slowly I inspect what I see. My eyes are so puffy, a translucent blue. I can see the ravages of the tears and traces of my strong emotions on my cheeks. The woman I see in the mirror looks frail and weak, but I find her beautiful. I smile at her and she smiles back, as if to approve of the beautiful turmoil of awareness taking place between us. *Me* and *her* are finally in sync. "We're going to start living again," I promise her.

A year later, I'm looking out at a magical landscape, my mind and my voice united in silence and stillness. It's five o'clock in the morning in Love Valley, Cappadocia, Turkey. Thousands of huge colorful hot air balloons had launched into the sky a few minutes earlier like a festival of floating giants amidst the clouds.

I'm in awe, losing myself in appreciation of the moment and thinking of nothing else. Not my past, not my future, not even my crippling fear of heights. It's just me and the endless possibilities of life. This lack of fear has brought me a newfound respect for myself and it's liberating. Two values I cherish the most, but haven't recognized in myself for a long time, come to mind: freedom and hope.

Floating through the void 500 meters above land in a small square basket is not at all an activity I would normally feel good doing. In fact, had anyone asked me a day before, I would have answered, "Absolutely impossible!"

I always wished I wasn't afraid of heights. The most captivating landscapes are always seen from up high and I'm a great nature lover. But until now, I had associated heights with fear. They triggered too much emotion and were too big of a risk. So, I avoided being lured by the beauty of landscapes. It was a trap. Well NOT ANYMORE.

The hot air balloon experience was only the first of a series of first-time experiences that I would make way for myself in the coming year. I felt like a child in awe of everything. It was like I was reborn and was discovering all things for the first time, like a filter had been removed from my eyes and my range of life had been expanded.

It was an amazing culmination of a year's worth of self-discovery and learning to embrace my Goddess Within. A year earlier, I had *stood up* off that bathroom floor in London feeling like a new person with a newfound awareness. I had packed my things and headed back to my Beirut, Lebanon, my home; full of fearless courage!

Although I was surrounded by friends and family that felt both good and warm, I was scattered like a million-piece puzzle. The road to recovering myself seemed long and foggy. I was aware I had to put my pieces back together and 'find my answers,' but I had no clue where to look for them.

Soon after my return, a friend suggested I look into life coaching as a means of self-discovery and change. I met Mayssa; she was soft, kind, and considerate. We would meet in the comfort of her house and talk about life, my philosophy of it, and how I wished I could live it. She would listen. Not listen to reply or give me advice; she just listened to what I was saying like it was the most interesting thing on earth. And every once in a while, she would hit me with a powerful question like, "In the best of worlds, what would your life look like?" She made things that seemed impossible possible again. Dreams were put back on the map, ideas flourished. In fact, she found my ideas brilliant and re-baptized my own inner judgments by framing them in new ways for me. She showed me how 'jumping around from job to job' became 'being versatile.' How my 'lack of depth in my relationships' was a 'lack of self-knowledge.' And how my unclear direction was more about being 'adventurous.' With this unconditional accepting approach, which could be identified as love, I slowly but surely started to *like* the person I was discovering: MYSELF.

Under a new light, I seemed fun, curious, adventurous, smart, and unusual! I seemed strong, full of life, and courageous. What else was hidden behind this person I 'almost' knew nothing about? What more could I achieve? Explore? And be in service of?

I was finally asking the right questions and the authenticity of my answers was like the sun on my face on a cold winter's day: warm, reassuring, natural. I soon realized I wanted to be a life coach myself. I wanted to do exactly what my coach was doing with me. I wanted to empower and encourage people to stop looking outside of themselves for fulfillment. In some way, I had always done that but was too afraid to label it. So to do that job right, I needed to do it with myself first ; and to do *that* right, I needed to love me again. This is when I began the most beautiful journey I've ever been on: the journey to me.

That trip to Turkey with the hot air balloons was the first exciting adventure I organized for myself and my mother to share. The adrenaline and courage I felt with such ease and stillness during that experience told me that I was doing the right things *finally*. My body was more grounded. I knew that I was exactly where I needed to be. Every decision I made was the right one and I felt a calm acceptance of that fact. I understood something in me had shifted. What else was I capable of doing? I was about to find out.

On that same trip, I rode a horse for the first time through the canyons and cliffs of the Red Valley. It was a five-hour ride of utter joy. The horse at times was literally walking on a very narrow little road between two mountains. When I looked on the right, there was a cliff. To the left... another cliff. It was right outside of my comfort zone, but instead of looking down, I let myself dive into the beauty of the scenery around. I was so ecstatic and proud. It felt as though I could do absolutely anything and all I wanted was to feel, feel, and feel. The stronger the emotion, the better! What else had I missed out on? Traveling with friends? Hidden hobbies? What foods had I not tried? What perfumes had I not smelled? I was hungry for life.

A few months later, I organized a trip with my best friend to Sri Lanka, where we spent three unbelievable weeks roaming the country and exploring its every corner. From the west to the east, the north to the south, we would park our luggage and spend a night or two wherever we pleased. We would taste all sorts of fruits on our roadtrip rides; we would sleep under the moonlight and spend days roasting in the sun attempting to stand on fishing sticks like local fishermen. We cruised rivers, climbed rocks, hiked trails, and met travelers. We laughed till we cried. My stamina and excitement knew no limits! More, I needed more!

Later that same year, I went camping with another close friend in the mountains of Lebanon. Me. Camping! In a tent on the ground. In the wild. I'd always loved the idea of camping, being one in nature. But the reality? Scary!!! Overnight, you are asked to revive all your animalistic instincts... and the bugs are everywhere!! Oh my god, so many bugs! But I said yes and off we were on a great adventure. Nothing could ever beat the laughs we shared under that tent and the refreshing morning we had waking up to the sounds of the river flowing beside us.

During that period of self-discovery, I also went on my first blind date, enjoyed my first crazy night out, met so many outstanding people I now call friends. I hiked three countries in my attempt to tour the Mont Blanc mountain peak and made it! I practiced my coaching skills with unbelievable human beings who became regular clients. I dove into so many exhilarating moments that I NEVER thought I would attempt because I was afraid. But my fear was long gone and my goddess was alive more than ever!

Looking back, it would be easy to think that for 15 years I wasted my time because I got in my own way. But it was so important to go through those years drifting away from myself before realizing I needed to find my way back. Now, I know the pain of not being authentic tops any fear and any pain possible. I feel so thankful to have met this wonderful person, this friend who has taught me so much. This person I have fun with and find solace in. This extraordinary human being who is never bored and always seeking her next emotional bouquet! This strong determined woman who is vulnerable in the most courageous way, a woman who is honest with herself: Me.

If you find some truth in my story, if you, like me, have allowed fear to guide your decisions, have faith. Faith that by trusting your inner Goddess, in holding her hand and letting her guide you, in embracing every feeling and every experience you can, in making space for yourself to run free, you will meet the most *amazing* person you have ever met in your whole life: YOURSELF.

IGNITE ACTION STEPS

Always be aware of when you are in tune with your gut versus when you are not. When you're in touch with your emotions and you let them speak to you, you will notice if and when something is not right and needs your attention and love. You will then feel calm, confident, and positive in making the decisions that will serve you most.

Say yes. To everything. And everyone. Stay open, be curious. Say yes to life, to opportunities, to possibilities. The more you make space in your heart for the light to go in, the more it will. In fact, where focus goes, energy flows so focus on you. **Get to know yourself better as you would with a friend: with kind eyes and an open heart**. Be your own cheerleader.

Seek help. Don't be afraid to go within. Change and self-discovery are roads less traveled and you might need guidance from a therapist, a life coach, or a spiritual guide to introduce you to yourself in a new light. The values, balance, and self-purpose you will discover will give you the resources to cruise through life with strength and courage.

Most importantly, have the courage to feel, fall, stand up, and feel again!

Nour Fayad – Lebanon
Co-Active Life Coach
www.thehappystop.com

INSIGHTFUL

HANNAH
WOEBKENBERG

*"In this space of feeling both and none,
one's greatest power arises, the inner Goddexx."*

**My hope is to demonstrate how shedding social and cultural constructs
can lead to understanding more aspects of Self, eliminating the need to
choose a 'box' already made. My wish is that my story is an example of the
rewards of liberating ourselves from being what we are told we 'should'
be to discovering our 'true' self. I want to Ignite you to become who you
authentically are so that you can share in the bliss that arises from the
synchronization of Self and this human experience.**

TREE RING

"Are you a man or a woman?" he asks as he sits next to me. We are both
facing the morning sun as it casts reflections of the trees and clouds above in
the pools below. I chuckle at being reminded that I am bald. It had taken me
a moment to hear him, as I was deep into Presence having just completed
Osho's dynamic meditation in Pune, India. When I look up and see this long
haired elderly man with wavy gray hair, a wild beard, and wearing a matching
maroon robe, my initial inclination was to jokingly banter about the irony of a
long haired *man* questioning my gender due to *me* being bald. Instead, I take
a deep breath into the question of who exactly am I?

I grew up in the Midwest, United States, filled with traditional acceptance of religion, the media, and history books. Growing up, my hair was treasured by my mother; she made sure it was perfectly brushed, braided, or curled every day for school… that is until my stepmother took me to get my haircut the day of her wedding to my father. I was in the 4th grade. I sat calmly as the stylist cut bangs in my waist-long straight hair. They perfectly matched my stepmother's heavily weighted and curled frizzy bangs, classic of the early 1990s. When I got home, my mother was furious, raging about missing my first haircut. She refused to fix my hair for months. I was confused by my mom's extreme reaction and that wasn't my only growing source of confusion.

Frustration and thereby confusion arose from not feeling in control of my own life, and also from witnessing incongruence between what I was being told and what I saw. This was exemplified by the experiences of being told I was a girl, yet not feeling like a 'girl,' as defined by liking the pink hearts and houses that danced on my bedroom walls. I didn't like the delicate dresses, dolls, or white boots my stepmom gifted me for Christmas. I had friends of all genders and enjoyed my time equally with all. I never wanted to be someone who I wasn't and yet I didn't fit well into the boxes that were presented to me by teachers, television, and family members. My mother and stepfather kept me on a tight leash, fearful I might get lost in the network of drugs and alcohol that was prevalent at my father's house and with all three of my brothers.

I was told how to behave by my parents, how to be saved by the Catholic religion, how to be successful by society, and how to be a *girl* by all of them.

In that restrictive environment, I turned inward, starting to ask questions of the generally accepted beliefs in my life. I turned first to the Catholic religion. I read the bible in its entirety; however, instead of finding clarity, I found more questions. Why do we personify this creator, this god, as having a gender when, if God created ALL things and all things funneled from this one deity, this god must be all things, all genders, or no genders. Of course, when I posed this question to priests or family members, there was no discussion; I was told to have faith and accept what I was being told. The end.

My next haircut came as I was entering high school. I begged my mother for months to allow me to cut my waist long hair back to my shoulders; I wanted change so much. Change brought me hope of something different, the possibility that my future was not limited by what I already knew to exist. I wanted the possibility of what I did not yet know. The negative reactions I received from teachers and classmates about that drastic haircut, now bouncing at my shoulders, would have sent most home crying but that small taste of my own power was worth every bit of criticism from others about not looking 'as girly' 'as pretty' 'as ....' — I felt liberated.

I dreamed of my own power. I wasn't the kid imagining their future partner, house, kids, or lifestyle. I was thinking, visualizing, and strategizing how I could find my happiness in such a confusing world. I didn't understand why life had to be so uncomfortable.

That discomfort and my desire for ease and happiness fueled my inner fire, illuminating hope for my future, and thereby enabling me to find appreciation for each childhood relationship. For example, my mother constantly drilled me about attaining ultimate independence (ironically while smothering me) while my stepfather infused the value of education as a source of freedom.

My independence didn't come with ease or without demand. I still needed to work for it. I was 17 years old the first year of college, so despite me being out of high school, my parents continued to exude dominance over me as I was not yet 18 years of age. That translated to telephone calls swirling in power struggles. The only times my college friends saw me cry was when my mother and I were on the phone. I felt so perplexed by our screaming fights. My mother, the most consistent part of my childhood, was the person I felt closest to and yet the one who triggered incredibly intense emotions in response to her ridiculing the decisions I was making. I was a good kid, a great kid in fact. I was valedictorian in high school, and attended a liberal arts school a few hours from home where I was on the pre-medicine track with a nearly full-ride scholarship. I had never experimented with alcohol or drugs. I had stayed focused and disciplined.

In the summer I turned 18, shortly before heading back to school, I cut 20 inches off my hair and started altering my clothing to create unique outfits. I was aching to fill a need to manifest my own reality. I felt like I was standing on a rock ledge overlooking a canyon. It looked dangerous to hike into the abyss, but I couldn't fathom to look behind me, from where I had come. I felt the furthest away from knowing myself and was ready to claim my life as my own.

I remember the day I started trailblazing down that canyon. I was staring at myself in the mirror in yet another telephone screaming match with my mother. I was livid and on the edge of a breaking point. As if the earth quaked under my feet, I discovered my inner will. Ready to claim my own life, I said.

"Janet!" (Yes, when angry, I call my mother by her given name.) "YOU ARE NO LONGER MY MOTHER! I am 18. You have done your job at mothering me, and now you are finished! You have two options: One, you can be my friend and I will continue confiding in you without receiving criticism and judgment by you. Or two, You can be nothing to me!"

I was serious. I didn't care if I had a mother anymore, nor did I want parental monetary support. I needed to be unleashed! She felt my seriousness and within a few moments, she said, "Okay... I choose to be your friend." I was relieved. I felt a sense of liberation and relaxation in my whole body. That moment was not only pivotal in my self-liberation but also in understanding the vitality of setting clear boundaries to cultivate mutually conducive relationships. Thereafter my mother and I grew one of my most valued friendships, focused on acceptance, support, and love.

That year continued to be groundbreaking in self-discovery. I took a class titled 'Christian Calling' to make sure my goal of becoming a medical doctor was really mine and not my mother's projection of her desire to further her own education in the medical science field. I read a thought by Frederick Buechner that said your life's calling is where your greatest joys meet the world's greatest needs. That quote triggered my first honest look at who 'I' was. What did I enjoy? What was I good at? And, what did I believe about the world around me?

The largest construct that dissolved into chaos for me was that of organized religion, particularly my experience with Catholicism/Christianity. This predefined construct didn't work for me if I wanted my beliefs to align with my personal experience and core innate senses. Clearing that rigid construct enabled me to develop a flexible belief system that was not only *relevant* to me but also able to *evolve* with me, in my life.

After that class I gained a wider perspective on my beliefs and also fully knew that continuing on the pre-medicine track was in alignment with my true self. By analyzing my belief system, I became aware of how to accept all others: that no two people live the same experience, therefore their belief systems *should* be different!

By having a construct that was just for me, I felt empowered to follow my intuition and in doing so, I fell upon a magical balance. I felt secure in my desire to be a doctor but also wanted to learn more about another interest. I switched from biology to an art major and continued in pre-medicine.

In exchange for claiming my own personal power through the full acceptance of all of my being, both my scientific mind and my creative mind, I was rewarded with the most joyous and productive year of schooling. Despite being in class from 8 AM to 8 PM most days, I found ease and flow, as they counterbalanced one another. When I was creatively stuck, I would swap to the hard factual nature of science and when I struggled to stay awake in biochemistry, I would shift to allowing my creative flow to travel through my hands into clay, plaster, or paint. I had felt a sense of imbalance in my childhood life and here was my first taste of balance. It was delicious! I felt ease, contentment, and euphoria as I teetered on this blissful state of equilibrium. Being shown that balance could lead to great happiness, I made this my goal for all aspects of self.

Over the years, I have continued to bloom into a greater understanding of my embodied self. I have been balancing life as art, seeing every aspect of how I live as an opportunity to create and find counterbalance. I'm working as a western Emergency Medicine doctor while studying eastern Ayurveda medicine. I confide and connect with beloveds and strangers the same. I artfully dress, eat, create, relate, and decorate my home because I am the expert designer of my life. I perceive every experience as an opportunity to integrate new information into my belief system as well as gain more depth of understanding who 'I' am.

At times I set aside dedicated time to further explore the query of who 'I' am, so after attending a medical conference in Sri Lanka, I extended the trip to India seeking a meditation center. Weeks before the trip, I was sitting in my friend's kitchen, watching the 18-inch strands of hair fall to the ground as she shaved my head. She had asked if I wanted to see it partially cut. I had replied, "NO, keep going!" as I knew I wanted to explore the world without the attachments of what my once long blonde hair had represented.

Moments after completion, I looked at a picture of us, seeing myself beyond my locks of hair. I looked different but somehow instantly more myself. I rubbed my head and it felt so soft. Suddenly all the attachments to my hair as a style, as a female identifier, and as a recipient of my power-wielding fell away. Soon to realize that through shedding the hair that symbolized societal, cultural, and parental expectations of my feminine, I could really feel and appreciate the alluring nature of *my feminine*. My head became lighter, my mind clearer, soul exposed, energies calmer, and my breath deepened in connection with all aspects of self.

Sitting peacefully in India, with the question of my gender still lingering in the air, I release a long exhale and drift down into my body feeling the warmth of the sun peeking through the clouds. My past prepared me for this precise moment. "Are you a man or a woman?" My eyes flutter open to see the elderly man waiting attentively and patiently for my response to his inquiry. I lock eyes with him and reply, "I don't feel like a gender."

I feel the honesty resonate within my deepest self as I acknowledge my female body on this earthly journey while also revealing my inner truth. I have both the masculine and feminine energies within, and when I accept and love both, I feel neither. I feel both and none and in this space, I come into my greatest power, my inner Goddexx.

The elderly man softly smiles as the light sparkles in his eyes. He accepts my reflection and we silently finish eating breakfast.

I feel an inner peace shower over my entire being as I celebrate acceptance of my authenticity. Removing the need to choose either/or enables me to see more of myself. After I changed the directive question, "Am I a girl or boy?" to an open ended, "Who am I?" I was able to see that I have both masculine and feminine energies, and I can't tease out what parts of my daily actions and personal successes are attributed to just my feminine or my inner Goddess. This is where *Goddexx* enters, a non-gendered equivalent to God and Goddess. I believe that we all are a blend of masculine and feminine. Not only did we each come from the masculine sperm and the feminine egg, but also, all humans share the same hormones, albeit in varying ratios. By acknowledging this union within self I not only heal thyself, I also heal external relationships with the masculine and feminine. Within acceptance of myself and others, I am liberated to be *me*! With further self expression, my root system grows, strengthening me to be empowered, embodied, and resilient to forces outside myself. It is in this space of stability I am able to grow tall and wide, accessing my gifts and joys, finding the bliss upon synchronizing myself with this experience.

When you are no longer being subverted to a set of human-created expectations of who you are, you become liberated. You can more easily express your truest, highest, and united self, finely woven in both the masculine and feminine: your inner Goddexx, a balanced, empowered, resilient, and dynamic creature full of love, clarity, grace, and peace.

IGNITE ACTION STEPS

Proclaim sovereignty of this human experience. Are there any relationships where you can claim a boundary to support your own personal power?

Create a personal unique belief system where your beliefs align with your personal experience and core innate senses.
- First, write out your current belief system, including any religious and social structures alive in your daily life. What are the knowns? What cannot be known?
- Then read your own writing. Do you agree with each aspect? Question everything.

- Take an honest look at self. Write out what you enjoy, what you are good at.
- Rewrite your belief system to account for your experiences, observations, and how you fit into your belief system. Make it work!

Extract what has been imprinted upon you. If in a debate over the source of belief or truth about myself, I find it helpful to meditate on that question or go to nature and ask for the truth to be revealed in nature clues. For instance, when I needed more information on what to do with emotions, I went to a local neighborhood park and found myself surrounded by 13 skunks. I sat in the midst of them and observed for two hours and as I became fearful of getting sprayed, I sat with that fear knowing that if I showed my fear with sudden movement, it would likely trigger them to spray me. I learned about separating emotional expressions from actions guided by emotions.

Discover your Goddexx. Identify how your ideals of the masculine and feminine have been influenced by your culture and society. Do they align with how you feel? Are there parts of you that you feel resistance to accept? Find a way to embrace that part of you. Love and stand confident in your truest self. By healing the division within us, we can mend the separation outside of us.

Create daily intentions/affirmations, in the format of "I am… " to help integrate new beliefs or desires into self. Read them daily until memorized. Stand in front of a mirror saying them out loud to self.

Hannah Woebkenberg – United States of America
Artist, Emergency Medical Doctor
Balancinglifeasart.com
⊙ balancing.life.as.art

INTEGRITY

Rev. Priestess Rose Amaru

"I will not fight violence with violence; I will stand and face my fears."

Have you ever felt like giving up and that there was nothing left living for? This story is about personal revelation, gaining integrity, and transformation through trauma. I want to inspire you to face your fears, discover who you are and stand up for yourself, allowing you to embody a life of Purpose, Power, and Pleasure.

Light Emerges through the Dark Night of the Soul

I was startled awake in the driver's seat of a dirty Ford Escort, surprised to find I was driving down a freeway. How long had I been asleep? Which day was it? Which month?

The sun beat brightly on the hood of my car as I surveyed my mirrors quickly and scanned my surroundings. My thug boyfriend was laying back in the passenger seat, passed out with the windows open, blasting us with the hot noisy air off Highway 80E as the four lanes merged with Highway 580 and curved down together from Richmond to Berkeley, California.

As University Avenue approached, my body knew what to do and flicked the turn signal, though my mind was slow to catch up. I made the assumption we were going to People's Park where I would take a nap or smoke 'crystal' and he would sell 'black tar.' My reality had become a blur of days, nights, and trips up and down that same freeway, and the landscape was cast with a sepia filter as I looked upon it.

I had to ask myself, "How long had I been asleep? Two hours? Two days? Two weeks? How often had I been checking out?"

I sucked in a deep breath as an electric spark of fear pierced through my contemplation… if I wasn't driving then who was?

Another disconcerting episode popped into my mind. My heart sank as I put together the puzzle pieces of something similar that had happened only weeks ago. A friend was sitting parked in the very same driver's seat I sat in, fumbling for tobacco to roll a cigarette from a crumpled bag of 'shag.' I decided at that moment to light some purifying white sage that was in the bottom of my purse.

As the smoke from the holy plant touched his body, he seemed to crumple and melt, leaning into the steering wheel. I steadied him back into the seat. His eyes were rolling upward and as I called him by his nickname, Screech, he said softly, "No, my name is Brandon." I drew in a deep breath and looked at him, bemused.

As I considered his words and the uncharacteristic soft way he had spoken them, he began speaking again as Screech, whining and cajoling pitifully. "Oh please don't hurt me, it hurts, it hurts." He sounded like a puppy who had been kicked. Lost in my own drug-induced stupor, I relented and put out the sage.

I hadn't thought about that moment again until I snapped back into reality while driving. I continued questioning myself, "If we are not consciously driving our bodies, then who or what is?"

I remember the first time I wanted to leave my body. I was 10 years old. I had a migraine that night, a particularly bad one; it was the mother of all migraines in fact. It robbed me of my vision, leaving only white light in my field of view. I doubled over in nausea and pain, asking my mother to kill me. Shocked, she rummaged in the medicine cabinet and fished out some pharmaceutical left-overs from a prescription she hadn't finished. I reveled in the glorious floating peace and euphoria her pills left me with. Later, after the doctors prescribed me opiates for the migraines, I came to depend on them. No one ever asked about my diet, habits, or environment. The doctors in white coats might have discovered the mold that permeated our house and had likely induced the mold toxicity which triggered the migraines. Instead I got a pill that allowed me to carry on and gave the doctor a commission from the pharmaceutical company. I had no idea at the time, but the opiates sparked a chemical affinity latent within the genes of an addict that would later haunt me.

I continued on prescriptions for migraines for years; the opiates my trusted savior. In high school, a neighbor boy used all his skills of persuasion to get me to 'robo' with him, meaning: drink an entire bottle of Robitussen cough syrup. There was no way I would do that; I was very smart and could read labels well enough myself to see it was way beyond the prescribed amount... was he stupid? No, he was persistent. He really wanted me to be *altered* with him and offered me some Adderall, and I questioned, "Why would I take that if I'm not prescribed it?" We argued for some time until he called a pre-med friend of his. My trust in conventional medicine was high and, as I remembered the euphoria of the opiates the doctors prescribed me, I listened intently as the 'would be' doctor described the buzz as well as the benefits for study and concentration that the Adderall would provide.

Adderall became a gateway into harder drugs and by the time I dropped out of college, four years later, I was not only using but dealing to support my habit. As the blur of days and months continued driving back and forth on the highways of California running drugs with the very same thug boyfriend, (who I found out was also a satanic priest) I decided I was ready to break free from the meaningless life of fear that I had been living.

For two weeks I disappeared, gathering the courage to escape from his net. I realized he would never allow me to slip away with his prized, dark possessions and that I had to return them.

The white lettering was flaking off the seedy Oakland motel's sign and beer bottles littered the parking lot. As I approached with his precious items in hand, I was surrounded by some tough looking characters, questioning my whereabouts and the text messages from rival dealers that had come through my phone that they had stolen from me. A police car passed by slowly, drawing everyone's gaze. Wafting over us was the scent of cheap grease from the burger joint across the street.

As I was surrounded, they accused me of betraying their trust. They questioned me about my actions, about the text messages I had not sent, and why I was trying to start a 'gang war.' One tattooed parolee with an inked teardrop by his eye, ominously suggesting his capacity for ruthlessness, asked who had any smokes. I said, "I have some in my car; I'll get them..." I responded, happy to give him what he wanted. Forcefully, he shouldered his way between me and the car, hissing "You. Can. *Not*. Go."

At that point my heart started racing, and I said that he should come with me. When I was told *NO* again, I flashed with terror and felt as if the ground beneath me vanished, and I was falling off a cliff. I began to run. My ex, the hoodlum, sent one thug to slash my tires so I could not leave and another, a female hoodrat, quickly grabbed me.

Beads of sweat dripped from her curly hairline and down her hard brown complection. As she began hitting my face, my chest, and my neck, something snapped in me… my fear dissolved. Everything became still and I was no longer falling. This was the crossroad, the veil between life and death. I realized who I was and refused to live in a reality where I could not live within my integrity. My entire Being filled with absolution, conviction, and tendrils of indignation; I became saturated with the knowing that there is a fate worse than death.

I accepted *All,* including the very real possibility of my own demise. As I opened my mouth, my true soul spoke profoundly. I lifted my arms wide like eagle wings, their breadth and strength denying her righteousness. I looked her in the eyes and stated:

"I will not fight violence with violence, and I will NOT run away from my fears!"

As her fists kept pummeling me, I noticed her looking back over her shoulder for guidance on what to do, a bit shaken and confused by my fierce surrender. Time then seemed to bend and stretch like a cartoon. She continued beating me in slow motion. Her fists seemed to take forever as they approached my face and chest. It was then a brilliant ball of white light appeared to me in the distance approaching on the right side. The energy felt more and more like a doting mother whose love-light energy bathed me and penetrated a piece of my heart I could not deny. And all my spirit and soul felt a profound YES!

To what . . .?

From the centre of the glimmering light, words were spoken. She said, "*Mija,* you can continue what you're doing if you want, or you can choose to serve me."

That hot and sticky afternoon, I discovered a piece of who I was. I stopped running, being afraid, and I chose to dedicate my life in service to The Divine Mother. At that time, I knew not her name as I had been an atheist up to that point. But what I awakened to in that moment was that a higher power does exist and loves me.

By the grace of Her miracle, I avoided near certain death. I'm still not sure how. The nondescript white van they drove was deprived of its duty to dispose of my corpse and instead I was exonerated of the sins I had been accused of. Standing there I felt for the first time an absolute certainty, a true clarity of what side I was on: *Hers*! My whole life and worldview shifted, although in that moment, I felt blissfully serene in the light of this huge shift. I settled into the sensation like a fish to water. It was like coming home after erroneously believing your entire city had been destroyed. I no longer had the deep aching desire to leave this wretched world. Now I had purpose; now I knew there was something worth living for. It was a moment of pure clarity, of absolute knowing and absolute faith. Of course those moments cannot last, but the base root and cause of my suffering... disconnection... had been cured.

As I slept, I would dream about using, and would always say yes. I didn't have the strength or control to say no in my dreams, and took it as a sign that I couldn't put myself in situations where there would be an opportunity for temptation. Finally, several years later, in one dream I said NO! It was a remarkable turning point and the beginning of realizing that I could trust myself.

Trusting and honoring my body was a *huuuge* factor in my growth. I began taking Pilates, yoga, and belly dance amidst working and putting myself through university. The connection to my own body temple as I was learning it awakened within me a sense of knowing, feeling, and trusting my body's wisdom... that I could know when something was right. At one point I committed to only feeding myself the best, blessed organic foods even though I was in huge poverty at the time. It was an incredible relief to have my faith confirmed. Somehow things always worked out after having made a stand for myself once again.

My dreams began to become inundated by messages, namely of the Serpent as an archetypal energy. I dreamt of hundreds of snakes pouring down my body, my arms, down my legs, and then a battle with a 40-foot boa who bit me before we could wrestle each other into stalemate. At that point, the Serpent said, "You would be a good dancing partner," then slithered up my arm and has been there ever since, signified by a huge serpent tattoo. The archetype of chiron, the wounded healer, the serpent bearer rang forth as a new piece of who I truly am. The messages about shedding and releasing that which no longer serves, the balancing of masculine and feminine energies, and activation of my sexual life force energies are all parts of the Serpent Medicine that I've come to treasure, embrace, and make part of my daily life.

Serpent, the healer, took me to the realms of the medicine holders, the Grandmother of Jungle, Madre Ayahuasca. Not only did it reinforce my developing sense of gratitude for the blessings and miracles in my life, but she also taught me forgiveness. Of all the dark twisted things I held close to me as a part of who I was, the forgiveness set me free! I could move on, no longer imprisoned by the repeating patterns of resentment. In fact, I began to take on a 'magical mindset,' and continue to be amazed to this day how the universe conspires to support me, send messages, and provide signposts.

As I write this story nearly 15 years later from the warmth and comfort of my large home with the giggles and squeaks of my young children running around, I cannot do anything else than give thanks for the grace, blessings, and hard work that have allowed my current success. Somehow I made it through the bleak times and found my purpose in life through service to the Goddess and am now her ordained Reverend Priestess, sharing my ministries in podcasts and through coaching, retreats, and workshops. I give back to my community and it is fulfilling to see women showing up regularly to transform and connect in the circles I am guided to lead. I've been able to work through my pain and hurt enough to allow a truly good man to love me. Dance, serpent medicine, plant medicine, and forgiveness work have been some of the most powerful tools that have allowed me freedom from suffering in addition to rewriting my story and sacred sexuality practices. My life is purposeful and more brilliant and vibrant than I could have imagined on my own. I'm able to move powerfully and be heard, gratefully enjoying life's pleasures and prosperity.

This was my journey. Many have been on a parallel journey. I've overcome this pain, separation, addiction, and hopelessness and you can too. If you don't stand for something, you'll fall for anything. If you are interested in reclaiming your power and enjoying a life of purpose, pleasure, and prosperity, face your fears. Discover who you are and then stand up for yourself. You'd be surprised how the Goddess, even in this Modern era, conspires to support you.

Ignite Action Steps

- **Face your fears! The way out is through.**

  Begin by noticing in the body when fear occurs. Is my heart rate faster, am I breathing more shallowly, is my body attempting to avoid something? If you aren't in real danger then begin the inquiry and investigation of the root of that fear. Does it serve you? What is it that you DO want? Start moving *toward* what you DESIRE, rather than *away* from your FEARS. Claim your space in your body. Who are you and what do you stand for?

- **Separate yourself from toxic situations, patterns, and people.**

  In order to change one's lifestyle it can be important to remove yourself from temptation or old habits until new patterns are firmly established. Create structural barriers between yourself and that which no longer serves, for example physically moving, changing your phone number, avoiding the ice cream store. A new pattern is like a baby, requiring lots of tender loving care. Expect this work to be hard until it can walk and talk on its own and even then keep nurturing it!

- **Create a Transformation Ritual**

  Create two pieces that represent where you've been and what you aspire to. It can be writing, a collage, or a drawing. Create a sacred fire. Give an offering to the fire such as tobacco (best), sage, or cedar. Bring the first piece representing the self you've been to the sacred fire and ask it to support your transformation, burning that paper. Place the second piece somewhere special that you will view often, until it no longer serves. The Goddess will then conspire to support that intention, sending physical and spiritual support.

- **Dedicate your life to the greater good.**

  It may be in service to the Earth and all living beings, to the Great Mystery, or to something much more specific, but once you decide to live for more than the ego's desires, miracles begin to happen as you begin receiving treasures you didn't even know to ask for. If you are interested in serving a specific spiritual energy, Goddess, or deity, then ask for their support and guidance by name. If you don't know the specifics, you might say, "I invite my guides that are here for my greatest alignment with the Most High, in the highest and best way, for the highest and best good, to reveal my ultimate devotion and service."

Rev. Priestess Rose Amaru – United States of America
Spiritual Counselor, Sacred Sex Educator
www.roseamaru.com

DETERMINATION

ANA PAULA GOMES

*"Nothing takes away your brightness when you
are connected to your inner power."*

**I wish you find your big 'why' that will empower you to move forward
despite any uncertainties. Find your inner Goddess. Be true to yourself.
Understand that once you step into your Goddess energy and are true to
your inner values, you will meet supportive friends in the transforming
moments of your life.**

CHALLENGING YOUR DETERMINATION

It was a sunny Sunday morning, my husband and I sat at a tiny table in our
kitchen, having our late breakfast. Our baby daughter was taking her morning
nap and my stepson was still sleeping. I clearly remember that it was 'decision
day', the most difficult of my life so far. I had to give my manager my answer
and I could not postpone it any longer. I had spent several weeks trying to
convince my husband to agree with what I thought I wanted — a life-changing
career move which would affect our entire family.

While we ate, I reviewed with him the options we had. The first option,
and in my opinion the easiest one, involved moving our family to a new city
so I could take the job. But this option would require my husband to travel
230 kilometers daily. I watched him anxiously, hoping he would finally agree
with me. He was uneager to make the long journey every day and was certain
it would affect his college classes. The second option, more demanding for

me, involved keeping our family where we were with me being the one to travel every day, but he objected to that also. His objections were of how dangerous it was for me to travel alone and the amount of time I would spend far from home. "Our daughter will call her babysitter mom instead of you," he complained. A deep silence hung in the air.

I knew this silence. I had felt it before as a young child, barely five years old. It was the sort of silence that made you hide behind the sofa, eyes wide and watchful as you tried to figure out what was going on. It was the silence of loss. At five years old, I had experienced exactly that same silence. At the time I didn't know what was happening; I was just missing my father's presence in the living room. The silence back then was broken by a discreet noise coming from the restroom. My mom was crying quietly in hiding. I approached the door and listened with my whole being, absorbing the fear and grief I felt coming from her body. I decided right there in that moment that I could not bring to her any extra worries. I knew I had to be the 'good girl.'

That belief was the basis of all my future decisions. My father returned from the hospital four months later. He had undergone a large surgery and was close to death. Life was not the same. My mom had some support from family and friends and she found the courage to become the leader of our family, eventually becoming a great wedding cake and desserts confectioner. Dad was her assistant, as well as me, my sister, and our grandmas.

My mom was always my source of strength, courage, and love. She drew her own fortitude from family and friends and was constantly surrounded by people. At her side, I learned the importance of true friendship and community. Life was not easy for her. She worked hard to raise me and my sister and provide us with all we needed, though we lived frugally and didn't have great luxuries.

As I grew older, I stuck to that promise to not be a burden on my mother — not wanting her to spend her money on private school. In Brazil, the good schools are private. Instead, I studied hard in hopes of being admitted to a prestigious public high school, and I was accepted. After graduating as a chemical technician, I was admitted to a chemical engineering program and moved to another regional city, far from family.

Life was always good to me and that time was no different. I got a job a few months later. Coming home from class one night, I stopped at a bakery when suddenly I heard someone calling me. I turned and saw a man who was wearing a t-shirt of the company I worked for. This chance connection grew into a relationship. We fell in love and, five months later, he became my husband. Life changed quickly. I was hired in my first professional role with a big chemical company. Sixteen months later, I got pregnant. Everything was perfect.

We created great moments while waiting for our baby boy to arrive. It was such an amazing feeling, life growing inside me. My mom was anxious to support me as a new mother so we decided to give birth in the city where my mom lived. The plan was perfect. My baby would arrive five days before Christmas. I would spend the holidays with my relatives and then come back home. My little baby boy was born late at night and, after the first breastfeed, I had my dad, aunts, and my sister come visit us, but not my mom as she worked every Friday preparing wedding cakes for the weekend. As I looked at my baby in wonder, the hospital TV was playing in the background. I heard the familiar chorus of a song sung by a popular Brazilian singer every Christmas that speaks about strength: *"That is why a strange force compels me to sing; That is why a strange force is in the air; That is why I sing — I can't stop."* Hearing those words, I felt the Goddess power awaken in me. Watching my baby's small movements and sounds made me miss my mother in that moment to complete the wonderful scene of love.

Many times in life, we need to change our plans. Sadly, my baby boy could not leave the Neonatal ICU. My husband had to return to work so I visited my baby alone every single day. I stayed with my loving mom and she was the one who saw me often quietly crying. She was my angel, taking care of me. My baby boy was brave till the end. I lost my soul at his funeral. I will never forget seeing my husband carrying the coffin in his arms. I wanted to give our little baby so much more love beyond those difficult 52 days, but it was all over and I had an enormous emptiness in my chest.

My husband was devastated but still tried to protect me. At home there were many things to deal with: insurance, maternity leave, and my baby's unused possessions. It was a long maternity leave without my baby to breast-feed. With the help of friends, I started teaching math and chemistry in private classes. I learned how to do tapestry. And underscoring all of it was the question: would it be possible to have a healthy baby? My husband and I both wondered, but this topic was put aside for a while so we could celebrate my college graduation.

Despite any suffering, my graduation was a dream, especially for my mom. It was the result of years of dedication, overcoming challenges, and personal growth. Everyone was excited to see me finishing this important step. I would be the first person to graduate and the first engineer in my family. My mom and dad were so proud of me. Relatives and friends came for the celebration. Of course, I was not completely happy. There were many moments when my thoughts drifted to my baby, and I wondered, what would life be like if he were there?

One month later, we visited a genetics specialist. The possibility existed that another baby would have the same genetic problem as my son. My husband said, "I do not want to suffer again; I prefer not to have another baby. How about you?" Lost in my fears, I just nodded in agreement.

Fortunately the Universe had other plans for me. One Saturday morning, I was not feeling well. My husband met me at the doctors and together we listened unexpectedly to our new baby's heartbeat. I had unknowingly become pregnant. I felt grateful but also tense. I had not paid attention to my body's signals and the baby was already eight weeks old. We lived with worry for weeks, but I reminded my husband, who was longing for a girl, that the geneticist said girls have a better chance of not having the genetic disorder, so we should stay positive.

A few weeks later, the tension dissolved. Yes, it was a girl! We were so happy! My parents dreamed of finally having their granddaughter. We planned her birth, with my mom close by and many specialists in a great hospital. When it was time, all my family, including my mom, were together at the hospital waiting for her arrival. She was a big healthy girl, and my heart was full of love and gratitude to have this new chance to be a mother. My mom came to stay with me. She was completely in love with her granddaughter and filled us with care, good meals, and rest. Two days later she had to return to her own home. I realized then how important it is to have someone who loves you no matter what happens and regardless of the distance between you.

The Goddess within me was resurrected. I felt a deep soul connection to my baby. She was a gift from the Universe to bring me back back to life. Soon enough I had to adapt to a daily routine and get back to work. I counted on my nanny to help me and she was more wonderful than I imagined. After a few months of me working and doing extra activities outside the home, my husband started complaining that the baby was spending too much time with the nanny. To add to my new life dynamics, my teenage stepson came to live with us and it was a lot of extra work for me to manage a baby, a house, my job, and a teenager. My husband put all the responsibilities on me and I felt like a single mom. I started explaining to him that I was struggling and stressed with having to deal with it all by myself. My Goddess energy was utterly drained.

Arguments started to happen, and after five years of marriage, I saw how much control he had over me. I felt frustrated and overwhelmed and finally convinced him that we should all take a break and visit my mom for a few days during our wonderful festive *Carnival*. My mom and I organized everything, buying a costume for my daughter that she would wear at the parade.

I prepared all our family's luggage and I could not wait to see my parents. Just a few hours before we were due to leave, I was resting on the sofa with my baby and the phone rang. It was my mom's number, but it was not her on the phone. My cousin was calling me to tell me that my mom had a fatal stroke and passed away in the living room. At first I had no reaction, numb. Suddenly I came back; I was screaming and crying desperately, such a big pain in my body. My mom was so happy and looking forward to having us there and seeing her little granddaughter. I thought about what I would do, alone. I just looked at my baby and cried. I can't explain my feelings at that time, but I can still feel them to this day.

I dove into the biggest black hole, the new worst moment of my life. My stepson came and helped me call his father. A few minutes later I had neighbors supporting me. They stayed with the kids and we drove to my parent's house. It took the longest time to get there. When we arrived, my dad was lying on the sofa close to my mother's body. He was destroyed. He had no tears and no expression. Once again I saw how important it is to build friendships and keep them. My three long-time friends were there with my mom's body, preparing her while my cousins dealt with arranging the funeral services. It was a long night. The most difficult moment was watching my grandparents come to see my mom. I couldn't believe my mom, so healthy and strong, my greatest inspiration ever, was gone. Yet even in my deepest darkness I could see the light of love. All her friends, family, and clients had great things to say about her. It was a beautiful and difficult farewell.

Determination made my sister and I keep my mom's agreements to deliver all her cake orders for the next few days. I was also stressed with all that I had to deal with at home. Conflicts became inevitable. As a couple, we were not close anymore and I was feeling overwhelmed. My Goddess retreated; it was the hardest period of my life.

Even when you are down, life can offer you new opportunities. At the end of that year I received the first professional proposal of my life, where I could work as an engineer and have a better income in a new city. I was thrilled and eager to share this with my husband. He was not as happy as me, but he suggested I research neighborhoods and schools before the final decision had to be made.

That morning in the kitchen at the tiny table, I broke the silence. "Are you asking me to give up this career opportunity?"

"You can look for another job," he replied. His response felt like a knife on my throat. In a flash, I remembered my mom and every sacrifice she made for me to become an engineer. I could hear her telling me emphatically to be independent and have a greater profession than being a wedding cake maker. I could feel the hidden strength of my inner Goddess bubbling up with determination. Her essence — *my* essence — surrounding and encouraging me.

Feeling empowered, I snapped out of my memories and said, "My mom will turn over in her coffin if I give up this job. That is not an option for me." I was stronger than ever, although I was also scared. Then, I said, "So, the option is... leave you here with your son and continue my life alone with my daughter." He tried to convince me to leave her behind, saying it would be difficult to raise my daughter alone in a new city with no relatives around. But I knew how strong and capable I had become. I could raise her alone.

I arranged everything to move to the new city, but never expected how hard that day would be. The movers took my belongings out of the apartment while my husband sat hugging the baby, just observing, no words, no questions.

The truck departed for my new apartment and I had to go by bus to meet it. My husband kept the car but had agreed to drive me to the bus station. The entire drive was spent in silence. He dropped us off and kissed the baby again, without saying a word. When I closed the car door, I felt like a portal was opening in front of me. I was nervous and scared about the future. From then on it was just me. ALONE. I was completely lost. For a while I just sat and cried desperately, releasing all my emotions, but then I thought of my mom and my determination returned — my inner Goddess reminding me of how capable I really was. I decided then and there to prove to myself that I could be whatever I wanted. Accepting the situation and looking for a solution was my first challenge as a single mom. I knew from then on, I would lead myself.

Looking back at those moments, I see how hard they were and how I overcame them. I learned determination from my mom and I use it. In life's path, my inner Goddess has shown me how important it is to build a community that supports me. I still feel alone many times, but I know I am not. All I need is to ask for help.

Who is around you waiting to 'lend you a hand'? We all have someone who inspires us, and although my mom did not have time to witness my wins, I know she is proud of how I faced my challenges. Being true to myself, to my values, and to my inner determination empowered me to move forward. And in stepping into my Goddess, I was able to surround myself with true friendships and loving support in the hard moments of life. I hope I can inspire you to be true to yourself and to believe that all you need is inside of you. When you really need it, the gift shows up. It is time to connect with your feminine energy and discover the gifts you have and how you can graciously use them in your life.

Ignite Action Steps

- **Look into your story.** Discover the gifts you received from the Universe and the skills you developed. How do you feel about them?

- **Build and maintain your community**. We came to this world to help each other grow up, so count on those around you to support you. Make friends and cherish the ones you have.

- **Choose to believe in you.** Every woman has her own journey and her own inner Goddess. You should not give up on yours. Do what you are supposed to do. Love that!

Ana Paula Gomes – Brazil
Trainer & Leadership Facilitator
www.perspectives.com.br

TRUTHFULNESS

CAROLINE OETTLIN

"Be Excellent in Your Perfect Imperfection."

The goal of sharing my story with you is to provide support in uncovering your soul's purpose. Knowing that there is a reason to never give up and to follow my inner calling led me to my personal truth. This is a journey of healing, raising self-awareness, and recognition of the divinity within.

FINDING YOUR DIVINE SPARK

At the tender age of three months, I was kept in the intensive care unit with twenty hoses entering my tiny body — on the edge between death and life. My soul wanted to escape my body. It was too much pain to bear. Due to that deep invasion early in life, my pain tolerance was very high. And the sensation of not wanting to be inside myself often oriented me toward numbness. Near-death experiences appeared many times in my life, experiences that would lead me to deep realizations and profound transformation.

Born on Christmas Eve, I had an inner knowing that I was a living miracle. Life tested me many times, none of which were coincidences. Being split by a fifteen centimeter scar that separated my upper and lower body, my emotions and my mind, made making wise decisions very hard. This disassociation of parts of me due to early painful experiences and invasions I suffered contributed to the pattern of not being able to speak or show up fully.

How could I make wise decisions if I could not feel myself due to the disrupted connection and my soul wanted to escape from the hostile painful reality?

A drastic incident one year later happened when I fell unluckily into a little pond close to our garden in the backyard. My mother was on the phone, while I was struggling to breathe for several seconds with my head under the water. It wasn't my time yet as destiny stepped in; my brother pulled me out by my diaper and saved my life.

Though I was *saved* many times, I didn't feel safe in my loving family and friends' environment and didn't know whom I could trust. My world was externally focused on those around me and how they were behaving — there was always a survival state neither being embodied or relaxed. Inner feelings of sadness and loneliness didn't pass by.

Fortunately, I had nature and animals close by, which kept me aligned during childhood. The glimpses of the *other side* made me know that another source of love exists, that we can access. Therefore, I escaped to my own fantasy — a world with all kinds of crystals and pink fairytale unicorns. It was a shelter from unpleasant aspects of life, where I had my peace, harmony, and my own imagination. With the years, this escalated to numbness in different areas of my life.

After high school, I left my hometown and worked abroad as an au pair in the USA. I handled the rising emotional challenges numbing myself with food. With every bite I put unconsciously in my body, I pushed down the emptiness along with the sentient part of me. My dissatisfaction, appearing from not having the words and courage to stand up as a *woman* in difficult situations, made me obnoxious. I took those feelings for real, bottled them in, and buried them deep in my shadows.

At the age of twenty-one I went to university. I was the first person in my family to have a college education. But, as I couldn't handle the pressure of the exams and the expectations of society, I got lost in workaholism, alcohol, and partying as my weekly routine. On top of that, I sought approval in men. These ways became toxic to a certain point, bringing on the first signs of depression and burnout.

I remember staring one day really close in a mirror. An empty face gazed back at me, asking " Is this all there is to life? And will I ever be truly happy?" I felt totally disconnected.

People around me didn't recognize what was happening. I was very good at protecting myself with a happy face, covering my real feelings from everyone. Through yoga practice and many self-exploration techniques, I tried to reduce the stress, but at this point the monster of unconsciousness was already too big, so it took over. Through the avoidance of feelings, I denied my life force.

On a normal Wednesday evening, when I was just twenty-seven-years-old, while driving home I suddenly felt my extremities falling asleep. I struggled my way through dizziness, crawled in the house, and called my brother. He saved my life again, calling 911. I woke up with the smell of iodine and the feeling of an IV needle in my arm. One hour earlier I was at death's door. I survived miraculously another intestinal obstruction operation. Now I had a second vertical scar from my belly to my pubic bone that made it hard to walk. The vulnerability and dignity loss in the hospital took me to my lowest point. I knew that I had to change drastically.

The book *Eat, Pray, Love* was a blessing in my path. I was amazed by the bravery of a woman traveling around the world to search, find, and discover love for herself. This inspired me to seek a life like that, a balance between the pursuit of spiritual devotion and pleasure. It set me on a quest of active transformation. Fueled by the knowing I was given a *fourth* chance in life.

Proactively I changed my job from business management to the non-profit organization sector. I took responsibility for my actions, my relationships, and happiness. Also, I converted from Christianity to Buddhism. I got out of another unhealthy relationship and met a great man. This connection healed huge wounds of my inner child that were covered by the fairytales I was seeking in childhood.

I started to be more courageous toward life; more daring and adventurous. So I followed the signs to go to India two years later, when my best friend introduced me to Palm Leaves Readings. I was sitting for hours, up to weeks even, in temples, listening to the sacred vedic chants of Himalayan priests. I let my soul lead and discovered the healing of food in my body through a raw-food journey and Ayurveda medicine. I drank less alcohol, quit smoking, quit taking the birth control pill, and I could finally feel the 'real Caroline' beyond any mood swings.

My inner fire was activated, fueled by many energetic healing classes. I took part in a 10-day silent retreat and connected with the *female Buddha* and goddess: Green Tara. I identified with her as Caroline which means 'the free' woman; Green Tara means *the Liberator*. I embodied her virtues of fearlessness, strength, and the active aspect of compassion. The silence made it possible to calm my mind and to invite a divine intelligence inside of me leading my actions and awakening my Goddess.

One year later, I made the wise decision to do a yoga teacher training education. A journey through the landscape of my body began. I experienced the ability to hold an inner communication with myself and my body. As Stephen, a yoga teacher I greatly admire once said, "May the inspiration encourage us to realize the hidden light in all beings."

In fact, the more I moved, the longer hidden shades were crawling up to the surface. My self-efficacy raised and my masks were shattered by the real me. I remember sitting in a meditation practice when my ego got confronted with its attachments, false belief systems, and longings. Being afraid of facing my self-ignorance, I suddenly ran out of the room. I did what I always did when I got challenged with the fear of losing the safety around me. But now I was aware of it.

Being able to face my inertia sparkled my divine light to a new level. My fear was naturally transformed by headstand posture, literally turning my belief systems upside down into curiosity. It was not all done — I would find out that this was just the beginning. The shades just started to dispel.

When I was ready, the concealed information started to appear. During a chakra healing session, an incident of sexual abuse in childhood came up. I felt dizzy, freezing and escaping at the same time from the core of my being. My breath stopped for several seconds, maybe even minutes. "Why would somebody touch me there?" I remember whispering to myself. It was an indescribable feeling of helplessness, powerlessness, and confusion. My cellular memory aroused different situations in the past and I was neither able to talk or to move nor to breathe. I felt shame, guilt, and fear. Hopeless that someone would believe me, I felt discouraged to tell it — so I swallowed it and pretended that nothing had happened.

Due to that unsolved injustice, I decided to protect myself to smile on the outside while some parts of me were dying on the inside. Only the faith in my innocent and strong heart made me process those feelings. Even when they arise today, I know that I can rely on my proactive bravery, which is able to visit those dark places and be okay. There, I can meet my feelings with compassion and empathy and connect with the pain of all the souls who have experienced the same violation. I could understand that the trauma left me, almost my whole life, alienated from my body. With this newly gained strength, my inner peaceful Warrior Goddess awoke.

My internal gut feeling called me two years later to do a shamanic education. Ambivalent feelings, traumatic patterns of power, manipulation, and codependency got squeezed up to the surface. With hours of tears in the darkest nights, the oncoming pain forced me to die within and surrender — for one good reason: to integrate and to heal. Through the connection of the shamanic rituals in deep alignment with the Universe, I released and forgave those parts of me which consciously chose those experiences. I could see past the illusions and the denial of my soul's mission.

The healing movements in ecstatic and inner dance were my raft during that time. I painted my story in a new way, trusting my intuition as my art director.

That inner knowing led me to my choice, when I took a holistic journey in Iceland — a place I had wanted to visit since I was six years old. Energy work, aligned with the raw and wild elements of nature, brought regeneration into my heart center. I embraced the feelings instead of denying them. What had been creating my suffering was my idea that feeling and expressing myself was wrong. It was definitely not fun to reconstruct my human story again but when you want a life full of clarity, fulfillment, bliss, joy, and playfulness, you have to put all your effort in and make it work.

Reborn like a Goddess, I felt empowered, pure, autonomous, and able to co-create the real taste of life. This prepared me for the climax of my journey which was to come next.

Back home, I was randomly invited by a friend for a healing vortex event and felt intrigued. I knew I had to go and couldn't wait to listen to the Akashic records open talk. I was astonished by the clarity and authenticity of the presenter — he spoke about Akashic Records Readings and the miraculous change which had happened since he started working with them. I had a strong feeling that this might be the ultimate breakthrough so I signed on for the initiation of becoming an Akashic Records Consultant. What has followed has been *way beyond* what I could have imagined. It Ignited my whole life.

A transformational practice started, and I worked seriously every day with the honorability codes and my divine connection. I focused only on what served me and dedicated consequently all my energy to my destiny. I received a glimpse of my higher mission and the magic of the probabilities of incidents which are available at any time. We just have to choose. Like an irresistible gateway, I was being guided beautifully and by free will; many course corrections into my new life took place.

Within three months I quit my job and my apartment to begin a new life in South America. I could finally embody my shadow parts and work with my ego as an ally. I saw all the beautiful mistakes I made. There are no wrong turns; it's a big cosmic game.

Through a very rare and exceptional, deep and divinely-oriented encounter, I met and connected with my partner in a truly mature and honest way. We have the blessing of experiencing our love in mutual adoration and truth with ourselves. That was and still is one of the greatest gifts I am experiencing in my life. This oneness has been intensified by our mission to bring alignment, harmony, and healing to the planet.

My personal truth, to master my energy with the muse of inspiration and acceptance of the pure divine goddess I am, didn't change my life. It SAVED my life. I never lost faith because I know I cannot fail when I am in service of the divine. Tuned in with the divine state, I created my platform from where I support the alignment of the earth and persons who seek a higher meaning and remembrance that we are eternal love.

I want to empower you to get in touch with your inner voice of wisdom, which guides you perfectly — when you allow yourself to listen to it. Everybody is a divine individual being. Be confident that it shows up in your personal way. To be truthful to yourself, trust in your own truth first. Recognize what matters to you. Strengthen your ability of discernment to develop clarity about what direction to take in life. Surround yourself with those who want to see you grow and be your own great Goddess from within.

Ignite Action Steps

- The willingness to take action changes the world. Do what needs to be done as best you can and then — let go.

- Develop a daily meditation routine: It helps to stay centered, to distinguish between feelings and emotions, to raise your creativity, and to focus on your goals. Know that you never lack; you only transition.

- Gain a daily exercise for training your *will-force*, focus on healthy nutrition for nourishing your body, and love yourself in a way as if life depends on it — because it does.

- Get a masterful, clear picture of your human mind and heart. Jack Kornfield is a great Buddhist meditation teacher who works with the loving awareness of the heart. Read or listen to *The Wise Heart*.

- Work on who you are and who you want to become. Stay always 100% true with yourself, your values, and intuition. Do only what Ignites your passion.

- Generate dance to get in alignment and into a deep relationship with your soul. Stay curious and discover where your movements want to lead you. Dance is the original language of our body.

- Be honest and truthful with your thoughts, speech, and behaviors. And with others. Vulnerability and emotional exposure opens us up for allowing, integrating and growth.

- Embrace and be kind to yourself. Be proud of yourself that you have chosen a spiritual path, which is not always easy. Create joy and bliss in all your actions.

Be Excellent in Your Perfect Imperfection.

Caroline Oettlin – Germany/Argentina
Hatha Yoga Instructor , Akashic Records Consultant & Intuitive Healer
www.we-are-eternal.love

INDEPENDENCE

ARIANE BARROS

"Miracles come from within."

I share my story for you to feel inspired to unleash your truest goddess self and embrace all that you are meant to be. May you feel empowered and courageous to connect with every aspect within you. To also express yourself in an authentic way, stepping into your true independence.

THE JOURNEY FROM BELIEVING TO LIVING.

This is the story of how I connected to my inner goddess, my independent spirit, and began to trust myself in a fuller way so I could follow my path.

Five years ago, I returned to my corporate job after being on maternity leave with my twins for five months. I was happy and eager to get back to work. I found a beautiful nearby daycare for my babies and felt relaxed knowing that they would be together all day. As an optimistic woman with all kinds of hopes and dreams, I have always been certain in my heart that I could have all that I wanted: a corporate career, a loving husband, a house, happy kids, health, spirituality, and fun! And there I was, building my life, family, and profession, just the way I wanted and believed I could.

I was entirely convinced this was possible. But I would soon find out that others didn't share my belief. At work, I was assigned fewer projects than I had carried before my maternity leave and was prevented from traveling or doing all the things I used to do before becoming a mom. "You just had twins," they said. "Take it easy this year; do more administrative work, research, or study." I didn't think there was anything wrong with any of that work or even with taking it easy, nothing wrong at all, and part of me knew they cared for me, but they weren't taking care of me the way I needed. I wanted to do *more* things. I love being involved in exciting projects. But every time I wanted to do something, I wasn't allowed to. I needed to make this decision for myself. I felt like I wasn't being listened to and that was frustrating. It was so clear to me — I should be able to decide what I could and couldn't do.

I didn't realize then, but I understand now that the problem was that this new scenario wasn't what my inner goddess wanted, and frustration started to creep into my routine. I felt like I couldn't make my own decisions. At times, I questioned my belief of the possibility of being a great mom and a brilliant career woman at the same time. "Was I a bad mother for wanting to work?" — would often swirl in my thoughts.

After several discussions with my boss, I knew I wasn't being given the responsibility that I craved and was capable of. So I decided to write a long email to him on how important it was that I got to decide what I could and could not handle. It wasn't easy to write, I was afraid of upsetting him and losing significance, but I needed to speak my own truth and trust my judgments. I reminded myself that I knew my own capabilities more than anyone else — I knew what I could and could not manage. My maternity routine and the weight of all the responsibilities depended on how everything was arranged and organized. It correlated with the support I had and how I responded to all the challenges. By stating what I wanted, I felt more connected to myself, and it reinforced the strong self-respect I had. I felt certain that by fully living the other facets of my life, I would also become a better mom to my kids. No guilt should exist in leaving for work or traveling for a meeting, as I was growing as a professional, a leader, a mother, a wife, a woman, and a goddess.

Speaking my truth worked for me. My boss completely changed his behavior and I was reinstated with all the responsibility and variety of tasks that I had dreamed of.

A few months later, my journey went from a place of believing to a place of intention. It began with me *imagining* what I wanted my life to look like. Then I *believed* that I could have that life, but I often second-guessed myself. The act of advocating with my boss had moved me to a new place where I felt pulled to go even deeper in my journey to my authentic self. Although I was challenged at work and loved being a parent, I knew that I needed to find my true purpose on this planet, my truth, and live it. With crazy routines and lots of joy, I filled my days with self-development activities, improved my self-knowledge with coaching and training, and started to surround myself with people who thought in a similar way. In that process, I learned that my main purpose was to help others, to contribute to their growth. I get so excited about helping individuals — I feel such joy when I see people improving and using their strengths — being better, stronger, and more successful. That is when I discovered my potential as a career coach and trainer.

I loved it so much that I started coaching some of my work colleagues and training some of the leaders. I traveled a lot and I was completely delighted to inspire others, to help, to spread the message I so deeply believe in — that we should improve ourselves, each and every day by looking inside to find our magic and excel.

In addition to my regular job, I began teaching at a local university and coaching professionals after work. I was filled with energy and I started to inspire people to do the same, to go after their purpose and dreams, and to stop procrastinating and blaming lack of time, money, or support for what they didn't have.

I remember in one class I was teaching, a student complained about not having time to take care of her health to which I responded, "I work eight hours a day, have twins at home, teach here some nights of the week, go to the gym every day, and travel regularly for work; there's no such thing as, 'I don't have time to do what's important for me'." Not liking my response, she fired back, "Then you must be a terrible mother." Her answer didn't bother me nor my goddess. It didn't bring up doubts about my feminine self. Moments like this are so important to show how much we have grown and the acceptance that not everyone is in the same place as you.

Being close to people who share similar values was crucial for me. I needed to surround myself with those who reflected who I wanted to be, who were hungry for life in the same way I was. I found a global tribe led by an amazing leader, Blair Singer, and started the process to be certified at his training academy. With regular virtual meetings and world-class training, I was able to feel energized and challenged to keep improving and growing.

I was going deeper in myself but still experiencing obstacles from people at work. I was often being questioned by my managers about my activities. I didn't feel their approval and that felt disappointing, but I needed to be true to myself. Several times I was asked to keep a low profile, to stick with my routine activities, and to serve only one team and not the entire company. I resisted, and without my manager's full support, was able to continue supporting people in my office, with coaching and training, until things changed. I took on a new role in a new department, thinking this would give me an avenue for helping others with the coaching and teaching that I loved to do. Quickly I discovered this wasn't the case. It got to a point where I was prohibited from doing these extra activities, "What you do is of great value for the company, but you work for me and I need you to just do your job here," my boss said. Once again, I was faced with other people's disbelief in what I could do. From their point of view, it was impossible to teach, coach, work, and be a mom. But in my heart, I felt it was not only possible but necessary. I knew I needed a new job. Every time I listened to the opinions that said I couldn't have the life I wanted, I was disconnecting from my goddess. When I couldn't do the work that I loved, I lost the energy and the will to do the tasks in front of me. I needed to do what truly fueled me. It was time I reclaimed my inner power.

Around that time, I took a few days off with my family; it was summer and we went to a perfect beach on the coast. I spent my days relaxing and having fun but also planning everything I wanted for that year and what my life could become. I was inspired and energized! I felt so happy and excited about the possibilities of what I could do. On my last day at the beach, while routinely reading my newsfeed, I learned my planning was all in vain. Unexpectedly, the company I worked for had a major environmental event that would impact me greatly.

I flew back home and very shortly was reassigned to another department to help with the crisis coordinating the psychological support for all the families involved. This important and necessary task made me put aside all the plans I had for teaching and coaching. Then, in the midst of it all, I found myself pregnant with my third child. I felt really lost in all of the uncertainty. I felt so anxious — it didn't feel like I had control and that I could make the choices to do the work I wanted to do. It was a turbulent year and the self-confidence I had built started to waver. At that time I was feeling lost, and disconnected from myself and my dreams. I felt like I had no control over my life. Everyday I would struggle to get myself in the right state of mind, to keep positive, to do what was within my control, and respond well to what was happening.

In the middle of that storm, a dear friend and mentor, Hanna Meirelles, invited me to her online course *The Family Business Expert*. She wanted my feedback on its content and structure. It was a great pleasure for me to help her, as I knew I would learn important things and be inspired by her ideas. What I came to learn from her would finally put me in a place where I could fully connect with my truth and step into my goddess self.

But before I share what she taught me, let me walk you through a little deeper what was going on in my life. Being pregnant in the middle of a company crisis wasn't fun for me. I felt like I had been sent to sit on the bench; I wasn't a player anymore. I felt disqualified from performing well in my new role. Before I shared my news about being pregnant, a former director offered me a management position in his organization in a different city. I was faced with a great opportunity, but, being pregnant, it didn't feel like I could even want it. So, I immediately turned it down. As the day went by, I texted my husband sharing the news of the job offer, and to my surprise, he asked me, "Do you want to move?" That simple question stunned me. I went home, thought a little about it, but still felt like I couldn't choose this path at that time. I went on with my normal activities and that is when Hanna's course began.

In her third class, she talked about how to *be* who we are *destined* to be and not who we *want* to be. She insisted that we need to find out who we really are and be clear about what we want and what we came to do in this world. It was about defining goals, making plans, and having support from people with effective tools. She encouraged us to become inspired by other fabulous women, and the most crucial thing was not to give up! I realized that I didn't need to give up. I connected to my desire and purpose and felt incredible energy from it. This was my Ignite moment. I realized, in the past few years, I had gone through a search for who I was but I had given up. I had taken myself out of the game, not seeing my choices and afraid I wasn't good enough. Somewhere along the way, I forgot my distinctive power, to be authentic, independent, respect my own truth, and value my goddess from within.

I was again empowered. Reminded of my strength, I called the director a few days later and made a suggestion, something that would work for both of us. I felt certain of what I wanted, who I was, and how I could contribute. However, there were still opposing opinions. I got a call from the HR Business Partner trying to convince me not to take the opportunity. She was empathetic and told me that she also had kids and couldn't see how I could handle everything. I told her that for some people stability and safety are their greatest values and what she was saying made sense for them, but not for me. Only a job with purpose and contribution could help me keep growing as a human being.

I began my new job. I spent the following four months traveling with my big baby bump, happy as I could be, respected by others and by myself. I felt important contributing to the leaders and their team's development.

After my child was born, I texted my director thanking him for the opportunity and sent an article about companies that were going against the market, hiring pregnant women. I was proud to be an example of such a rare situation.

He responded that just like the article's example, he had focused on my talent and not on my pregnancy, and thanked me for being up for the challenge.

Before all of this happened, my father once wrote a letter about me for my coworkers, which I can see now showed that he saw my inner goddess all along. The letter was for an end of the year celebration meeting and each coworker received one. Mine started like this:

"AUTONOMY - Perhaps that is the word that best defines your qualities as a human being. Autonomy here is understood as the value and the taste for discovering yourself and the mysteries of life. But also, autonomy as a sign of courage in the face of the unknown and an intolerance of dependency. You are a person who never says "I don't know" or "I can't" because your willingness to do what is necessary and required is also an opportunity to grow and learn.

OBJECTIVITY - Is another word that suits you very well. This is sometimes mistaken for impatience and a strong personality. But what marks you is your focus, your sense of optimizing the means so that the ends are reached sooner and in the best way. That is why, in your academic training, you specialized in the behavioral, education, and training areas, which ended up opening space for you to work in the areas you thrive in.

JUSTICE - The third tripod of your virtues. You have an absolute commitment to doing and administering justice, what each one does to qualify their merits and their needs. That is why, despite being demanding and direct, you are always trying to be helpful and consistent with your actions."

I reread my father's letter while writing this story. It confirms to me who I really am and it reminds me to keep being true to myself.

To live in our truth and find our independence is to find the goddess within us. It has always been there, whispering to us; we just have to listen. Finding the goddess within us is a journey, an inward journey. It's all about silencing the world for a little while and hearing your intuition, finding your purpose, and living with passion for what you believe in. The magic comes from within and after we connect to it, it drives us to live our purpose every day, in everything we do. The *way* we do things matters more than *what* we do. I learned that from my great mentor, Blair Singer, who taught me how to facilitate memorable training experiences and, more importantly, taught me how to take responsibility for everything in my life and live in alignment with my beliefs.

Today, I find myself surrounded with love from my children and husband, playing games with the twins and cuddling my little one. Every day I wake up and I feel connected with my goddess. My husband has said that being apart was hard, since I stay three days of the week in a different city, but that he is happy for me that I am doing what I love. Even apart we are still a team, helping each other take care of our family and, at the end of the day, my smile coming home makes everything worthwhile.

Finding and living your truth and being independent are daily exercises; some days are easier than others, but the important thing is to stay aligned to yourself. The journey in listening, honoring, and connecting to your goddess can only happen when you do what you believe in, embracing all the wonders that life brings you. I wish that you find your goddess self, enjoy her, and look within your soul so that you can live with true authenticity and happiness always.

IGNITE ACTION STEPS

Look inside – get to know yourself, take every opportunity to learn more about who you are and what you believe in. Write down five of your strengths and five things you enjoy. Honor those.

Write your dreams – set goals that are aligned with who you are — forget about the goals that others expect you to have and write about what is truly important to you.

Be true to yourself – with every decision you make, take a moment and reflect if what you're doing is what you believe in. Focus on what you love and schedule it into your day. Make your Goddess a priority.

Ariane Barros – Brazil
Coach & Trainer
www.elevconsultoria.com.br

STRENGTH

KERRY PATON

"Claim your life!"

My hope is to inspire all future generations of Dragon Goddesses (especially my granddaughters). I want to encourage women to be their most feminine, powerful selves, and direct their own life's path, asking for what they want and need. Do not let life pass you by; seize hold of the joy within it. My story is not about regret; instead, it unearths how life's lessons build strength. It is through years of experiences that we all gain strength, creating a vision of hope in our hearts.

IT'S NEVER TOO LATE

The bathroom door shook from the incessant pounding. His voice, an angry stream of threats, striking fear into my very being, into my heart. I prayed the thin white-painted wood of the bathroom door would hold. My sweet innocent son lay sleeping in my arms, his long eyelashes casting small spiky shadows on his cheeks, unaware of the drama playing out around him. I was shaking uncontrollably, tears streaking down my cheeks, dripping down my neck, and soaking into the collar of my pyjamas as I knelt, my hands clenched together in prayer. "If I make it through this night, I will do anything to keep him safe, to keep us safe… I will find a way to escape." The spotlessly clean linoleum floor was cold beneath my knees. I looked around wildly, my breath coming in great ragged heaves, searching for an escape and knowing that the tiny window, two stories up, small and black with the night, was the only option. My thoughts raced, "Could I jump with my son if I had to?"

The house finally quieted around me, the stillness echoing the frozen posture I had been holding for hours, tucked into the corner as far away from the door as I could get us, my son still sleeping peacefully tucked up against my heart. My racing heartbeat settled into something steadier. The adrenaline of the situation left me feeling sick in the pit of my stomach. I was trembling with the uncertainty of what would happen. Would it start all over in the morning? Would my son and I get out unscathed and whole?

I slept then, right there on the bathroom floor, tucking my son into a nest of towels in the tub and pulling another over myself for a blanket. I woke in the early morning hours, stiff and cold, to find us alone in the house. Laying there looking up at the cracked light fixture in the ceiling, l could hear the unrelenting drip of water from the sink tap. Why did this happen to me? I wondered how my life had come to this point. The sight of my son, still asleep in the pink tub, broke my heart. He was an innocent child and I needed to find a way to keep him safe. As I watched him, he began to stir and I realized there were things that needed to be done to secure our safety.

I carefully put my hand on the doorknob, pausing to listen before opening it. I tiptoed over to the window at the top of the stairway where I could get a glimpse of the driveway to see if his car was there, if *he* was home. Relieved to see an empty driveway, I dressed quickly and frantically threw some things in a bag for the two of us. With the phone tucked under my chin, I called a trusted friend to come collect us. Driving away in my friend's car with hardly more than the clothes on our backs, I felt relieved to have escaped with so little physical damage. I would not take a steady breath until we were many miles away; but I was grateful that my son was too young for memory, that he would never remember that night in the bathroom where our lives hung in the balance.

My son would have likely grown to have an unhappy childhood if I had stayed with his stepfather. My childhood, in contrast, could not have been more idyllic. I had loving parents and siblings. I was raised on a farm in a small town in rural Manitoba, Canada. The farm was a busy place. My mother always had a garden. There were horses to ride, sheep and pigs, and beef cattle, too. My parents' farm was in the community that they were born in and remained in their whole lives. There was a deep connection to community, church, friends, and most of all, family. I loved to sit at the chrome table in Mom's kitchen after school, eating fresh homemade bread hot out of the oven. And it was at that table that I discovered my love of sewing and creating from my mother and grandmother. That love turned out later in life to be a saving grace for me.

It became my 'happy place.' A place where I could escape from the troubles of life but also one that gave me a great sense of accomplishment.

I graduated high school with some of the same kids I went to kindergarten with. I was involved in community clubs, church choir, school clubs, and sports. I had a childhood that most children could only dream of. If my parents had troubles, they would never let on to us kids. I do not recall them ever having an argument. My circle of life was a loving, safe place to thrive and I had assumed that everyone's life was like that. I am sure that I went through my youth with rose-colored glasses firmly in place.

I went off to college a mere hour from my family home. Living in my own apartment in what to me was a huge city, so different from my hometown, I thought I was so grown up, so worldly. How naive I was! My sheltered youth had in no way prepared me for this new stage of life. Removed from the safe cocoon of my childhood, I soon found out just how unforgiving and hard life could be. You know how every girl has that 'bad boy' in her life? The summer I turned 19, I found mine and a few short months later, I was pregnant.

Had it been the 1950s, public opinion would have dictated that a pregnant young woman like myself marry the baby's father. In my small farming community in the 80s, while not so rigid about the matter, there was still some expectation of marriage. When I told my son's father about the pregnancy, he immediately disappeared, abandoning me and our child. I was alone, unsupported emotionally and financially. And I was scared to death. How would I support myself and my son? How could I build a life for us? I was forced to make choices about my future — choices that I was ill-equipped to make.

About six months into my pregnancy, my cousin introduced me to this guy, a man's man, tall, very polite, and well-spoken. He was charming and sweet, and I stood there with my belly sticking out between us, wondering what he would think of a young pregnant girl like me. Meeting this man who would soon become my husband was like waking up on Christmas morning, finding everything I had ever thought I wanted. He was kind, he said he loved me, he was a good provider, and he found joy in watching my pregnancy progress. My heart would skip a beat just by being near him. But he was not entirely who he portrayed himself to be. By the time I figured that out, we had married and had become a family of three.

I had no idea about marriage, no notion that it was a lot of work and full of compromise. I thought it just *happened...* my parents made it look so easy. I was unaware that there was a darker side to committing and trusting your body and soul to another. That betrayal, control, and abuse could happen... I had no idea. It was a foreign concept, out of my realm of reality.

When the abuse began not long after we were married, I went down the street to his mother, seeking help. Her life was a mirror of my life and I thought she might have insight for me. My husband, her son, should have been my safe place. Instead, he enforced fear, abuse, and cruelty. "What should I do? How should I handle this?" I asked her. She said to me, "Just stick it out like I did, because look what I have now!" I knew she was referring to how her husband had sought help from AA and changed significantly, but I was still stunned by her advice. She had no compassion, nothing. I had expected her to be sympathetic and supportive. Instead, I felt rejected. My safety at the hands of her son didn't matter to her. I knew I would have to find the inner strength to cope... and do it alone.

My coping strategy for life had always been to not rock the boat. It turned me into the 'go along, get along' girl, the one who was always pleasing everyone else before herself. I would escape to my sewing room when everything became too much, letting all my troubles disappear and finding my place of peace again. In this way, I had many years of happiness and contentment, even joy. I carried this escape of mine into a second marriage and then a third. In each relationship, the promise of change held me in the situation until the situation became unbearable. It was easy to stay because it was not too uncomfortable. Somewhere deep within me was hidden a belief that somehow 'this time' it could work. I kept hoping in my heart that each time it would be different, but it never was. Before I knew it, 35 years had passed.

There were many moments during those years when I felt that I was missing something. That this couldn't be how we were expected to live life. Looking back now, I wish that the moment when I was locked in the bathroom with my son would have had a different impact on my life. It was a moment of tremendous strength and courage, yet I did not continue to carry that self-determination through the next years of my life. I *should* have been able to rise up from the wreckage of that situation and been stronger...

What?... I was strong, I coped with many difficult situations. More adaptable?... I was a freaking chameleon. What was it that was missing? I wondered what it was that I continued to search for and couldn't find through three failed marriages, that essence that stopped me from moving into my full self. My Goddess self! Where was she? If I had appreciated and respected myself, and demanded the same of my partners... If I had insisted on their positive attention, sincere affection, and strong support of who I was, my life would have looked very different.

When I met my last husband, I thought he was the 'one.' He gave me a feeling of being home. In the beginning, I thought he was so different from my previous choices. He was a hard worker, steady, and always had time to spend with me. With the Dixie Chicks big hit *Cowboy Take Me Away* playing on the radio, we fell into our life and marriage. I gave him my whole heart and soul. I took the chance, the leap of faith. There were years of hard work: head down, ass up, getter done to build a strong financial future but little time for anything else — including my husband's inability to make time to build a relationship with my child. Major family milestones got missed. My own relationship with my son and his family suffered. I missed out on so much because of my 'go along, get along' attitude. Because I didn't take a stand for what was important to me. It was a huge price to pay.

And then my husband was diagnosed with cancer. Surgery and treatment was a stressful time for us, and we had already been struggling in our marriage. If any life-changing experience should give a person the incentive to live their best life, this health scare was certainly it! For my husband, it did not seem to register that way. He didn't step up and embrace life at all. But I did! For me, it was like a thump on the side of the head! I thought, "Life is not never-ending, life does end. Is this how I want to live MY life for the rest of the time I have here?" I was Ignited.

In my efforts to save the marriage, we started attending couples therapy. One day, my counselor forwarded an image to me, an image that touched my very soul, inspiring me to finally step into my feminine power. The image was of a Goddess warrior seated on the root of a tree deep in a forest, her sword standing tall, point in the ground, her hands resting atop it, and her face turned to the heavens as if in prayer. She was dressed for battle, ready to fight. At the same time, I could feel the peace and grace emanating from her. Her strength. Her softness. Her resolve that she could and would face anything that life could throw at her. In the background a ghost dragon, wings spread, gazing down on his mistress as if waiting for her command. The caption read, "She needed a hero, so that's what she became." I felt inspired, compelled to finally make the decisions that I needed to make. I could feel it settling in, creating a warmth of infinite wonder and hope. I knew I wanted to be like her. To possess the strength and grace that she had. To handle anything, with power and confidence, all drawn from within.

And then my mom passed. I had made every effort to spend as much time with her and family as possible over the last couple of years as she battled dementia. It meant a lot of travel, a lot of time away from my own home and family. My marriage was already strained at that time and my absence did not help, yet I felt so privileged that I could be there with her when she passed, spending her last moments with her.

My son and husband flew in for her funeral. From the time my husband stepped off the plane, everything was about him. At one of the most difficult moments of my life, instead of making things easier for me, he made things more painful, giving me more things to deal with. He could not put aside his wants and needs and just support me. I so desperately needed him to be my best friend, to help carry the load, to be my soft place to fall. I was crushed, wounded beyond repair. During the funeral, there were many family and friends who came to pay their respects and offer comfort. A man who I had known when he was young gave me a hug in comfort and friendship. He and his family had been neighbors and longtime friends with my family, and he had just buried his own father only a few months earlier.

My husband portrayed this comforting, friendly hug as a dirty, sexually-charged encounter. It was an innocent hug meant to bring shared solace. I thought to myself, "What the hell!!!! Why could he not, just once, give me the benefit of the doubt and support me in my time of need?" There I was, barely holding it together, burying my mom… ENOUGH! It was then that I chose, after months of couples therapy, to no longer trust my husband of 21 years with the care of my heart or soul. I may have not got the download from my Ignite moment the first time, maybe not the second or third either, but in the end, it hit me like a ton of bricks, square between the eyes. In that instant, I said to myself for the first time ever, "NO MORE. I choose me". Like the Dragon Goddess, I claimed my life! Loud and clear. I stepped into my strength, I found my dignity and embraced my courage to move forward. Upon arriving home from my mother's funeral, I immediately packed my things and moved out.

This journey in writing my story has been very healing for me. This is a story about me not reclaiming myself and who I was, that young girl of 19 who never had the chance to become who she could have been. It is about me finding myself for the first time. So here I am, still on my journey. Working on sewing my life back together, on finding a way to show up differently in a kinder place of grace, in a softer and more grateful way, all the while staying true to myself, honoring myself, and honoring the other people in my life. Taking time and space for me. Living the kind of life I want to create for me. Taking responsibility for my own happiness. It may have taken 35 years for me to step into my fierce, beautiful self, but here I am, ready to live my life out loud, filled with hope, insight, reliance, and determination. Now is my time! I am claiming my Dragon Goddess. Don't let 20 or 30 years go by; live your life now! Celebrate your life! Realize your dreams and seize life with both hands. Be your own Heroine. Be the Dragon Goddess of your own life: sword, shield, and heart.

Ignite Action Steps

If I could gift you with the one thing that I did to help me get through this time, it would be journaling. You may think that is lame; I certainly did… until I actually tried it. Before I talk to anyone, before I check Facebook, before I even have my first morning coffee, fresh from my night's sleep, I take 30 minutes every morning. I have a favorite chair beside a window where I can watch the sunrise. I set my timer for 20 minutes and I begin. I write about anything and everything that pops into my mind. It might be a single word, a phrase, or a rant that has been circling in my head about a situation I am struggling with. It can be uplifting or my deepest despair. It doesn't matter what I write; it only matters that I commit it to paper. This helps me process what is happening in my life. Good or Bad. It doesn't need to make sense; chances are I will never read it again. It only matters that I download it. After 20 minutes, I reset my timer for 10 minutes. I start a fresh page and write five things that I am grateful for in my life.

Kerry Paton – Canada
Mother, Grandmother, Dragon Goddess
kj.paton@yahoo.com

SURRENDER

Kristen Appenrodt

"When you let go of any idea of who you are and commit to the discovery of who you are destined to be, life meets you in the most magical of ways."

My hope for you, dear sister, is that you commit to the discovery of your body and your womb. To come home to the sensations of your physical being and live in harmony with nature and with yourself. May you know and trust that you are deeply supported and a life of magic awaits.

Sacred Journey Home

"... And allow yourself to receive."

I remember those words as if they were spoken yesterday. They melted through my mind and into my heart, touching the parts of me that had been denied the ability to feel and to truly be seen. What began from that sweet space of 'savasana' has since evolved into an exploration of the depth of those words' meaning. I was once asked what the most significant memory in my life has been thus far, and I responded, "When I started to get to know myself." Quoting Ram Das, "Once the seed of awakening sprouts in you, there's no choice — there's no turning back."

I was 18 years old, a freshman in college at the University of San Diego, United States, when I found out I had multiple blood clots in my lungs. My breathing had become sharp and painful, each inhalation a daggering pain in the back of my ribcage. It had happened unexpectedly; after multiple weeks of having an increasingly challenging time breathing, the pain in my lungs had gotten so intense I panicked and submitted myself to the Emergency Room in the middle of the night.

While in the ER, the doctor in his white coat calmly told me that the blood clots had originated in my legs, and traveled up to the lungs. I was lucky to be alive. However, at the sweet age of 18, I didn't register the trauma of this experience. After further testing, we found out that I tested positive for Factor V Leiden, a blood condition that makes one predisposed to getting blood clots. In other words, I have sticky blood.

It turned out I inherited this condition from my parents, but unlike the majority of Factor V people who only have one expression of the gene, I have two. Genetic Jackpot — definitely not. Divine Planning — I would later find out — yes.

Emerging from the hospital with that diagnosis was strange. I was very excited to return to normal college life and fun times with friends despite the lifestyle restrictions from taking blood thinners. It felt easy to pretend that a traumatic experience had not just happened. I went on with life as though everything was normal and didn't speak to any of my friends about it. My dear mother, on the other hand, was not ignoring it. She was concerned that I was not fully understanding the gravity of my diagnosis. She came with me to all my appointments and kept track of all my files. One day as we were sitting in the parking lot at yet another doctor's appointment, she looked at me with tears in her eyes while clinging to a binder full of my medical records. "Don't you realize you could've died?" she expressed through trembling lips.

In that moment, a rush of warmth went through my body as I felt her deep love for me. It was quickly followed by a tightening in my chest as I finally registered the seriousness of what I had been through.

It was as if the emotion of my mother and her sharing with me invited me to pause for a moment and feel. Starting in my high school years, I became very skilled at disconnecting from what I was feeling. As a young child, my emotional passionate self thrived through playtime, creative imagination, and time outdoors. As I got older though, my creative outlets diminished and responsibilities grew. I had no awareness of how to be and live as an emotional person. And so I did the only thing I knew to do; I pretended I didn't feel anything. I found a myriad of ways to numb myself. Eating disorders, drug use, and gentle lies were my way of controlling and disconnecting from any emotional experience. At the same time, I had a supportive home life, excelled in school, had many different circles of friends, and was on track for a 'successful' life. From the outside, everything was 'perfect.' On the inside, however, my sense of passion and joy was beginning to dwindle into an internal emptiness.

During college, I told myself that when I made the '*30 under 30*' business magazine cover, which would finally reflect my potential, I would feel happy. And so, my system revved up, tainted by an unsettling sense of rushing.

All the while, a dawning awareness around the blood clots was beginning to be revealed.

From the moment the blood clots appeared, my menstrual cycle started slowly drifting away. First it disappeared for a month, then a couple months until it disappeared completely. During that time, my mom took initiative in planning different appointments with doctors and gynecologists to determine what was wrong. I felt extremely uninterested by the process. I had no desire to spend any more time meeting with doctors, getting blood tests, and never feeling like anything was getting resolved. Doctor after doctor came to the same conclusion, "Go on birth control."

But due to the blood clotting disorder, I couldn't.

Eventually my mom stopped making appointments. Any hope we had had for a conclusive answer had dwindled. So it all came to a halt; I didn't care much that I wasn't getting my period. I was actually quite happy about not bleeding every month. And so it continued like that, until one day, five years after I first had blood clots, I went to a yoga class that would change my life.

Although I had been practicing yoga for over three years, my practice had geared toward hot, fast, and athletic. But a new type of yoga was beginning to enter my life, and that particular class was slow, sensuous, heart opening, and breath oriented.

Standing on my mat in a comfortably full room, I felt so at ease. Oh, the feeling of being present and embodied... lost in the breath… every transition from standing to sitting to stretching felt so luxurious and meditative. My mind was completely still. I could feel my chest rising and falling with my breath, immersed in the rhythm of the movements as I fully connected to a sweet space within.

As I was lying in savasana, the teacher prompted the question, "What allows you to receive?"

My belly lifted as I took a deep inhale and felt an opening in my chest. It was as though I was breathing love and presence into the tender parts within for the very first time. Tears trickled down my face. I felt so incredibly touched by that question, and I didn't yet understand why.

Following that class, I began to live life through a new lens: "What allows me to receive?"

That question brought me from my mind, into my body. *How does this feel?*

And with that question, my life began to change drastically, and fast.

With the support of somatic therapy, breath work, and yoga, I began to feel myself in a way that I hadn't for a long time. I was learning just how deeply I felt, how sensitive a body system I was living in, and how much was inside me that was longing to be expressed. I was learning to be with my 'human-ness' without numbing or running away from it. I saw clearly how I had been spending my time — throwing dinner parties, working in real estate, and how socializing with certain people was creating a feeling of emptiness within me. I was longing for something different, something deeper.

And so, I chose to spend my time differently, and my reality started to shift.

I began spending my weekends at yoga retreats and workshops, and enjoying meals and walks with the soul-centered people I had met. The collection of individuals I was spending time with started to blossom into a beautiful community of healers, yogis, and holistic health practitioners. Possibilities were becoming more abundant and life was feeling more open and exciting.

Synchronicity after synchronicity guided me to purchase a one-way plane ticket to Peru. It was a magical moment of clarity as I was divinely guided to put my things in storage and begin a grand adventure of self-discovery.

I left my phone, computer, and camera behind and flew off to Peru enroute to a yoga teacher training with a feeling that anything was possible. I let the wind and fire *within* guide me forward, listening to where I was being guided, to what tickled my heart and appeared as a sweet opening from Spirit.

That time revealed itself to be a period of deep re-learning. After many years of numbing myself from feeling anything, I was retraining myself: practicing the art of feeling and listening, flowing with life rather than forcing. For the first time in my adult life I was tuning in, rather than tuning out.

Through listening, I was discovering who I truly was outside of who I was taught to be.

Over and over again, I was learning to relax, to trust, and to know that in every cell of my being, I am supported. In my journey I was meeting the parts of myself that were addicted to knowing and controlling, that had felt more comfortable contracting and resisting than relaxing and allowing. I was guided to go deeper at women's gatherings and trainings where the beauty of the feminine way was beginning to melt the jaded edges that I had built around my heart.

When I returned home to California after that year of travel, the most incredible thing happened. I started to bleed. It was the first time in over four years. That was precious blood! A sign from my body of restoration and well-being. It was a surreal moment of disbelief. Something that had felt so far away and so confusing for so long was being registered by my system with greater understanding. I knew in that moment that the body speaks a subtle language, that *she* is always listening and yearning for connection. It marked the beginning of a very sacred relationship — a growing respect and lifelong service to *womb wisdom* and our feminine expression.

Connecting with my womb, trusting in my own intuitive guidance to lead me, defying the medical system, and relying on my own inner knowing was powerful.

In the Sacred Journey of returning home to my body, there was a message that reverberated deep within my cells: "Let Go and Let Goddess."

Let Go and Let Goddess is my invitation to 'trust fall' into the support that is always there, in full surrender to the beautiful discovery of life. When I let go of any idea of who I am and commit to the discovery of who I am destined to be, life meets me in the most magical of ways. I was guided deeper into my study of the womb, of the menstrual cycle, and its connection to the voice and our creative expression. A feeling of resourcefulness, of being sweetly settled in my being, met me. It was completely new, almost foreign but familiar. I was intrigued by this new realm of learning about feminine energy, creative potential, and honoring the Goddess.

What I learned about my feminine cyclical nature through my own intuitive feeling was that in order to alleviate my menstrual discomfort, (which had plagued me since its return) I had to first really feel and embrace the intelligence of my body. I had to be present to the tension, to fully understand and integrate the messages my womb was trying to communicate. I committed to creating sacred space in my calendar, giving myself full permission to slow down and to be with whatever I was feeling, no painkillers included.

When I took the time to listen, the feeling would echo through my being, "Slow down, sweet Kristen."

Oh how hard it was for me to slow down! I dreaded the 'time of the month' because I knew it was a time to rest, to turn away from to-do's and to listen deeply. This slowly began to change as my commitment to creating space and honoring my body grew. It was so powerful to feel fully dropped in, in deep respect to the wisdom of cycles and to the process at play. With every passing month, the cramps eased and my relationship to taking care of myself and honoring this sacred time deepened immensely. I now appreciate and cherish these days of self-reflection and personal restoration.

She, *the womb*, is teaching me in so many ways. She is my touch point for connection. She inspires me to look toward the wisdom of cycles and seasons and invites me to surrender more deeply into the support of life. She shows me when I'm ignoring my sensitivity and disconnecting from the richness of my emotional landscape. She encourages me to plug into the wild, erotic, and everchanging nature of my feminine ecology. She gifts me with the feeling of connection to the Earth, and to the divine web of women everywhere.

Throughout my relationship with the womb I've been reminded again and again of the importance of rest, integration, and becoming acutely aware of patterns of rushing and forcing. I call this Journey, the Path of Pleasure: of slowing down and luxuriating in the moment-to-moment magic of life. Understanding that pleasure is not just something we create in certain moments with another, but that it is an immersion into the present moment, into the feeling level of our experience. A continuous home coming into the breath and the sensations of the body. It is not always easy, but it surely is rewarding. In the Path of Pleasure, we know that a life that feels inspiring and filled with beauty is not just a fairytale dream, but our birthright.

I walk in full trust that this is how life is intended to be lived, and that I am always supported in my Journey Home. Thank Goddess for the blood clots.

I can now say that I am living life truly IGNITED; the sacred fire which has once burned me is now lighting my life up in the most magical ways. I am beyond grateful. I hope that you, too, feel the familiarity and intelligence in the wisdom that is carried in your womb. The primal and intricate intelligence of the Earth gifted to us, as women, to carry. May we find great honor and hope in this gift, and feel empowered to be a voice for this wisdom. To breathe into any shame around pleasure and our sacred anatomy, and let it fuel our passion for exploration and expression.

I hope that you, dear sister, feel inspired to honor the beauty and perfection of your body, exactly as it is, and to become lifelong friends and lovers. To take time to cultivate a relationship of respect and deep listening. Magic will meet you, I promise.

Ignite Action Steps

Honor and connect with the elemental being and wise woman that you are. In understanding the natural forces which we are made of, we create more space for our Goddess to be and thrive.

- *Earth.* Cultivate a relationship with the Earth and your Body. Take time to listen to the messages. Touch your body and the Earth. Witness how she shifts from season to season.

- *Water.* Honor yourself as an emotional being. Where are things not flowing?

- *Fire.* Honor the passion, the power, the sexual fire that lives within you. Create space for this aspect of your being to explore, express, and play.

- *Air.* Honor the presencing power of breath. Take time to witness how you're breathing, and that you're breathing. Explore your range and relationship to your voice.

Kristen Appenrodt – United States of America
www.kristenappenrodt.com

SENSUALITY

Embodying the Goddess
SHARING FROM AN EXPERT

SEDONA SOULFIRE

"Your body is a temple and the Goddess lives within."

You are an Earthly representative of the cosmic creative force. As you stand in the midst of a majestic and awe-inspiring naturescape, know that you are a sacred reflection of this perfection. Your body contains the wisdom of the Universe. It is a precious and perfect *micro*cosmic expression of the magical *macro*cosmic cycles of life. It is a portal of ecstasy! The blissful pleasure we experience as we revel in sounds, sights, tastes, scents, and feelings is a pathway to divine communion. This bliss is your birthright. You deserve to experience sumptuous embodied fulfillment; in fact, your body was designed for it. Your body's systems and functions are governed by the same innate intelligence that animates all of life. You are a chalice, a container of divine and miraculous creative energy. This energy can be amplified, directed, and expressed as you desire. This is your power. The brilliant ray of your unique beauty is an integral part of the whole. True beauty is diverse. We are living in an embodied reality and your sacred earth body is the gateway to Igniting and uniting with the goddess within!

Take a moment, dear one, and breathe in these sacred truths. Allow them to bloom in your consciousness and soothe your soul. Can you imagine if you had been told from the very start of your life that you are a divine miracle and your body contains all the wisdom of the Universe? What do you think your relationship to yourself and your body would be had we all been raised in a world with systems, structures, and cultural constructs that were shaped by the aforementioned statements of truth? Close your eyes and imagine such a world. Sink into the feelings of empowerment and relief that this world inspires.

Unfortunately, we did not grow up in a world that truly honors the diversity of beauty, the magic of our body temples, or the creative power we contain within ourselves. Instead, we have had to navigate through the muck of body abashment, sexual shaming, and violative dishonoring. Right now, there are 'beauty' industries playing out their own manipulative million-dollar agendas designed to make us feel imperfect, flawed, and not as beautiful as we are. I don't think there is a woman on the planet who has not felt the repercussions of this. But times are changing. We are currently emerging from a dark period of feminine discrediting and disempowerment, rising like a phoenix from the ashes, reclaiming our power, listening to our wisdom, healing our hearts, honoring our bodies, celebrating our womanhood, and Igniting the goddess within! This book in your hands is part of this radiant re-emergence. Women all over the planet are raising their voices, sharing their stories, and reconnecting with their true essence as wise, loving, creative, powerful beings. We are turning the tides, rewriting the story, and coming home to ourselves and our bodies in self-loving acknowledgment and celebration.

The ancients celebrated and revered feminine presence and the womanly vessel. We can see this from the many paleolithic Venus figurines bearing large breasts, round bellies, full buttocks, and heavy hips.

In times of antiquity, women were celebrated in their procreative power; the impregnated and ripe expression of a woman's body was a collective focus of worship and celebration. Women were revered as human incarnations of The Goddess and the way in which women served life through incubation, gestation, birthing, and nurturance was honored as the miracle it is. This ancient reverence toward women, our bodies, and the way we fully serve the continuation of life can be a strong inspiration to women of this modern age. It offers an illuminated perspective on how we can connect with our goddess gifts and honor ourselves.

Through the magic of our women's bodies, we create space and seed creative potential. We hold, incubate, and nurture that which is being created. We bring it through the chalice of our *being* and then we offer sustenance, protection, guidance, and support. Whether you choose to have children or not, whether you are able to or not, as women at any age in any circumstance, we all hold this powerfully encoded blueprint of creation. Through the magic of our monthly cycles, our bodies purify, clear, and create fresh space for life to bloom. In the same way in which our womb creates space for new life, so do our spirits create space for creativity. Ovulation offers forth a spark of creative potential in the form of an ovum. In a similar fashion, we can be hit by the spark of an idea or creative inspiration. If the spark is fertilized, our bodies provide nutrients, shelter, and optimal circumstances for new life to be fed, fueled, sustained, and gestated within. So too do we offer forth our feminine nurturance that our most fertile ideas grow. Then, with the utmost courage and strength, we open our bodies in an act of all-encompassing surrender to birth the new life through. Amazingly, the miracle does not stop there. Instead, our bodies generate nutrients and food for the new life. Whether we receive the seed spark of inspiration to make a meal, redecorate the bedroom, plan a fundraiser, Ignite passion in a relationship, create an artistic offering, open a small business, or create a family, we offer ourselves and our lives as the space and energy needed for manifestation. Through our feminine presence and devoted intention, we bring the formless into form and then, from the depth of our hearts, nurture these manifestations in love and support.

This is where the ancient goddess worshiping traditions and our bodies can guide the way. For it is in the act of doing what is actually quite natural to so many of us that we are embodying the goddess and expressing our divine feminine superpowers. This becomes a more empowering goddess embodiment process when we open our ancient eyes, engage in our creative pursuits with intention, and experience ourselves as incarnations of The Goddess of Creation.

Embodying the goddess is understanding that this creative blueprint is a power. It is a gift. It is here to serve the world and not by just the continuation of the human species but by filling the world with offerings born from your creative, loving feminine presence. What's born of this creative blueprint offers the world the medicine of inspired connection, beauty, fresh expression, protection, spiritual heart nourishment, and LIFE! We are able to connect with our goddess gifts by perceiving and receiving the wisdom that lies in the blueprint of our womanly creative potential, but also in seeing how the larger cosmic cycles of the moon and mother nature's seasons are also reflected in our bodies and our life cycles.

It's no coincidence that the average menstruation cycle is the same length as one lunar cycle. Dark new moon is connected to the bleeding time when we are fallow and empty. The waxing moon as it ripens to full is when we make our way toward ovulation. Ovulation symbolizes full moon time when we are ripe, luminous, and filled with potential. The waning moon is connected to when our bodies again make our way toward menstruation, turning back toward the new moon. Our womb cycles are a fractal of the larger pattern. This applies to our entire lives as women, too. Our maiden time aligns with the beginning of the cycle and the season of Spring, a time of youthful innocence, exploration, growth, and blooming potential. Summertime, like the full moon, is our mother phase, a time of sacred ripening, of fulfilling our creative callings, of shining our brilliance through our manifestations. Like a lush summer garden, a woman's mother phase is a time of rich and radiant expression, a time of experiencing and connecting with the fullness of ourselves and our lives. Autumn and winter, the crone's waning moon seasons, see the force of life draw deep within and manifests as powerful inner gnosis. It is the time of shedding extraneous and outworn ways of being, and embodying the knowledge gained through living a full life. It is a time of drawing one's energy back to center to rest in the sanctity of well-cultivated heart knowing.

When we honor and acknowledge our incredible innate connection to Mother Nature and her cycles, we can understand our divinity and embody our connections and the wisdom contained within them with confidence and clarity. This holds the seeds of our awakening and guides us into a sacred space of knowing ourselves, knowing nature, and thriving in the awareness and beauty of our intimate interconnection.

Our miraculous bodies not only link us to the wisdom of nature and the cosmos but are our most powerful tool for transformation. In tantric and yogic wisdom traditions, our connection to the entire matrix of life and its energetic building blocks (known as archetypes) is invoked and experienced through ritual embodiment practices. These traditions viewed the body as a microcosmic expression of, and link to, the larger macrocosm. Movement, breath work, sacred sound, energetic practices, and other rituals would be performed to attain a high vibratory state and invoke and embody archetypal energies personified by a specific deity. These techniques coupled with devotion and intention enabled dancing priestesses in ancient temples of India and Nepal to evoke, contain, amplify, and transmit the chosen deity's energies that it may serve as an empowerment to the collective. The Natyashasta, a 2500-year-old text on divine dance and drama, tells us the purpose of temple dance and other temple arts is to offer a transmission of divine energy and universal truth to awaken and elevate consciousness on the planet.

Archetypes are energetic blueprints that provide intrinsic structure to life. They are collective constants that expand beyond time, space, and culture. They give order to what otherwise would be chaotic. We can easily see archetypes as expressed in the tarot and in different goddesses and gods through various cultures and traditions. Carl Jung referred to them as underlying forms within the collective unconscious which emerge as images, motifs, and qualities such as the Mother, the Lover, the Queen.

We see the archetypal energy of fierce love and fiery transformation in the Hindu Goddess Kali and the Buddhist Goddess Vajrayogini. We connect with the archetypal energies of sensuality, beauty, fulfillment, and sustenance through the Hindu Goddess Laksmi, the Greek Goddess Aphrodite, and the Latin American Goddess Oshun. We can see the foundational frequency of gnosis, higher knowing, expanded vision, awakened intuition, and connection to magic and mystery in the Tarot card of the High Priestess, in the Egyptian Goddess Isis, in the Gnostic-Christian Goddess Sophia. We can think of archetypes as they permeate all of life, ourselves included. These dancing priestesses of antiquity were not tapping into something that was outside of themselves necessarily but instead awakening something that lies within. They opened themselves as transceivers as they embodied these energies and anchored them into the earth grid for planetary healing and elevation.

Women's ritual embodiment was an integral part of sacred rites in India and beyond. In Greece, Egypt, Babylon, African, Algeria, and Latin America, priestesses danced the sacred stories of creation and offered embodied enactments of goddess mythos. They accessed the wisdom of other planes of existence and shared this wisdom through their dance. They brought forth the embodied blessing of the gods and goddesses they portrayed. Through their ritual artistry they served as living temples that they and others may commune with the goddess energies that flowed through them.

These temple dancers, sacred artists, and ecstatically embodied priestesses were honored and revered. Their service was seen as valuable and integral aspects of a harmonious thriving whole. Their spiritual embodiment enlivened and empowered the community, nourishing the spiritual hearts of all.

Now, whether temple dance or priestess arts resonate with you, I am sure you may have drifted into a heightened and rarefied state in which you felt altered, more expansive, and connected to something greater than yourself, perhaps during love making, dancing, singing, gardening, hiking, swimming, surfing, breastfeeding, doing martial arts, or working out. These are the moments of true goddess embodiment, and something that is accessible to all of us. It is why there are different goddesses with unique attributes and qualities, Goddesses of earth abundance and harvest; Goddesses of love, sexuality, and sensual pleasure; Goddesses of wildness and nature; Goddesses of water, flow, creativity; Goddesses of unconditional love and nourishment; Goddesses of protection and providence; Goddesses of strength, strategy, and will power.

This is where connecting with the archetypes through the goddesses offers us a world of inspiration in knowing ourselves, our strengths, weaknesses, and most of all our potential. When we view the archetypes and the various goddesses and their qualities as relevant aspects of ourselves we can more readily embrace our full spectrum nature and navigate through the wild tides of life armed with our arsenal of goddess attributes. We are offered an opportunity to better understand ourselves and know what face of the goddess needs to rise within and through us to best meet life's ever changing sea of experiences.

Perhaps we need to embody the fiercely compassionate demon slaying Hindu Goddess Durga when we need to meet ourselves in a more compassionate loving way and slay our inner demons of self-doubt and harsh self-criticism. Maybe we are called to embody Artemis, Greek goddess of intention and independence, as we honor our own autonomy and set self-protective boundaries on our time and space. Perhaps it is Polyneisna Goddess Pele of volcanoes and primal power that quakes through our body as awakened passion and untamed creative expression.

When we see our bodies, our hearts, and the entirety of our being as the playground for the goddess to express her many facets, we activate our present day priestess power and are able to experience ourselves and our lives as divine. This also offers wonderful inspiration to take care of ourselves and our bodies as the vessels and channels that they are. The more clear and cared for your body, the better it will serve you in being able to access and connect with the goddess energies that lie within.

I once read a quote that said something along the lines of "honor the goddess by honoring women." This touched me deeply. When we honor and care for ourselves we are honoring the goddess within. Embodying the goddess looks like radical acts of self love and self care. It is a sacred self honoring that goes beyond what the outside world could ever give us. It's a deep respect for our feelings, our desires, our inspirations, our bodies, and a rich understanding of our innately multifaceted nature. It is allowing ourselves to fully enjoy the gifts of being in a vibrantly alive body of sensual delight and primal prowess. We all have a powerful opportunity to be a force of feminine awakening on the planet now. Freeing ourselves of self-imposed limitations frees the feminine force for one and for all. It is a revolutionary act to dissolve the self-judgment and harsh criticism and transform our inner dialogue to one of praise, compassion, caring, and celebration!

Our goddess worshiping ancestors saw women as powerful human emanations of the creative power and universal wisdom of The Goddess. Can we see ourselves in that same light? Could we relate to ourselves from this sacred viewpoint, walk it, talk it, live it, love it, express it, embody it? What would that look like to you? What do you feel moving and responding in yourself as you sit with this inquiry, as you read these stories of awakening and transformation? One by one, like in the stories you are reading here in this book, women are Igniting the goddess within, coming home to themselves in sacred acknowledgment, love, and acceptance. It's a movement, a force, a flow. It is bigger than just one woman and yet it takes each one of us to create and sustain the momentum. It is the call of the goddess beckoning us to return to her that we may know her love, commune with her grace, and unite with her power within her most miraculous and majestic temple. The temple of the human body. The temple that is YOU.

Sedona Soulfire – United States of America
Priestess, Ritual Artist
www.sedonasoulfire.com

RECEIVING

Ruqaya Kalla

*"What you bring to the world from inside of
yourself is what you empower others with."*

**I want you to see yourself truly as you are. There is so much more to
you than you have ever imagined. You have the power within you to do
things that you never expected you could. My wish is for you to realize
that anything is possible when you focus on your inner power. Being a
Goddess is about focusing inwards, embracing your strengths, accepting
your weaknesses, and knowing that you are perfect just as you are. We
are all Goddesses in our own way.**

The Power of Receiving

I was in Pula, Croatia, at the opening party for an event I was attending. My
white high heeled shoes were hurting my feet and making walking extremely
uncomfortable. Some of the attendees who I had met earlier that evening decided
to stroll along the beach. I wanted to go with them but I dreaded walking all
that way. I stood there undecided, my desire to join them heavy from my dread.
It was at that moment a young girl came to me, went down on her knees, and
replaced my shoes with her own more comfortable ones. I was speechless and
thinking, "What is going on here?" When she finished, she looked up at me
and simply said, "Welcome, your majesty."

That gesture of kindness and compassion shocked me. I realized how sweet
that act was, especially coming from a complete stranger. All I could do was

say, "Thank you!" One of the things I know about myself is that I'm terrible at receiving things. I have had to continually work on my ability to accept: a compliment, a random act of kindness, or even treasured gifts from the Universe... but it took me a long time to grasp that idea.

Twenty years before that moment on the beach, I was newly married and had my first child. I recall feeling like I hadn't yet achieved anything significant. Most of my friends had been at university, but I chose to get married and did not pursue any further study. After my second child, I remember telling my husband, "I feel I am not going anywhere in my life. It is as if I am postponing my career, denying my profession." It was true that I felt this way, yet I would always find a justification why it was never the right time for me to pursue my professional dreams. Having grown up seeing my father running his businesses, I made several business attempts of my own, always going into business with partners, which usually ended in losses. I was never in charge and had no control over the outcomes. I thought that I needed other people to help me and that I was not able to do it alone. After multiple attempts over the years and five children later, I found myself in the same place — lacking in fulfillment.

From a young age, I always felt the need to help other people. As a family, we often attended self-development workshops; my first was around the age of 12. I remember telling my father one day that we needed to gather the schools in my community together so we could learn how to prevent bullying and how not to judge others but rather accept them as they are.

As an adult, this idea of healing others stuck deep within me. For years I had been interested in a healing modality called *Body Talk*. Every time I tried to look deeper into it and study it further, I used excuses that prevented me from continuing. But now, after child number five, my husband said he would support me in my studies, so I enrolled in my first *Body Talk* training course.

I was still breastfeeding when I went to my first class and, every break, my husband would bring the baby for me to feed. The training was happening in the same city where we lived, which made things easier. But for the next module of the course, I had to commute to another city one hour away. Even with the complicated logistics, I still had full support from my husband who would bring our baby each day to be nourished during my break times. We managed that quite well.

Helping others gave me a sense of purpose. I was passionate to support people to change their lives. Learning and going to courses to grow my skills in this field became a positive addiction for me. It was not just the skills I was gaining as part of the process, it was how I was growing as a person myself.

I enjoyed every part of it. I was a very dedicated student, asking as many questions as possible. I remember when one of the instructors was annoyed at me because I was very curious, wanting to expand my comprehension and understanding continuously. I wanted to see the *full* picture, not just parts of it. I wanted to go deeper and become knowledgeable. I craved learning and doing more. I was always yearning for the next bit. I kept pushing and studying harder. In record time, I was ready to take my exam and became a certified *Body Talk* practitioner.

While my kids were growing up, I started studying other healing modalities such as Access Bars, Cranial Sacral therapy, Neurolinguistic Programming, and others. Along the way, I heard people telling me that I couldn't do it, that moving so fast was too much for me… but I am the type of person who, if you tell me I cannot do something, that will only make me want to do it even more. I persisted in my dream to keep learning and gaining qualifications so I could help more people in their journey through life.

All that dedication paid off not only with knowledge that I could share with other people, but with the tremendous personal growth I experienced myself.

Before starting this journey, I was very conscious of not allowing my ego to show up. I wanted to be humble. Every time something resembled my ego, I would pull back. Somewhere in all those trainings, I finally realized that it was not about me being egocentric; it was about authentically sharing my gifts with the world. I then had the clarity, understanding, and a grasp of who I was, which allowed me to accept that I had much more potential than I had ever given myself credit for. I felt like anything was possible. Whatever I put my mind to, I could achieve if I chose to. Making that connection to the powerful Goddess that was within me, not outside of me, represented the beginning of a new awakening.

The Universe wasn't done teaching me how to rely on my own personal power. I was attending many different courses and they were all very practical with live demonstrations where people in the audience were called up to work with the trainer right there in front of everyone. Every class the instructor was always calling people to come to the stage, but I was never the person they requested. I would ask myself, "Why not me?" If there were classes where they picked absolutely everybody, I was usually the last one to be chosen.

I finally gave up on being called upon and then, to my surprise, on the first day of a new class, for the very first exercise, the instructor pointed directly at me and asked me to come to the stage. Being front and center and fully exposed was a new experience. As I climbed the steps to the stage feeling awkward and nervous, the weight of everyone's eyes on me was heavy. Despite my nervousness, I realized that it was all okay; the Goddess was in me and would guide me.

After that process, I was more open toward that healing modality and felt lighter about being vulnerable in front of people. I realized I had been harder on myself than those watching were. I didn't need to be perfect, I just needed to be myself. Despite this new realization, my nervousness crept back during my next class.

I called upon my Goddess energy to guide me and show me the way. For many months I had been searching for the best in neurolinguistic programming training and after much consideration, I decided to fly across the globe from South Africa to Orlando, Florida, to take the course with the co-creator of neurolinguistic programming.

The class was larger than any others I had been to before. I was in a different country on my own, and I did not know any of the attendees. Despite my trepidation, during that class, something magical happened. The instructor asked who was afraid to come to the stage. I was obviously thinking "Me!" but I wouldn't dare to raise my hand. Hands all around me went up in the air, but it didn't matter. He must have felt my energy among all those hundreds of people. He pointed right at me and said, "You! Come up here."

I couldn't believe he had chosen me and not one of the dozens of people with their hands waving high in the air. My immediate unthinking response was, "No." As I sat there, the instructor then proceeded to take me through a short process to make it easier for me to accept his invitation. It worked, and I mustered up the courage to join him on stage. As we worked together, he saw that I needed to step into my *own strength* when I'm facing others, especially when in front of a crowd. When I stand on stage, I should be able to look at people like I own the room and I deserve their full attention. I should radiate confidence and power whenever I need to. At some point during the session, he asked me to face the room and say, "I own your ass!"

I did. I said it over and over at his command. With each time I said it, I felt the fear of facing everyone releasing from my body. My chin lifted and my eyes finally rose to meet those in the crowd. With every repeat, I felt more and more empowered. After that process, I had so much more confidence. There was a huge shift in the way I looked at the audience, but more importantly, there was an even bigger shift in the way I looked at myself.

I went to several other courses on NLP, traveling frequently to the USA to qualify myself as a trainer. Each certification I earned made me eager to learn more and more.

In the USA, I met a gentleman. In the process of learning together, we started doing business together. In the past, every time I started a new business, I was *not* the one in charge. Now, I felt more knowledgeable, more experienced, and more empowered and I stepped willingly into the lead role in our business. Through that partnership and with all the learning I was acquiring, I started to see in practice that I was capable of doing much more than I ever believed. When my partner decided to no longer be involved in the business, I considered for a moment running to my family for support. My family had several businessmen in it, but deep down I knew I didn't want to rely on them in my business. I felt I could handle all the problems by myself. When I sat down with my accountant and we ran through the numbers, I thought, "If I could make it once, I can make it again." I had bad moments, but I never looked back at the losses. I kept going. I worked hard at both my business and continued to attend trainings and gain more certifications.

After having experienced all of this, I realized that I had more potential than I ever gave myself credit for, more than I was willing to acknowledge. I saw that for years something in me resisted my worth and was unwilling to grasp it. I had to ask myself why couldn't I believe in my own potential? Why couldn't I believe in myself fully?

This thought lingered in me until one day, I was in Washington, DC, at a class when one of the presenters paid me a compliment. As I usually did, I thanked him and then immediately paid him a compliment in return. He looked at me oddly then and told me that I hadn't acknowledged what he said. That I struggled to receive. I opened my mouth to reply, then stopped. I thought of all the times I had negated or brushed away and not received such a gift. This awareness started an unravelling in my mind, and for the first time, I said nothing in return. His words resonated perfectly with me. I always felt I had to immediately give positive feedback bigger and stronger. My focus was on the other person. Receiving was not a natural or welcomed instinct for me.

I realized then that this major quality of the Goddesses was missing inside of me. Receiving is one of the characteristics of the feminine. Although I was a female, a wife, a mother of five, a business woman, and a dedicated daughter, my focus was mostly on doing, serving, giving, performing, and assisting. Not on receiving at all. With this new awareness, I wanted to learn, starting with the basics of how to say thank you when receiving a compliment and being accepting of that.

Several people had to come to my life to help me to see the power that indeed existed *inside of* me. There was something in me that still said, "I couldn't do it on my own." But little by little as I stepped into my own power, I felt more independent and capable. And then, I went to Pula, in Croatia, to spend two weeks learning from different personal development teachers. I immersed myself in the opportunity to practice *receiving* and began to challenge my own belief systems.

The opening celebration of the program was a theme party and we all had to dress in white. This was a challenge for me. I thought wearing white clothes would emphasize my darker complexion — something I had been teased for as a child — and I was terrified by that. I never, ever, ever wore white.

This event brought the opportunity for me to break that cycle. And I wanted that. I ended up planning not to be completely in white. As a Muslim, I always wear a scarf in public over my head, so I had planned to wear a gold scarf instead. But my luggage, where my outfit for the party was, didn't arrive with me. I had to buy new clothes and everything that I found was white, including the scarf.

Arriving at the party, I was very uncomfortable. I kept looking at myself using the camera on my phone and thought I looked terrible. And then somebody said to me, "Oh, I have seen you in pictures. It seems the camera loves you. Our photographers said you are very photogenic." I started to talk to him and had the courage to express that I didn't feel good wearing white. He replied, "What are you talking about? Brown people look the best in white. It highlights their beautiful skin color." His words made me start looking at myself differently. I could feel the Goddess coming forth as I started to feel comfortable in my own skin.

Others came to me at that same party with similar words of admiration and I couldn't believe it. Why would they say those things to me unless they truly meant it? Days later, I realized they had seen in me the true Goddess Within before I even saw her in myself.

I had not expected to leave that conference with so many new friends who made me feel loved and appreciated. I didn't expect the friendships to last beyond the glorious days and nights in Pula. While I was back in South Africa, some of my dearest new friends sent me a video saying, "When are you coming back to us? Your chair is waiting for you. We miss you!" Their video made me tear up. I felt loved, valued, respected, and that changed everything! One more belief that was transformed. To this day, we keep connected and our friendships only grow. They have changed my life, as they have made me receive love and allowed me to see myself even more. They opened doors in me that were closed in the past. Now, I am open to receive whatever comes my way.

As a result of being connected to my Goddess and to who I truly am, after all those experiences, I grew both professionally and personally. I expanded my business, I started helping people through healing, I was invited to conferences and retreats to represent organizations. I even went to the United Nations. One thing I realize now is that I don't need anyone else. All I need is me and my Creator. I am not dependent on anyone to step up into my real power. I realized I have a choice.

As a modern woman and Goddess, there is so much more we all can achieve. Even when times are hard, I still feel that whatever is going to come will be beneficial and powerful to us. Be open to receive it all! Self-doubts may still pop up, but you have the clarity and power in your hands. Embrace your strengths and love your imperfections. Be present. So much has changed and it is still changing. Whatever happens, be grateful and accept what *is* with Goddess grace.

IGNITE ACTION STEPS

- Love life without expectations — be unconditional in the way you love.

- Be in the present — focus on the now. Leave the past in the past and the future in the future.

- Focus on your strengths — when we pay attention to our strengths, we are able to receive more of what the Universe wants for us.

- Give openly — The more you give, the more you receive.

Ruqaya Kalla – South Africa
Entrepreneur, Holistic Healer, NLP Trainer
@ @ruqayakalla

ENDURANCE

JENET DHUTTI-BHOPAL

"You are divine feminine energy personified; let no one diminish your spirit."

I am sharing my story with you to inspire you to take action and work toward an imperative goal. I want you to *encourage* young girls and women so they may know that their existence and their voices matter. At the same time, I wish for us all to continue to *encourage* young boys and men to *empower* HER. My ultimate wish is that all understand that their feminine energy should never, ever feel diminished.

ENCOURAGING & EMPOWERING THE MODERN GODDESS

When I was 11 years old, my mother gave birth to my baby sister, Nisha. She was not the only sister I had — I was one of four in our female-dominated household. I remember going to school that day happy and excited, but also a little worried. This was not the first time I had seen my mother pregnant, but the 11-year-old me saw her worrying and praying a lot more. I wondered then if it was because she had fallen on the stairs a few weeks earlier, but a niggling thought in the back of my mind hinted that she might be worried about having yet another girl.

The day my sister was born, my father came to pick me up from school. Stepping out of the car, he had the biggest smile on his face. My two younger sisters, Sarika and Monika, cheerfully yelled out from the back seat, "We got another baby sister, Didi." I was absolutely overjoyed at the news.

Dad drove us to the hospital. The whole drive there, I was mentally taking notes on how I would plan my days ahead, adjust my schedule, and help out more now that there was another little human joining our 'party of five' and making it 'the six of us.' My happiness at having a sister was slowly being overpowered by worry and I couldn't connect it to any event that may have taken place.

I had been to the hospital a year before to get stitches in my knee, and my gut tightened with an instinctive feeling of unease even though I knew we were there for the happiest of reasons. After having a cesarean section, Mom was resting in bed with all sorts of tubes attached to her body. She looked exhausted yet managed a faint smile. I was anxious to go near her, afraid I might pull on those tubes and harm her. Right next to her, the nurses were bathing my newly-born sister and joyously admiring her delicate features. At that very moment, it was just the six of us and it felt like heaven. Any worry was overshadowed by contentment and joy.

A little while later, four women from our community circle entered the room — the 'mean ones' as I used to call them and, quite frankly, still do. As soon as my dad stepped out of the room to grab juice boxes and cookies, their criticism started. These women should have been admiring the baby and asking Mom how she was feeling and offering support. Instead, they started crying and, in Punjabi, questioning God and his decision to punish my parents by giving them another daughter. "Why couldn't He have gifted you with a son, Rani?" "What are you going to do now? You will need to prepare and save lots of money and jewelry to marry off *four* daughters!" "Are you being punished for something you both did in your past lives?"

Exhausted and overwhelmed, Mom burst into tears. With each tear, my own heart's conviction grew stronger. My mother had just endured not only a cesarean birth but also a bit of reconstructive surgery to correct stitches from her previous birth. Lying there on that bed, she was a hero and I knew it. The words she was absorbing were cruel and unjust, and her tears represented her knowledge that these callous comments would continue to come forward, perhaps for the rest of our lives. It was not fair. Watching her cry, I was panic-stricken for her. I tried saying something to help take the sadness away, but I felt overwhelmed too and the words would not come. I stood by the bedside and caressed my mother's hand, saying, "Mom," over and over. There were no words to express the tumble of emotions in my 11-year-old heart. What could my parents have done to be punished? Was I really such a burden on my family?

I was not the only one to feel the injustice of those four women's cruel words. My mother's dear friend, sitting quietly at her bedside until then, stood up and berated those mean women, announcing loudly that all babies are a gift from God, no matter their gender, and that this child, as her sisters were, was a blessing.

Her words echoed through my body with a strange power. This was the intuition I was dismissing all along. At the tender age of 11, hearing the 'mean ones' words, I started to worry too, about things that I shouldn't have, like how my parents would manage to fund our schooling and eventually our weddings. I stood there in silence, trying to block out the 'noise' that was made up of sheer idiocy, but this one friend of my mother's had given a voice to what I was thinking. My sister *was* a blessing. She, like all of us girls, was a gift from God, not a burden. I offered a silent prayer and made a quiet promise to my mother — little did I know it was a promise that would become my moral compass and impact every decision for the rest of my life.

After a few days of recovery at the hospital, Dad brought Mom and my baby sister home. We lived in a cozy, homey two-bedroom apartment in Manila, Philippines, that was filled with love and laughter. The first floor consisted of the living room, kitchen, dining room, and a small open area next to the bathroom. The night before, my sisters and I helped Dad rearrange the furniture and living room so that a daybed could be placed on the first floor in close proximity to our only bathroom so my mom wouldn't have to take the stairs repeatedly.

Pushing furniture around that night, though I did not know it at the time, awakened my inner Goddess. I discovered, piece by piece, the nurturing aspect of my being. Call it instinct or an innate maternal feeling, but that very moment was when I embraced my Goddess. I knew I had to grow up and be the protector and role model for my sisters. Mom was on complete bed rest until her stitches healed and I knew that I had to step up and care for all of us. I knew that, as girls and women later on, we would be facing many challenges and I wanted to prepare, but in that precise moment, the challenge ahead of me was more immediate: Who will cook for us?

The answer was my whole family. My mother's brother and sister came that day to help us out. From the moment my aunt walked through the door, my body shuddered with a release of tension. It was a relief to have someone who genuinely cared for Mom's holistic health, not just the family's status or social standing. She trained me on how to do a few tasks while my maternal uncle coached me on what to do if any of the 'mean ones' came back. The entire apartment was flooded with the rich aromas of spices from the curries and chicken adobo, the smell of soy sauce and vinegar teasing my nose and making me hungry. My aunt cooked sufficient batches of food for us for two or three days. I felt a sense of sadness when they had to leave. Sarika was nine years old and Monika was not even eight years old yet. I knew I had to be the 'adult' for both of them. The nervous feeling and weakness in my legs was unbearable. I remember running to the bathroom, vomiting, crying, and vomiting again. After purging, I felt a surge of relief and sense of readiness. I have never told a single soul about that until now.

Over the next few days, I discovered what a great cook my dad was (he still is). He taught me how to knead dough to make chapattis. He also demonstrated how to use a pressure cooker and told me it was the most important tool in any Indian kitchen — second only to the various spice mixes. My sisters and I all contributed to ensure the household functioned as efficiently as possible, dividing tasks in the kitchen, caring for the baby, and helping our parents. I was given the additional task of ensuring my sisters were completing their home-work, helping them get ready for school, and completing my own schoolwork as well. When I found myself getting overwhelmed by it all, I would think back to the words of my mother's friend, and recall my father's constant reassurance, "You four girls are such a blessing to me." With that thought foremost in my mind, I toughened myself to face any challenges ahead and told myself we'll be fine. The six of us will be alright.

When my mom was physically and emotionally stronger, she didn't mince words. She loudly voiced her dissatisfaction every time someone would attempt to shift the topic of conversation toward her challenges in having to raise four daughters. She had no tolerance for anyone who criticized her situation.

When I turned 18, I got my first marriage proposal. Someone from India called my mom to arrange my marriage to a young man who was working as a teacher. I was sitting with her when she answered the call and my throat tightened with uneasiness. My mother's wise eyes looked at me and she stated clearly, "Jenet is too young for marriage and is focused on her studies."

A huge sense of relief flooded through me at her words. Later that evening, I eavesdropped on my parents as she told my dad about the call. My dad was furious with the caller and shut the whole marriage thing down. When my mother spoke with me later, relaying the full content of the conversation, what bothered me the most was that the caller had announced, "Unmarried young girls are a burden to their parents. They should be married off and leave to build their own life. They must have children and continue the cycle of life." I quietly cheered for my parents and their determination to do right by us and, smiling broadly, went to bed. "It'll be alright," I told myself.

When I graduated from university, a few so-called concerned relatives began to harass my parents about the importance of getting their eldest daughter married. It was apparently 'now or never.' My parents responded to the collective 'concerns' of those people by sending me to the United States for post-graduate studies, which was a rather progressive move for those in my culture. Many raised apprehensions and called my parents irresponsible for sending a young woman to the western world all alone. Dad was nonchalant; however, Mom was a little worried — not because of the 'now or never' comment. She was worried about my safety and survival in a country that had just been massively attacked. I was too, and so were my sisters because my flight to the United States was scheduled just 10 days after the 9/11 attacks in New York.

Adjusting to the western world without my parents and siblings at my side was challenging. I was homesick. It was manageable because I had visited the US in the past and had an idea about the way of life in that part of the world, but it was still an adjustment. My parents had always provided my sisters and me opportunities to learn about other countries, regions, and their cultures. We were encouraged to embrace diversity from a very young age. They were rebels in that way. Others expressed their concerns because exposing girls to a world outside of the four walls of their home was seen as a dangerous precedent that may have negative repercussions. As always, my parents refuted those unwarranted concerns and followed their own path.

My life in the US taught me a lot about independence. I traveled, lived, and worked in India, moved to Canada ten years later, and got married to a marvelous man of my own choosing. Everything was going great until I was in the second trimester of my first pregnancy when I had a miscarriage and lost our son. I was broken and devastated. Despite the tragedy that befell my family and me, I held onto my faith and leaned on my family's support to see me through that dark phase. A relative came to visit and offer her condolences. She shared her own heartbreak over losing a child. I felt so cared for and supported until she uttered the following words, "Had it been a girl, you both wouldn't have been this devastated." All of a sudden I was struggling to breathe. I attempted to sit up on the couch. I was appalled by her comment. My husband Parmjit is a reserved man who only speaks up against idiocy when it is crucial to do so and, at that very moment, it was warranted.

"I didn't care if it was a boy or a girl. All I know is we lost a child. I don't agree with your viewpoint where you diminish the significance of daughters." His words came into my heart as a breath of fresh air. There was something so energizing about what he had said about daughters.

I smiled at my husband, excused myself from the conversation, and went to my bedroom. I was physically, mentally, and emotionally exhausted after the miscarriage, but whatever energy was left in me was not going to be expended toward an ignorant woman who reduced the importance of daughters. What I did want to do was to not let that awful experience deter me from my knowledge that girls and women are an equal part of this world. I knew then and there that my life's mission would be empowering and honoring the feminine. It Ignited in me the determination to continue the feeling I had as an 11-year-old, that every female fundamentally matters.

Growing up, my parents continuously reminded my sisters and I about the importance of education. My parents see their dreams fulfilled through our accomplishments. They have a great sense of pride in seeing their daughters educated and independent. Having a progressive father who believed in empowering his daughters from a very young age (and continues to do so even now) helped build my confidence and inspired me in identifying and structuring my principles. By keeping his last name, I have forever sealed that legacy to which I belong. Meanwhile, having an empathetic husband who cares and supports my advocacy work to raise the importance of educating and empowering girls, is helping me continue conversations and take action. By adding his last name to my last name, I have permanently conjoined the legacies of the most important men in my life.

Presently, I work with marginalized youth in various capacities, especially with girls coming from parts of the world where they don't have a voice or are in fear of using their freedom of speech. I strive to open up their hearts toward embracing their passions and carving a career path for themselves from a young age. I focus on teaching them professional and personal development skills to aid them in improving their proficiency. I also help them define their modern goddess by encouraging them to maintain their authenticity and nurture themselves and others. These skills empower them to live their life independently, strongly, and without fear.

When 11-year-old Jenet's inner goddess awoke and gave her the strength to make a promise to her mom, it unleashed a fierce determination that would persist her entire life. All girls deserve to be empowered and connected to or re-acquainted with the goddess inside of them.

Loving yourself, your goddess, and your chosen gender teaches you the value of Self. You have the ability to make changes that will positively impact you. Your presence as a confident individual uplifts others. I am counting on you to *engage* all women, all goddesses in conversations to help change the rhetoric on female descendants. I ask you to always *encourage* families and communities to celebrate daughters; I need you to *empower* HER — and the many girls and women you will meet along the way.

IGNITE ACTION STEPS

I am sharing a few essentials I have consciously been following which have helped me overcome challenging situations. These are habits I continue to practice. I hope these tips can help you as well.

- **Allies:** Identify genuine people who appreciate, love, and respect you wholeheartedly. They are the superheroes you need when you're at your lowest point in life and cheer for you when you accomplish milestones. You don't need a whole battalion.

- **Network:** Connect with like-minded people who share your vision. You may or may not have the same story or objectives; however, if the conversations foster mutual respect and understanding, place yourself in those circles. Keep your distance from those who weaken your essence.

- **Explore:** Aim to visit new places as much as you can. Don't pressure yourself with a time frame. Be spontaneous; try it even if you are the most structured planner. There is so much to explore on this beautiful planet. Start off with your city then countries and continents. It will help you understand human experiences and perspectives from various lenses.

- **Self-care:** Take care of yourself, your holistic well-being. Nourish your heart, mind, and soul with constructive activities; you owe that to yourself. Nurture your heart, body, mind, and soul with books, thoughts, places, and people you adore.

Jenet Dhutti-Bhopal – Canada
Youth Ally & Mentor
in @jenetdb

STRENGTH

LAUREN CUTHBERT

"A wild, blazing fire can start with one single spark."

Firmeza — a feminine noun — meaning strength, stability, steadiness, endurance, resilience. **My prayer for you, as you read this piece, is that you can feel into my mirror of strength, recollect your own sense of empowerment and inspiration, and receive my story as a reminder of your inner *Firmeza* goddess.**

MY STORY OF FIRMEZA

Throughout my childhood, the 'normal,' happy, calm family dynamic never seemed to last for too long. My family loved to travel a lot across Outback Australia and to islands in Fiji. After my parents' messy separation, there were spontaneous trips with my Dad to his mistress' house and destinations that added to his CV.

My dad was full of passion, charisma, energy, and love although he suffered immensely with bipolar disorder. This led him to years of confusion, cheating on my mother, finding himself in huge debt, experiencing manic ups and downs as well as mental health challenges that progressed to an attempted suicide when I was only eight years old. Months later, on Father's day weekend, he had a boating accident and his body could not be found. As a little girl, confused and shocked, I was reassured with words like, "Let's stay positive. We might find his body. It'll all be ok."

His death was elongated to an agonising five years. When I was 14 years old, his body was found by a fisherman on the shore of the lake where he went missing. The reality of his death sank in and I had certainty that I would not have another day with him.

The last time I saw my father, he said, "I love you." At nine years old, bitter and angry at him for cheating on my mother and wanting to leave life on earth, I slammed the car door on him. My confusion and pain were dressed up with so much projected anger and frustration, but underneath all of this, I knew there was love and I hoped one day there would be forgiveness. Forgiveness for my reactions as a child in response to my Dad's actions and release of the pain I had felt from him.

When Dad went missing, death became a regular occurrence in my life that was as common as celebrating my birthday. At 15, I had attended 15 funerals. This cyclic pattern synchronistically seemed to stop only when my father's body was found. I know that experiencing so much death at such a young age fertilized me to grow into a human who is incredibly grateful for the gift that it is to be alive.

Feeling angry and confused as a teenager, I started to rebel by running away from home. My destructive outbursts even resulted in a hospital visit. Waking up with a drip in my arm and disappointment in my mother's eyes, I longed to learn how to befriend my inner shadow and the dragons that were haunting my mind… and reality. Emotive punk music and thrashing my guitar was medicine for my soul at this time.

Simultaneously, at 11, I began to channel my energy into dance, music, and acting. This gave me a place to express myself and allowed me to enter new paradigms and landscapes. Acting gifted me the illusion of a place where I could manufacture my own life. My creativity soared and became a gateway for me to process and unravel all that had happened. I felt very misunderstood and, as I started maturing as a teenager, my empathetic ways attracted lovers with manipulative qualities who introduced me to drug taking, alcohol bingeing, and patriarchal, porn-inspired lovemaking. Although creative, loving, and visionary traits were heavily present, my lack of boundaries and desire to increase my serotonin and dopamine levels were firmly in the driver's seat.

I witnessed my mother fluctuate to a couple of different men who were clearly not 'the one.' Then, around seven years after we lost Dad, she met a man who at the beginning seemed lovely and supportive. He was the closest thing to a father I had known since my Dad's death. This seven-year relationship, however, became a toxic engagement ending in his prison sentence for domestic violence. I knew my mother felt like a prisoner in her own home, but she attempted to hide her reality from me to protect me. I constantly begged for her to confide in me, desperately wanting her to know that she could choose another way. She then found an unbelievable amount of courage to break free from the chains she was living in and left him to create a new life.

One of the triggers that empowered my mother to leave was acknowledging the effect her relationship was having on her and me. His actions were so volatile that both our lives were at risk. This experience, my mother's and my own strength, and our family's support have taught me that unconditional love and trust always wins. Witnessing my mother's infinite source of strength, vigor, and determination for justice was life changing for me. She connected with a community, found her heart's own medicine, remembered her inner knowing, and listened to her truth.

The realization of how precious this sacred life is, coupled with witnessing my mother's strength, fueled me to explore what was outside of my reality. I asked myself, *"What miracles can be made when I have trust, open my heart to more love, and let myself fill with gratitude?"* When I allowed nature to nourish and hold me in her embrace, I started to notice the undeniable beauty here on earth. I began to travel far and wide, and I noticed and appreciated what was around me outside of the clouded perspectives and dark experiences that life had previously offered me. When I traveled, experienced other cultures, and immersed myself among the trees, my focus became less on the dark. I learned that positivity can start with one single spark and spreads like wildfire. Spending time in nature made me passionate to explore environmental conservation, though I learned quickly that when I wish for healing to occur on this planet, it must first start with me.

My perception of life was cultivated through my choices of how to respond. It was built on becoming curious whether I choose to react, break out of the mold, and use this awareness to go beyond the constructs — on what I'd been taught what is right and what is wrong. I was curious and continued to ask, "What is the meaning of all of this? How can I use these experiences to inspire others? To keep on keeping on?"

My *firmeza* goddess was Ignited with fire to live life like everyday was my last. At 19, I began a journey — traveling to 40 countries in six years. I hiked for 30 days straight in the mountains in New Zealand with no technology; only a backpack and sand flies for company. One of the most powerful, healing, and profound parts of this journey was emptying my hands of my comforting possessions and letting the path through the trees lead the way. Part of my traveling journey involved healing in the Himalayas where I dove deep into yoga and meditation, constantly asking the question, "Why?"

Meditation and yoga became a practice I was
guided and gifted by spirit to apply
to my tool box, to allow myself, to practise more conscious goodbyes.
I began to feel high from the new oxygen supply.
My views, beliefs, attitudes shifted.
And so did the strategy, in the way I let myself cry.

Profound connections with new friends was a constant source of strength for me as I began working in Sweden, the United States, Canada, and then Kenya in the volunteer and outdoor education industry for youth. These connections and environments offered my soul a chance to inflate. I had moments where I was beaming with joy, so happy that nothing would feel unaccomplished if I had died. I became aware of how my body was influenced by the moon and the tides. My mind, body, and soul connection deepened as I saw the earth and me as one. Looking back, I know that the experiences from my past and the support of my loved ones fertilized me to grow into what I have become.

As my *firmeza* goddess, my inner truth, and my strength was embodied and recognized by myself, I found epic moments — like flying off of mountains with a parachute in Austria, saving baby turtles in Malaysia, busking on cobbled street corners in Portugal, and joining in wedding dance parties in the streets of India — were becoming regular occurrences in my life. In my early 20's, I became qualified to work for a company that supports young people from Australia as they travel to developing countries to explore the outdoors and get out of their comfort zones. We built schools in poverty-stricken rural locations; we cleaned up plastic-filled beaches; we planted trees in the Amazon; and we consciously observed what other cultures could teach us. They taught us things like how to thread leaves to make baskets and gave us awareness of our environmental impact. These minimalist tribal cultures showed me the importance of our connection to nature and the potency that a loving and simplistic lifestyle holds.

Energetically, I held my students hands as they taught me what it means to be a leader. I learned that leadership was at its best when I provided a space for not just one person to be at the front, but for us all to step up equally so that together, we all rise. On nights in South East Asia, sitting by a golden red fire baking fresh roti, I would commonly hear students say things like, "It's clear that it should be our global birthright to be loved," and "We should all respect each other equally." All they wanted to do in their lives was give back and make a positive impact. Hearing young people have these profound realizations about equality and environmental needs made my heart dance and overflow with love and gratitude. I encouraged the students to be inspired by one another; to be guided by the laws of nature, by our ancestors, and to listen to their own inner teachers.

I feel, when we strengthen our trees, our animals,
and our seas, our inner worlds mend.
And vice versa, the exchange is mutual.
Moving from a strong place of fear, this opening can feel unusual.
As our hearts remember the innate love we have inside,
This can feel like we are exposed, naked, without a place to hide.

As my yoga journey began to take the steering wheel, I was noticing the flame I had inside of me was highlighting the vision I had to start up my own purposeful yoga travel business. *Karmic Journeys* was birthed; a yoga journey that is more than just learning about the technique of falling out of a handstand and landing in a cartwheel. These yoga retreats travel to nature, support small communities, and empower people to love our unified home. I wanted to give back in a way that could amalgamate all I had learned. After first doing business in a very yang way and burning out my adrenals, I learned that it's best when I lead with my feminine and allow my intuitive wisdom to be the main guide. My passion and commitment to act as a voice for the voiceless wove in my *firmeza* goddess; a consistent thread of strength.

At 24, I fell in love and the walls I had built throughout my life started to disintegrate into rubble. His masculine energy opened into the cracks in my cave and dripped sweet honey, pouring a message to my soul that it was safe to let go of the structures I'd built. I explored deeper, in between the gates, and was curious to learn about the magic, the keys, and the codes that we hold within as women. I wanted to know more about the messages my body was trying to express and explore the sacred space that alchemizes stars into human form.

I know I was his muse; and when I surrendered, liberation and ecstasy emerged. I saw the fragments of what once was my life desperately attempting to lure me back into the past. These places had previously given me nightmares, triggering memories that would bring me pain and destruction. Independently and together, we worked on unravelling the programming of our minds. We could see the patterns that our hearts were urging us to unlearn, letting the multigenerational lessons drift away. We restitched the way in which we weaved as we journeyed through new portholes and consistently redefined our relationship.

His presence whispered sweetly to my essence,
the remembrance of loves' reverence.

Though sounding poetic and heavenly, one of the biggest lessons was in letting go. After two years, we realized it was time to have space so that we could both fly high and not be chained to our pasts. I pulled *firmeza* from the base of my spine to cut the energetic chords, contracts, and visions of an alluded family and future together. The disconnection from our intimacy gave me an invitation to separate from the karmic wheel and realize the reality I was painting from my previous experiences of sorrow. He showed all the parts of me I had not yet healed. We found ourselves, multiple times, smiling, crying, and reflecting on our love story and the comical truth that we both were mirroring all that we had been running away from.

I decided to step back into my power, claim my sovereignty, and choose to align my values to my actions. As I began to feel more empowered from remembering my own self-love, I organically remembered my purpose and my drive and realized there was no lack. In my self-love practice, I found a rhythm and saw the angels that have always been here with me, stylin' in not only white, but also black. I learned that the more I unravel myself into a space of love and forgiveness, the less I see life as an attack. When loving myself first above all, I can let myself dance with the flow of life and feel empowered to give back. I learned if we don't take responsibility to heal the painful experiences we deeply feel, they are dished up to those around us like a poisoned meal. Choose what magic you keep, and to what magic you say farewell.

For all earthquakes have to teach us. These significant sacred lessons
For without them, there would be no movement,
and who knows how we would find
our essence. Gratitude can be the prayer that takes you out of your hole.
Connection to breathe, has taught me there is no need to control.
Love can be the medicine that reminds us that we are whole.
Life and death, the teachings that remind us of impermanence,
and that present moment awareness is the most certain of all goals.

The journey of my *firmeza* goddess continues to teach me the art of connection and that our strength lives in the spaces where we choose to stop and listen. Sometimes it can feel lonely to be on a leading edge, but it's at the edge of our discomfort where we grow. Evolving by breathing into resistance, our seeds will sow. I was strengthened and transformed by holding the hand of my goddess within to welcome all of me to be seen in the light; by embracing my pain with love and allowing the supportive self-embrace to alchemize what was a struggle, into lessons. The merging of my inner shiva and my shakti, and walking this blue and green blob in space with curiosity of the creation and destruction process offered me a more playful, pleasurable, and fluid response to life.

In beautiful reverence, my mum, sister, and I have grown and loved through thick and thin. We are the three musketeers bound together like a fierce pack of wolves. Life has completely transformed for us. Our family expanded with them meeting their kind, supportive husbands and the arrival of two beautiful babies alongside remembering the strength that lies within, and from giving and receiving unconditional love and trust. Although we went through pain and tragedy, the love we have for one another — and for life — is unbreakable. This love mirrors how I see humanity and the earth.

My *firmeza* goddess metamorphosed into power and fierceness. She was at times messy and disjointed, but ultimately wildly transformative. We can all let our pain be transmuted into love, curiosity, and adventure. From this place, we are led to gratitude, pleasure, peace, and contentment. The strength we have within us deepens as our courage to visit places of vulnerability grows. Remember, a wild blazing fire can start with one single spark

Love from Lauren x.

Ignite Action Steps

- Stand in the mirror, naked; start by looking at yourself in the eyes.
- List 10 things you love about your instrument.
- Without judgment of what arises, surrender and let yourself be surprised.
- Be with the intimacy that is there when the corners of your mouth lifts; when your smile arrives. Look into the mirror, tune into your heart, and see the inner child inside of you. She is asking to be seen; to be loved. Can you give her some nurturing advice?

Lauren Cuthbert – Australia
Movement and Meditation Teacher, Leader, Creative, Coach, Adventurer
www.lovefromlauren.co ; www.karmicjourneys.org
www.artofconnection.community

JOYFULNESS

UTE BENECKE

"Your biggest wound can be your biggest gift.
It's a decision; it is your decision."

My wish is that my story helps you to trust and believe in yourself so you can step into your full power and be the wonderful goddess you truly are. No matter where you are in your journey, everything has two sides. Your biggest wound and healing can be your biggest gift. Instead of judgment, choose compassion for yourself and for others. Trust and believe in yourself; everything is always working out for you!

WHEN YOUR BIGGEST WOUND BECOMES YOUR BIGGEST GIFT

I was lying in my hospital bed and there was one question in my mind which gave me a stab in my heart. Am I still a *real* woman? Let me start at the beginning.

I am just a Catholic girl, who grew up on a farm, next to the church. I have a brother and sisters, and I never talked about my womanhood or sex until I was 37 years old. Not with my parents, not with my sisters, not with friends, or my partner. Sex was just something you had and not something you talked about.

I was in a relationship for 17 years and, after it was over, I moved out of the house we shared into a new apartment. I still remember sitting on my bed looking at the new pink fluffy carpet in my new place, excited and wondering what else was out there for me in the world of intimacy. Up until then, sex had just been something that I *had*. I had been in the same relationship since I was nineteen, and did not have much sexual experience before that. I was curious to begin a new sexual journey. I had no idea, but I knew that I wanted to uncover more. I had started to explore my feminine self and then my life changed.

I had to go into the hospital for what was meant to be a routine surgery. I always went to my annual checkups because I had fibroids in my womb which needed to be watched. A recent MRI test revealed that the fibroids were now seven inches long. My doctor told me I had to go to the hospital immediately. I tried to find a doctor who would do this surgery and preserve my womb. I was 36 and I still had my dream of being a mother and having children. I finally found a physician in Austria who was a specialist and professor in this kind of surgery. The surgery was made under the full understanding that I still wanted to have children — that's why I chose this surgeon and the hospital in Austria.

It was a routine surgery, so even though it was far away from where I lived in Germany, I didn't ask anyone to come with me. I arrived at the hospital alone and the next day I had my surgery. When I came out of the anesthetic, the doctor came in and told me "Ute, we are so sorry, but we had to remove your whole womb." I was shocked. My dream of being a mother and having children had just burst. I felt terrible and broken.

That is when the one question in my mind began, giving me a stab in my heart. Am I still a *real* woman?

I felt devastated, all by myself in that white, cold hospital room, lying on my back, staring out of the one window, trying to cope with what had just happened. Then I had the awakening that changed my whole life. At that moment I made a promise to myself. I promised that I would change my life! Until then I had been focused on my career as a financial advisor and worked incredibly long hours every day. I decided that I would not continue the way I had been until then. I wouldn't go on with just working hard and focusing on little else. I didn't know what my life would change *to*, but I knew I wanted it to be different and that I wanted to be in charge of what would happen next. Little did I know all that this promise would mean to me.

I left the hospital and traveled home to Germany for six hours on the train pondering what this question now meant. I felt exhausted, lonely, and sad. It was a challenging trip to make by myself; I was my entire support. That was the start of my own healing journey.

One of the first things I did after my recovery from surgery was to find a personal coach. The most important advice I got from my coach was, "Ute, this is as though somebody you love passed away because something in you did die." This made so much sense to me, so I started to do a lot of grief work to deal with my loss. The work helped me to understand and to process all the grief and the emotions that came up. Especially since whenever I saw a mama with children, I had a stab in my heart and a voice in my mind reminding me that motherhood would never be possible for me. It took months for the stabbing pain to fade.

After 11 months, when I had recovered from the surgery, there was another profound moment for me. I was sick at home with the stomach flu, lying on the sofa, drifting in and out of sleep while the TV flickered. I faintly heard the last few words about a female sexuality workshop in a documentary. I woke suddenly, jumped from the sofa, and wrote down the name. Three weeks later there I was, me the Catholic girl who never talked about sex, sitting in a workshop about female sexuality — a whole new journey began.

This was the journey I had started when my long-term relationship ended but had been interrupted by my surgery. The journey to explore my own sexuality. The self-exploration from being full of shame, fear, and limited taboos, to questioning myself if I was still a real woman, to a place of liberation where I unleashed my Goddess to become wild, sexy, and free.

What you don't know yet is that I wasn't only a Catholic girl from the farm who had never talked about sex; I was also so ashamed of my body since I was a teenager. I wasn't even able to be naked in front of the other girls in the school changing rooms or the other women in the dressing room after the gym. I always went home to shower because I was so embarrassed by my body.

Awkwardly, I glanced around the room at my first workshop about female sexuality, observing all these beautiful women. Oh my God, I almost wanted to leave. You know these beautiful women: tall, blonde, slim in a wonderfully toned body where all men turn around and stare after them. I always thought if you looked like this, you must be happy and have no worries.

Slowly my opinions of these women began to change. I was sitting on my purple linen meditation cushion, with my eyes and ears wide open, while I listened to the problems these beautiful women were openly sharing. Problems I never thought they would have. This was the moment where I made another decision. I made peace with my body, choosing love and acceptance; no matter how much I weighed or what I looked like. It was freeing and liberating. My whole body was at peace because I embraced *all* of me.

I came away from that workshop with a whole new level of understanding and compassion for my body. I stepped into the true Goddess in me. I learned that if you want to have better sex, it is very important that you are at peace with your body. Otherwise, you will always be in your head thinking, "How do I look right now, is this a good position, what does he think of my belly or my butt"... and you are missing the best moments while wondering if you are 'good enough.' You are missing the touch, the sensations in your body, all the good feelings that are happening while having sex.

I learned that we have to love our bodies no matter what. Your body is what keeps you alive; that makes it precious. Judging it keeps it closed and shuts down you and your power. I had been doing that for all my life. Now I stand in my power. My journey to better sex started from being a Catholic girl rooted in traditions, who never talked about sex and was ashamed of her body, to being devastated after surgery and overcoming tremendous disappointment, to being wild, sexy, and incredibly free.

The biggest surprise on my journey was that better sex not only led to even better sex, but it also led to so much more. Other areas of my life began to change and expand.

I had my most successful year in my entire career as a financial adviser and also decided to leave that field, which was a part of the promise I had made to myself to change my life, lying in the hospital bed after surgery. I reached six figures while working at least 30% fewer hours — since I was busy having better sex… It was just amazing.

I went from being the 'better man' — a woman in a sea of men in the financial world — to being the *Goddess* I truly am and I have enjoyed it ever since. Yes, I don't have children, but I am a *real woman*, more than ever, and I own this!

It took me a while until I was able to talk about my loss and surgery in public. When I started sharing it, so many other women were touched by it. Many women were shocked and thanked me for being real and raw. My honesty helped *them* be honest and authentic. It helped them to feel better because they realized they are not alone.

The standard in many societies is that a *real woman* has children. This left me feeling judged and unworthy many times. Society tells women that being a mother is the standard. If you are not a mother, there is something wrong with you and you are not a real woman. No matter what the reasons are. There is so much judgment and shame around not being a mother.

We know women judge other women for not having children even though they don't know the reason why. This happened many times to me. Both women and men will ask me, "Do you have children?" and when I say," No", there is this look, this opinion, this judgment. I quickly realized it's not about the words they say. It's about the energy and expression behind it. Many have an opinion of me or assume they know me, but most just shy away from asking to know more. They assume that I am a successful business woman and that must be the reason why I don't have children.

Through my work now, I see many women who have faced this experience. Many feel hurt and judged while still healing and learning to cope with their loss. I want all women who don't have children, for whatever reasons, to know:

It is ok!
You are loved!
You are a real woman!
Let nobody else, including yourself, tell you anything else.
You are a true goddess no matter what.

I invite all other people to think about this. Next time you ask a woman if she has children and she says no, take a deep breath and give her a moment of compassion, not pity, instead of judgment. Because you don't know why she doesn't have children. As you can see in my story and, in the end, it doesn't matter at all. There is no reason for judgment because a woman is a divine human being, who deserves to be worshiped and accepted.

What I discovered after I had healed is that everything has two sides and that there can be a big gift for you in being a woman and not a mother.

In the beginning, the other side of this loss was that I could enjoy my sexual journey a lot. I didn't have to search frantically for a partner to have children with, fearful of my biological clock. Later, out of my healing and sexual liberation journey, out of my biggest wound, came my purpose to inspire and support women to unleash their sexual power so they could have more and better sex. Without surgery, my life would have been very different. I would have never chosen this path and this path wouldn't have chosen me.

So many times I have been asked, "Ute, how did you get into this work?" My answer is always the same, "It found me and I had to be brave enough to say yes to it." When I started my own journey to explore the power of my own sexuality, the teachers told me, "Ute, you've got a gift; you need to do something with this." My answer was, "Yeah that's a good joke." So no, I didn't wake up one morning or ever dream of being a Sexual Empowerment Coach.

I am aware that I cannot give birth to children in this lifetime. But, I am also aware that I gave birth to so many other things. I birthed my calling into this world. I help other women to birth whatever theirs is, into their world.

I know deep in my soul that I am here to help women, to unleash and liberate their sexual power so they can own it and be the *goddesses* they are meant to be.

Without that surgery, without that Ignite moment in the hospital, without making that promise to myself that I will change my life *and* follow up on it, I would never be who I am today and do what I do. This is my contribution to this earth — to stand in my full power as a Goddess.

Your biggest wound can be your biggest gift and it is a decision; it's your decision. You get to open your heart and listen to your inner Goddess. Maybe you don't always feel it, but there is a gift inside of you, wanting to be seen, to step into the light, and be brought out into the world. I would like to encourage you to listen to your heart and allow it to step into being you. What do you choose, Goddess? What do you want to birth into *your* world? What makes you a *real* woman?

With all my love,
Ute

Ignite Action Steps

How to step into your power so you can be the Goddess you are:

Take a deep breath. Inhale through your nose, exhale through your mouth. Put a hand on your heart. Then inhale through your nose, exhale through your mouth, and connect to your heart. Do this five times so that you get out of your head and into your body, connecting to your heart. Take another deep breath and ask yourself: Where in your body can you feel your power? Breath deeply, inhale through your nose and exhale through your mouth, listening to your body. Put one hand on the part of your body where you can feel your power. Then breathe deeply into it and feel it. How does it feel? Is it already powerful, is it low, is it high energy? No judgment, just allow yourself to feel what is.

Then take another deep breath; inhale through your nose as deeply as you can and then exhale through your mouth. Ask inside, where in your life do you give your power away? Allow yourself to listen and hear it and just breathe deeply. Feel it, hear it. To clear this out, let's do some Ho'oponopono. Ho'oponopono is a very simple yet powerful Hawaiian forgiveness ritual with which you can clear blocks.

Take another deep breath, inhale through your nose, exhale through your mouth, and then speak out loud, "Whatever it is in me, that holds me back from stepping into my full power as a goddess, I am sorry, please forgive me, thank you, I love you. I am sorry, please forgive me, thank you, I love you." Repeat these four phases until you feel a shift in your body. Maybe you will feel lighter or a release. When you're done, take three deep breaths and shake your body.

Feel into your body, how does it feel now? Take three deep breaths and connect to your power again. Where in your body do you feel it, how does it feel now? Put a hand on that part of your body and connect and feel your power. Breathe deeply, take it all in, soak it in. Remember the part of your body where you feel your power. Whenever you feel powerless, put your hand there, take three deep breaths and connect. You can do this whenever you need it no matter where you are.

To complete this, imagine you are taking a shower of golden light. Breathe, filling yourself up with the golden light, in every cell of your body, until your body overflows with golden light, from your toes to the top of your head. Breathe and take it all in. You are now showered and filled up with golden light. You are loved, you are radiant, you are a true goddess in her power. Enjoy.

Ute Benecke – Germany
Sexual Empowerment Genie
www.utebenecke.com

GRACE

Alida Del Bianco

"Dance to the Rhythm of your Heart and sing the Song of your Soul."

I share my story with you to contribute to the healing process of your Divine Feminine energy. Having inner balance of yin and yang will freely radiate your light and support our Mother Gaia in the Great Awakening. I hope that by reading my story you will be inspired to look into your own deep wounds and heal them completely.

Rise of the Divine Feminine

The wish to travel to India had been growing in my heart for years, but I always felt that India would come to me when I would be ready. In the core of my being I knew that the right time would arrive and I surrendered to that knowing.

A good friend of mine from Delhi, India invited me to the wedding of his son and it was the greatest celebration of love that I have ever witnessed. I would prefer to share with you all the traditional ceremonies and the beauty of that gathering of souls from all around the globe, but this time I choose to write about another trip to India that shook me profoundly and showed me again and again the hidden meaning of every encounter in my life.

Throughout my journey I have been thirsty for knowledge — as a child reading books, then later studying literature and linguistics, healing arts, Ayurveda, and yoga. It seemed to me that knowledge was the key to my growth and expansion of my consciousness. As a yoga teacher I was learning all different yoga traditions, modalities, and the heritage of Vedanta sacred scriptures, searching in all of them for my unique expression. I wanted to go to India to expand my awareness even more.

On my trip to India, I chose to explore deeper into Tantra yoga and I found one ashram in the holy city of Rishikesh on the sacred Ganga river, known for being the place where the Beatles™ rock band were inspired to write and study Transcendental Meditation. My heart was beating fast when I arrived at the Delhi airport and I was feeling the excitement of my feet touching the holy ground of Mother India again. I hadn't planned every detail of my time in Rishikesh and the unknown was now unfolding in front of me.

The greedy taxi drivers trying to sell their services, police officers looking at me with the gaze of "Why is this lady traveling alone?", tourists overwhelmed by the long hours behind them, and experiencing the cultural shock of my 'first time in India' took my attention. At a tiny kiosk, I had a nutritious Indian breakfast with masala chai and I felt grounded and ready for my adventure. I chose a calm, older taxi driver and started the beautiful but dusty drive to the world's capital for yoga: Rishikesh.

It was the end of April, the hot season in India, and the taxi ride was long, taking almost eight hours to travel 150 miles. The driver was relaxed and composed, talking with me about Indian gods and goddesses and the worship of Goddess Parvati and God Shiva, the gods that are embodying the female and male energy. We stopped for lunch in a Parvati restaurant where delicious spicy food, happy families, and bright, sparkling children's eyes were giving me that welcoming warm feeling of home.

We finally reached Rishikesh, the city where you literally breathe the spiritual energy with Ganga flowing from the Himalayas, purifying my soul and accelerating my karma. I absorbed the energy as I watched the mountain shadows outside growing longer in the late afternoon.

Slowly, the taxi came to a gentle stop as the road in front narrowed, bougainvillea bushes and rounded rocks covering it from each side. The driver turned to face me and said, "Madam, it is not possible to drive you up to the Ashram by car; do you want to walk?" It was almost dark outside, too dark to walk the rest of the way with my luggage. I decided to stay overnight in one of the cute hotels nearby at the base of the majestic mountains.

The hotel was in a beautiful natural setting on the river, immersed in tropical gardens with mango and banana trees. I had a nice room and friendly service. I enjoyed another amazing, colorful Indian meal and went to sleep. As I drifted off, I felt happy, content, and excited as I had arrived at the destination that soon would bring my transformation.

In the morning, leaving the luggage behind, I went walking to the Ashram alone. The sun was burning on my skin, so I protected myself with my favorite pashmina and walked for about an hour on the narrow pathway that was sometimes covered with water streaming down to the Ganga River. I was in the jungle surrounded by high trees that were guiding and protecting me, showing me the way. When I reached the Ashram, they were just starting the Puja, the fire ceremony, outside in the garden and they invited me to join them. I was honored to be there, and humbled by the presence of such an amazing place and all the dedicated monks.

It was the first day of Navratri, also called Durga Puja, a major Hindu festival that is held in honor of the divine feminine; it occurs over nine days and all the aspects of divine feminine are celebrated and honored: Goddess Durga, Goddess Lakshmi, and Goddess Sarasvati. I was aware that everything was divinely orchestrated for me to be there in that precise moment and receive the Blessings of Maa Durga (Divine Mother). After all my efforts to arrive, I felt blessed and joyful to have come at that special time.

When we finished the ceremony and chanting sanskrit mantras, I was introduced to the Ashram Guru. Everyone in the Ashram considered him an enlightened Master, but in my heart was a feeling of 'something is wrong here' and I said to him out of the blue, "I am not staying for the Tantra class, Namaste." I walked away from that place not understanding why, but I felt like I had just avoided something that was not good for me.

On my way back to the hotel, I passed by a modern and unique-looking yoga school and I was unexpectedly pulled to go inside.

It was lunchtime and all the teachers were sitting together at a very long table enjoying the flavorful Indian food. One of the teachers approached me and we started to talk. He was extremely loving; his voice was soft and his presence was resonating with my energy. He told me that a course had just started today and that I was welcome to stay with them and take the class. It was not Tantra yoga, as that was my wish and goal for coming to India, but instead, Ashtanga yoga, a tradition that I never was attracted to, because it was the most masculine principle of yoga. Physical strength and discipline were core aspects of Ashtanga yoga and I had never practiced it before. It was an advanced Ashtanga course and I was just recovering from a shoulder surgery and rebuilding my muscles in my rotator cuff. Despite all of the challenges, I felt "this is my school, these are my teachers, and this is my class!" So I stayed and took the class.

In fact, I moved my luggage there and signed up for the full month of training with them. The next morning at 5 AM my day started with cleansing practices, meditation, pranayama, yoga practice, philosophy, anatomy, teaching practice, more yoga practice, alignment, and, at the end of the day, mantra chanting and meditation. I was exhausted after my first day and I felt soreness in all of my muscles, but my energy was high. In the evening I went into the town of Rishi-kesh to visit my good friend Alok. I first met him when I was in Rishikesh two years before, and from the very first moment we connected, we became good friends, sitting for hours in his small shop drinking chai and talking about life. Seeing him again felt comforting and he made me feel at home.

My course was very challenging and some days I could not walk from the pain, and often I asked myself, "Why am I here?" Even one day, when the whole school suffered from food poisoning, I kept my practice. In the evenings I was spending my time talking with Dany, a fellow yogi from Lebanon, who became my soul companion from the class.

One day when we were going to the town on our lunch break, a beautiful French girl, a student who had arrived that morning, asked to join us as we walked to town. The fragrance of Paris was still on her small black dress and her skin was shining with purity. She was smiling with innocence and Dany and I both invited her to come with us. We walked down on the narrow rocky pathway between cows, motorcycles, and cars — the harmonic Indian chaos was a celebration for all of our senses.

Just before we reached the shop of my friend Alok, Dany and I saw a huge black bull, untethered on the street, slowly coming our way. We quickly crossed the road to avoid him. I didn't notice at first, because I was convinced that the French girl was right behind us, but suddenly, I looked back and I saw her standing alone in the middle of the road visibly in shock. She was locked in place, still as a statue, and I saw distinct fear in her eyes. The locals were all staring at her and I knew that something terrible had happened. I ran to her and she told me, "I was just hit by the bull, but I am okay." She was holding her pelvic area with her hands. I looked down and I saw that she was bleeding. I realized that we needed help and quickly asked Dany to go to Alok's shop and call the ambulance.

In the meantime the girl and I went to the portable toilet on the edge of the road to see where she was hit. It was on her yoni. I was overwhelmed seeing her wound — her skin looked blue, swollen, and deformed and there was blood coming from everywhere. She started to cry pleading, "Don't leave me, don't leave me..." I promised to take care of her and that I would not leave her. She kept bleeding, her pulse was very slow, and she was slowly losing consciousness. I felt very strong and knew it was my complete responsibility to help her. I went into survival mode, quickly reacting and assisting her as if she was my child and needed motherly support. We had an instant bond despite only meeting one hour before, as I had to rinse her feminine area with a bottle of water and assess the wound.

All I could think was, "Oh my God... where is the ambulance?" Holding her in my arms, I was talking to her, trying to keep her with me... waiting for the sound of the sirens. I realized she was fading and possibly didn't have much time. Dany rejoined us and we scrambled to get the girl into a taxi that was just passing by. Secured in the taxi, we started weaving through the crowded Indian streets, rushing to take her to the hospital that was not far away, but felt impossible to reach due to the congested streets and noisy Indian traffic jam.

I don't know how long the drive was... but during the ride, the girl began sharing. She felt afraid and compelled to open her heart and started telling me about her heartbreak — the man who she loved deeply had betrayed and abandoned her the night before, when she traveled from Paris to India. She was lying in my arms and holding my hands . . . from time to time she was losing consciousness, her Parisian dress was covered with blood and her skin was turning pale.

I was invocating Maa Durga, praying for her, and we were all crying — even the taxi driver, realizing how precious the gift of life is and how this adversity was giving us the opportunity to heal on a very deep level and understand the magnificence of Creation. Her life force was fading and we were doing everything to keep her present and with us.

In the hospital she was medically treated, and a few days after, when she was able to travel, left for Paris to recover. Before leaving, she told me that the pattern of being abused, betrayed, and emotionally manipulated from significant men in her life was repeating continuously and that only now did she recognize herself as a victim and that she had been feeding her soul with this pain. She also told me that she had wanted to impress Dany by showing how brave she was, confronting the bull. The experience with the bull had taught her that it is better to listen to her own voice and be herself — she realized that there is no need to impress anyone else and especially not when we forsake ourselves to impress others. I completely understood — in my past I had always wanted to impress everyone by fulfilling their needs. By being successful, attractive, and socially acceptable, I was compensating for the lack of love and acceptance in my childhood. In this way, with time, I had disconnected from my own authenticity.

I understood from that experience, on some level, all of us are manifesting a victim energy. It is our collective feminine wound caused by manipulation and oppression since the beginning of time that perpetuates this. Centuries of patriarchal domination have suppressed the female energy. It is the DNA *shadow* in women and men equally — dominant in our sexual energy as the creative force and the renewal manifestation here on Earth.

I recognized that aspect in the Tantra Ashram, when my soul knew that the sexual energy there was used to manipulate. Both men and women bear this deep wound as it is manifested here on our Earthly plane in both roles: victim and perpetrator. My amazing soul friend Dany ultimately helped awaken my transformation from this dramatic event, showing me his compassion and vulnerability.

Later Dany shared that during our taxi drive, as he witnessed the collective feminine bleeding and healing, he understood that he needed to heal the wounded Warrior in him. This was so important to me, because I finally could see the big picture from the male perspective. I realized how helpless men can also feel. I saw that reflected in the male yoga teachers and how much guilt and shame was tormenting them, when they came to the hospital to support us not knowing how to give relief to the French girl. When I sensed their helplessness, it helped me understand the male and female wholeness of us all, as I was also feeling so helpless and yet so strong.

My Ashtanga yoga course also brought me closer to my feeling of *Oneness*. The practice reconnected me with imprints held in my body by the lack of flexibility in my torso that had functioned as a way to protect my heart from being wounded again. As much as I felt that my heart was healed, I confronted myself with the Truth that I am a great giver of Love and Healing to everyone but not to myself. And, that my strength was a result of resistance to vulnerability and my fear of being hurt again. Developing my physical strength through vulnerability on the mat, I shifted my awareness and I could recognize the male and female principles in me merging into Oneness.

I finally realized that my Goddess Haurvatat, the Sumerian Goddess of Healing and Perfection, was invited to rise in me and witness my wounded Goddess, Mother, and Lover to heal and rise again in her humble Power within me. I completed the Ashtanga course a few weeks later and Dany and I could clearly see God Ganesha, the remover of obstacles, in our closing ceremony, smiling at us and giving us blessings for our journey. Our teachers were so moved from all that we had been through during this Navratri festival that a deep bond and friendship formed between all of us for life.

My intention for healing through sharing this story is directed to all of us, especially now more than ever. Our Mother Gaia will recover and heal when the aspects of suppressed female and male pain are healed and we claim our power back — our freedom to express who we truly are. When we let go of all restrictions and limitations caused by collective trauma, we allow the Kundalini to rise and create the Unity Consciousness.

Ignite Action Steps

DNA shadow of pain is manifested in victim behavior and to see it clearly we must look deep within and recognize our addictions to certain emotions and states that are repeating themselves continuously. The ultimate abuse is when we separate ourselves from our Soul and our true self... this is the separation from the Source!

I invite you to dive into a meditative state and observe yourself with the intention of recognizing and releasing the wounds from the child in you, the woman or man in you, the ancestors in you, the collective in you, and allow the Source Energy to heal you.

Namaste!

Alida Del Bianco – Croatia
Energy Healer, Ayurveda Therapist,
Yoga and Meditation Teacher, Founder of Surya Soul Temple
www.surya.hr

COURAGE

ARIADNA CRUZ GROBERIO

"Make decisions with courage, expand your awareness, and listen to the sounds of your heart."

I dedicate this chapter to you because I want to inspire you to have courage and faith in yourself. What are you exchanging your life's hours and minutes for? I hope, with this story, that you water the roots of your courage. And that it inspires you to persevere so that freedom will spring in you, revealing your Goddess Within that is capable of changing your life. Believe that you are the captain of your destiny, face your fears, overcome them, and feel the strength in your modern-day goddessness. You will feel abundant love and satisfaction, along with the unshakable power of faith.

UNSHAKABLE

My goddess journey started in Brasilia, under the scorching sun of the central plateau where low vegetation and beautiful waterfalls prevail. It is also where Brazilian power and politics are concentrated. I was born in 1976 in a small town in Minas Gerais, Brazil. Since then, I have explored the beauties of the world by making my own story.

I shared my childhood years with my sister Adriane and my mother, 'Tita', who was a seamstress, a hairdresser, and had the enviable skill of being able to work miracles with the little money we had. I was an ambitious and competitive student, a trait that I got from my father. My father, Sinval, was a sales genius. In his hands, even the worst products were easily sold. I remember always seeing the book *The Greatest Salesman in the World* by Og Mandino on his bedside table as I was growing up.

My family, unlike me, was very conventional and I grew up surrounded by limiting family beliefs. As a rebellious teenager, I determined that I would not allow limiting beliefs or differences to define my destiny. I have a wonderful skill of remembering images that my eyes photographed into my memories. I have always loved creating those onto canvas and paper, using my charcoal pencils and brushes as a time machine and a dream printer all in one. As a teenager, I fell in love with the art of calligraphy, dance, and painting. I had a whole world to explore and I was ready for that.

I started working as an intern at a major bank in Brasilia upon high school graduation. I passed the entrance exams for a University of Technology degree and was moving out to live on my own when I found out that I was pregnant. Everyone's reaction was one of shame. Many around me felt that my early pregnancy would ruin my dreams — but it was exactly the opposite — a new Ariadna was born when my light, my son, arrived. I was still struggling to enter university but I was determined to make it all work. Felipe's birth was the first day of my strongest battle. I felt encouraged and empowered by him.

At that specific stage of my life I understood the importance of honoring my story, my son Felipe, my roots, my parents, my sisters Adriane and Karolinne, and being my own self-rescuer. I had the feeling that I was about to *give birth to wonderful possibilities* and wanted to experience something new every moment. This helped grow my most genuine characteristic that I have achieved in my life, which is my constant passion for life, for people, the world, and the Universe.

The simple act of making a decision is one of the best medicines in the world. I decided to be *happy* when I went to university, became a regular employee at the bank, and moved into my own home with my son, as I had previously planned. I also decided to change from studying law at university in São Paulo and enter the computer program at university in Brasilia, realizing that a lot of what I was doing was to please the people I loved instead of doing what was best for me. I knew the world needed my best. I left my mother's house on a sunny afternoon, with her blessing. She stood in the door, fragile and crying, knowing what I was going to face and that the world was not for the weak. I had the power to plan and decide my own life. I was not at all fragile. My eyes were like that of a tiger and I couldn't look back. I knew that life's great opportunities arise at exactly the most difficult moments.

My many years of waking up at dawn to utilize more hours of the day benefited me with the grateful gift of watching many spectacular sun rises. The sky of Brasilia is, for me, one of the most beautiful in the world. One particular morning, I felt it shone especially for me. I had launched myself into a career as a leader and project manager while juggling the demands of a child at home. For a young woman, this held many challenges; each would change the direction of my life and open a new door for me.

I had won a very important role in a new company, which raised the intense pace that I already lived with. I was living at the extreme, a high-performance machine, and my sleep was more and more limited. I challenged my physical body daily, starting my day at 4 AM and only going to bed after 2 AM. Due to lack of sleep, headaches became normal, but the combination of enthusiasm and love for my son generated an unfailing fuel and allowed me to do everything I needed to. I was tireless, listening to an internal voice saying that I could change the world. I frequently wondered if that was the 'right' way. I felt constantly exhausted and depressed with too few hours of sleep and many hours of work and study. I knew I was on the edge, but I was determined to keep going.

The day that made me rethink and restart my new destination was marked by an incident. I was late for a meeting, exhausted, and pushing hard to get everything done when, rushing to get to the meeting room, I suddenly fell.

I woke up and saw not the sky above me but a bright square of fluorescent light over my head. I was in a cold, white place lying on a bed, alone. I looked around and saw my handbag and laptop that I always carried with me. That little instant was an eternity, enough to drain tears from my eyes. The blurry vision of my father entering the door scared me. I felt muddled and confused, wondering what had happened, unsure of where everyone had gone.

At that moment the immediate rescue of my own needs took place, transforming me forever. I realized I had an accident because I had allowed myself to be worked to exhaustion. I knew my life had to change. I needed to be more assertive, confident, and place more importance on myself and my son. My complex nature was eager to mature and launched me into new challenges but I knew my true value needed to come forth.

When I left that hospital, a new chapter was born. I was the fearless female protagonist for a new life experience. My thoughts turned to my son, to what I was doing, and to the strength I knew I had. I felt like I breathed in a different air, one of light and gratitude for having a cycle of existence with such divine generosity. With each minute of life, I saw myself better and stronger for the simple fact of existing.

I kept asking myself, "What are you exchanging your life's hours and minutes for?" and the answer was not satisfying. I knew I had to have the courage to expand my awareness and listen to the sounds of my heart.

As I started paying more attention to my desire for a better, more meaningful life, the Universe started answering me. I achieved professional recognition. I was invited to work in other cities and countries. Everything flowed as I kept my spiritual connection and pioneered with great courage and resilience the new lands and cultures that I experienced. After working in Canada, São Paulo, and other cities around Brazil, I was now working for a new project in Maranhão, Brazil. When Felipe and I arrived at our hotel, I received a phone call with a proposal to work in Africa on a project of the International Monetary Fund, which would change my destiny.

I embarked for Africa before my thirtieth birthday, fearless, with luggage full of dreams and many uncertainties. After almost 20 hours of travel, the plane flew over the city of Maputo in Mozambique. I was watching every detail carefully: the architecture, the streets, the greenery, plus the immensity of the super blue Indian Ocean filled my entire visual field. I didn't know anything or anyone. The company was sending someone to meet me at the airport to welcome me.

I landed in the heat of Africa focused on my professional achievements, without looking back, stronger than I have ever been before. Stepping out of the airport, I was being swarmed by people wanting to help in exchange for money when suddenly I heard someone call my name. I looked over and saw an Italian man standing among the locals. He approached me. "Ariadna? My name is Nilton. I came on behalf of the company to welcome you."

We drove along the coast on the way from the airport to the hotel and he started teaching me a few words of the local dialect, always patient and good humored. I felt surrounded by and embraced by the Universe.

My first day in Mozambique, I was alone in my hotel room. In that country, I knew nothing and nobody. The sounds coming from the mosque woke me up at 4 AM. I sat on the balcony and felt the sunrise warm my skin. I heard the sounds of the beasts passing by below, of mothers carrying their children in brightly-colored capulanas and big bundles on their heads. They walked with long strides and a firm, upright posture. I admired their strength and determination. They were beautiful! I did not see any signs of sadness or discouragement in those women; many were extremely young but always with an exuberant smile and a sparkling energy. These women's smiles, white and beautiful, showed me they were true Goddesses. I had no doubt. The women of Mozambique are fearless. They are romantic. They are souls who dance when they are born, when they marry, and when they die, and there is no time for drama. That moment in the dawn of my first day, I knew I would learn much from those Goddesses.

Moving to Africa opened a special chapter in my life. There, I was allowed to be who I really was, abstracting from the fact that I was a woman alone in search of her full freedom, with a child, facing a completely new world and a peculiar culture. I expanded my capabilities, experiencing magnificent professional leadership challenges, unleashing my deepest goddess instinct, opening up myself to the possibilities that I had no idea I had. There I learned the importance of having a story and confirmed that we have so many differences, but that we are all the same!

I felt a deep connection to the goddess power within me and knew that from that moment, life was going to be infinitely better. Even so, I never imagined that that good-humored man who met me at the airport would, a few years later, be standing beside me in Venice, Italy as we married in the chapel of Santa Chiara.

Our daughter Clara was born in a Mediclinic in Nelspruit, South Africa, 18 years after my firstborn Felipe. Four years later my daughter Helena was born in Brasilia. She came as a divine gift right after my mother's death. She was a blessing for everyone. All my dreams were gradually delivered by God and the Universe through divine hands.

My natural euphoria of inexperience was opening up slightly to maturity. As stated in Ecclesiastes 3, "Everything has its time." In my 'new time,' I found the strength and beauty in raising my self-esteem, which is directly linked to gratitude. Practicing gratitude is much more than a habit and cannot be an obligation; it has to be natural and profound, a lifestyle. When you look in the mirror, feel gratitude, smile, be sure that you are connected with your Goddess. Today, when I see myself in the mirror I understand the strong link between physical appearance and internal power. In my strength, I am beautiful. I now know I have become the modern Goddess I always believed in.

The greatest gift of a mortal goddess is having the power to shed her pure inner light by giving birth. By birthing a child, we are goddesses with goddess powers. We are creative beings. We generate a complete Being that already has its own soul. This phenomenon is the greatest proof of the unshakable creative power of a female goddess! We can create lives, generate and deliver them into the world in a new form, transforming the power of the Universe.

Today I see life as a composition of beautiful learning cycles which I face as precious opportunities for personal and spiritual evolution. After long years in Africa, I left Mozambique with full gratitude and tears in my eyes for a last meeting with my mother who was terminally ill with cancer. I would close all other cycles again to share the moments of her physical body's transition overflowing with love and gratitude. The mother Goddess left, leaving her legacy stuck in my heart.

My mother's Goddess was now assisting me, and I needed to recover my faith, my work, and preserve my other loves that were nourished by me! My beloved firstborn son, Felipe, who has always been the reason and fuel for my soul; my two daughters, Clara and Helena, who came after and hold some of the best pieces of me in their existence; and my husband Nilton.

Great skills and genius minds can come from experiences of mistakes and successes. I am aware that it is useless to hold all wisdom and deep knowledge in any area if not adjusted to the spirituality and lightness of maturity. Alternating my mindset and molding myself from the inside out transformed me into a more complete professional, a better leader and mentor, promoting much more relevant and striking transformations for companies and people around me.

I have the habit of glimpsing, thinking ahead. I am a visionary, but my experience showed me the importance of harmonizing feelings, bringing your feet into the present, and living the fullness of the moment. When I discipline myself to get the best out of my 'waking up moment,' it is restorative. I start each day getting in touch with my inner Goddess. I practice conscious breathing in a meditation and prayer exercise that allows me to dream of the best every day. I project joy for everyone, the achievements of my day, the health of my body, and visualize my family overflowing with love and joy. Waking up early and taking this time just for myself works miracles in my day!

When you discover the beauty and strength of the Goddess within you, you will be able to find courage and have faith in yourself. While some get tired and give up, by connecting to your Goddess Within, you can face your fears, overcome them, and draw on the strength within to always keep going. You will feel abundant love and satisfaction along with the unshakable power of faith. Make decisions with courage, expand your awareness, and listen to the sounds of your heart.

Ignite Action Steps

*My journey made me recreate my feminine essence,
reconnect to the natural rhythms and cycles of the feminine experience,
and helped me Ignite my Goddess Within.*

Be the owner of your soul and journey, lord of your destiny; never leave it in someone else's hands. There is a time for everything — if your intuition shows you are not on the right track, change it!! Life always gives us an opportunity to start over. You can come back, retreat, change, and resume at any time. Don't be too terrified with the consequence of a change; decisions are necessary and require all your courage.

Take full control of your life; only you know where you want to go. Drive yourself.

Ignite your intuition and you will discover the magical paths that will lead you to synchronize the most perfect vibration of your sound. Be daring. Many times things go wrong and then work out.

Take the responsibility. Do not wait; do not regret what you didn't get, what wasn't given to you. If you didn't come from a perfect cradle, make your own story,

Listen, listen, and listen. Always be ready to listen.

*Ariadna Cruz Groberio – Northern Ireland UK
Digital transformation coaching. Speaker.
Leader by nature and Project Manager by profession.
CEO of CodeVoyager. CTO of Xerofone. Chair of PMI NI UK.
Eternal entrepreneur and Investor in the franchise sector
www.ariadnacg.co.uk
thecodevoyagers.com
ariadnaacruz@gmail.com*

PERSEVERANCE

ESTHER LÓPEZ

"Embrace your feminine power."

Every girl is born a Goddess. The challenge is how to remain a Goddess, how to live your divine essence, stand in your power, stay true to yourself, and reach your full potential. Sometimes the challenge is how to find your way back to her, your way back home. My wish for you is that you embrace a strong connection with your Goddess and let her lead. It is not a coincidence that you are reading this book. The time is now.

FINDING THE WAY BACK HOME

I don't want to live. Do I want to die? No. I don't want to die... but... I don't feel like living.

The sunny yellow walls of my living room are in direct contrast to the dull gray feeling in my chest. There is an intense pain in my back, a pain that does not allow me to walk or move normally. This pain and the physical limitations of it are familiar to me. I've lived this before and I got over it. However, this time it is not just a matter of focusing solely on the recovery of my body… I know that this time it is something more — it is my soul shouting at me, through my body, to stop, to make changes, to end this self-deception, to listen to my true pain. I know in this moment that I need to listen not to the outer pain, but to my inner anguish.

It is an inner void, a cry for help from my Being. A fist squeezing my chest and hindering my breathing. A cloud of tears forming above my eyes and drawing a frown. A sad look. My footsteps move me forward one day after another with no purpose, dragging me through life.

I look at my existence and I feel guilty about my apathy, as if I have no right to feel this way. Outside of this physical limitation, I am healthy. I have a job where I am valued. I have a nice house in a nice area... and yet... I don't have a life. I have no purpose, no passion. I don't have a social life. I feel alone even with people. I am bored by the stressful routine, choked by my uncompromising self-demand. I feel like life is slipping through my fingers and time is fading away... I've been so focused on work, trying to fill a void that hurts to look at, trying to fit in, to please others by placing their needs or desires above mine, above myself. I have been neglecting my total well-being.

Paradoxically, at the same time, as if I wanted to rebel against that self-imposed humiliation — that denigration of my Being — I show a false strength and self-confidence. This strength is detached from any emotion. Unable to enjoy. Cold. Demanding. Robotic. Apathetic. Anorgasmic.

Looking back on my childhood, I realize I miss myself... What happened to that strong, positive, proactive, dreamy, independent, curious, questioning, activist girl? What have I done to her? How can I make her come back?

These were the questions that were on my mind when I was 35, during a long year of medical sick leave spent largely on my comfy blue couch. I was living a year of pain and agony, both physical and emotional, and I was desperate to break free of it. I was very far from my Goddess... so far in fact that I had not the slightest awareness of her.

The year began with a recurrent pain and physical limitation, but it hid a much-needed healing. I am now grateful for it, as it gave me the space and time to descend into hell. To raise my own awareness. It was the beginning of my journey back home, back to my essence, back to my Goddess.

I was spending hours in medical offices and at the rehabilitation center. Although my physical recovery was the primary focus of the doctors, they also suggested I look for psychological help to deal with my stress and my emotional state.

I got help. During the next year, I spent many hours in a tiny yet lovely little corner office with my psychologist. She helped me uncover something significant that happened to me when my mom passed. I was 21 and her passing had a more significant impact on me than I first knew. Grief overtook me, pressing on my throat, choking me, suffocating me. At the same time, I felt this incredible sense of relief, the lifting of a weight, knowing that she had been released from her suffering. It was a complicated blend of feelings and

I hardly knew how to deal with it. My mother's death was a major turning point. I began to engage in life in a whole new way. Suddenly, I had a lack of self-confidence and I lost my voice. I began to live from guilt, unconsciously punishing myself for my mom's passing. I imposed on myself an extreme level of self-demand, not allowing myself to enjoy, to love, to shine... as if I no longer deserved any of that.

Despite identifying that turning point, I was still far from understanding that it meant the disconnection from my Goddess. And nothing would really work to its full potential until I connected with her again... until I returned back home.

I remember clearly recognizing the Goddess within me as a child and as a teenager. That strong, positive, independent, assertive, curious girl who would observe and question with the honest interest of learning. I was forever asking questions... Why this? Why that? I drove my parents crazy with the constant barrage of childish curiosity.

I remember a conversation with my mom when I was 14. We were seated on my bed, close to the window, my feet feeling my pink carpet. She was sharing that she was not happy, that she had given up many things to be a mother, which she did not regret at all. However, she did not feel totally fulfilled in her professional vocation, nor was she happy in her personal life. While we talked, it was hard for her to be open and she wasn't expressing it clearly, but I could see in her blue eyes how she wanted to talk about divorcing my father.

From the assertiveness of my Goddess, I asked, "If you are not happy, why don't you get divorced?" She was surprised at my question. "I didn't do it before because of you and your sister being so young." Her response felt to me like she was asking for my permission. "Well, we're not that young anymore, and you don't do us any favors if you're not really happy," I replied in a matter of fact way. I wanted to support her. I wanted her to put herself first — to make a decision that would make her happy.

Two years later, we went to court for the trial to determine our custody. I was 16 years old and my sister was 10, and according to Spanish law regarding our fate, only I was old enough for my declaration to be binding. Again from my assertiveness, I declared in favor of my father and we would see mom every alternate weekend.

I have a very intense memory of my mom in court after my declaration. We were in a long dark corridor. Her lawyer was with her. The memory of her words may not be literal or even real. She may not have said these words, but what I have imprinted is a message, "You will regret it."

Everyone in the family had a difficult time during the divorce, but the truth is, piece by piece, my dad built a new life. My mom, on the other hand, fell ill with cancer a couple of years later. Many hospitals, a surgery, and a kidney later, it seemed that she had overcome it. However, two years later, a metastasis on her lung ended her life at the age of 46.

I consciously know that I was not responsible for her death. Nonetheless, that does not change the internal interpretation I created, the guilt I unconsciously felt, nor how I handled my life from that moment on. How, little by little, I lost confidence in myself, turning off my voice, ceasing to shine. I focused instead on working, on doing, doing, and more doing... as if I were serving a long penance in which fun, passion, and love were not allowed. I was my own judge and my own executioner.

That year, that long period of being on medical sick leave, was extremely difficult but incredibly enlightening. It allowed me to understand how I had got to where I was in my life. Feelings of release started to bubble in my subconscious, a tiny speck of relief from that guilt. That was when my pain started lifting. I felt stronger emotionally and my physical recovery started progressing faster.

Once I was physically healed, I went back to work feeling ready. I wanted to make up for lost time. However, a few years later, I would realize that consciously identifying that turning point and its consequences was not enough... the journey back to my Goddess had just started.

A year after I returned to work, I felt I could no longer play the role I had been playing for so long. That I was a different person, with new interests and aspirations. So I quit my job. I started that new phase in my life with enthusiasm and optimism. Yet one after another, the setbacks came. I felt uncertain, vulnerable, alone... until I finally collapsed two years later. Once again, it was my back that stopped me. I couldn't move. I could not feel my leg. I called a friend to come help me, unshed tears making my voice wobble as I asked him to take me to hospital. I had completely lost the use of one of my legs and I had to undergo surgery.

I was not afraid of my physical recovery. I knew how to deal with it, but what about my life? This collapse and the time needed for physical healing was just one more stop along the way to reflect... I thought understanding my story was what I needed for my life to change, and I thought this had already happened! I thought I had already done the work. But I hadn't. I felt lost, aimless, with no direction and no compass... What was I missing? What was I doing wrong?

An ancient Zen proverb says... "When the student is ready, the Master will appear."

After recovering from the surgery, a new phase began that represented a quantum leap in my self-development and personal growth, and in which I had many and diverse Masters. During the three years that followed, I went through a multitude of high-impact training in various areas of personal development, in different countries, sharing my growth experience with people from all over the world.

I started to navigate life in a completely different way. I was feeling that strong, positive, dreamy, curious, and questioning girl coming back. At the same time, I still had a lot to process and integrate. I knew the journey was not quite over, that something was still missing. Perseverance is without doubt one of my virtues, so I knew I wouldn't give up in what turned out to be my pursuit of the Goddess.

I returned to work for the company I had left five years before. Although it was a comfort zone to me, I was faced with the challenge of not getting completely absorbed. I didn't want to be trapped in my old workaholic ways. The challenge was to show my new self, to act authentically, and to be able to set limits while I continued searching, studying, attending seminars and high-impact training sessions, traveling, and always growing.

I became certified as a Life and Business Coach, a Health and Nutrition Coach, and a Wingwave Coach. I became a Neurolinguistic Programming Master and Hypnosis Master, a Psych-K Practitioner, and a Goal Mapping Practitioner. I felt myself being called to support others on their journeys. Even so, I caught myself procrastinating, doubting, feeling that something was still missing. That 'something' always seemed to be the next certification, the next course, the next training, more experience... but it wasn't that... With my job as Project Manager, I also told myself I had no time for all of this... but it wasn't that either...

One day, while working on my limiting beliefs with one of my mentors, it all came together and made sense. I found the missing piece. That piece was making *peace* with my feminine essence. The feminine energy inside me had been blocked since I was 21. All that false strength and self-confidence I had shown in my life, that energy with which I had shielded myself when I returned to work after my sick leave, the same energy that had helped me rise from a hospital bed after surgery, the one that so many people recognized in me, and that even seemed to scare and intimidate others... It was an emotionless, tough energy, with a mostly male vibration. My energy was completely detached from my essence. I was acting like an angry and aimless warrior on the warpath for no reason. This was not my true Goddess self.

That attitude had led me to disown everything that could identify me with women. I even went so far as to perceive femininity as *weakness*, to the point of rejecting women and isolating myself completely from the sisterhood. In doing so, I had also disowned my intuition, my creative strength, and my enjoyment of love, beauty, and sexuality.

Removing that block allowed me to embrace and integrate all the virtues of my essence. It empowered me to live and vibrate from my Goddess, recognizing, accepting, and honoring the Goddess in me. I was finally back home, energized and able to shine and unleash my full potential.

I am a firm believer in the fact that every girl is born a Goddess, but then life gets in the way… In my case, an internal interpretation of an event that marked my life blocked my Goddess without me even realizing it. In many cases, the collective external social or cultural expectations of what a woman and her role in society should be disconnects us from our Goddess. "Be a lady," they say… These pressures — internal or external — can easily lead to conditioning, limiting beliefs, and a need to fit in, frequently diminishing ourselves in favor of men, often even fighting among ourselves. For some women it can also lead to the opposite extreme of fighting with men, using masculine energy to prove we can do everything they can… Either way, we are detracting from our greatness, diminishing our power, and definitely disconnecting ourselves from our Goddess.

Herein is our challenge and our responsibility. How do we remain Goddesses? How do we find our way back home, embracing all the archetypes contained in a Goddess? How do we live our absolute essence, stay true to ourselves, and reach our full potential?

Being a Goddess… living the virtues of the Goddesses… is to feel and to be complete in yourself. Independent. Belonging to no one. Expressing your truth with assertiveness. Doing what you do, not out of a desire to please, to be liked, to fit in, or for approval; but because it makes sense to you. Because it motivates you to follow your own values, regardless of what others say or think. Living your Goddess is not a quest for power or for someone else's interest or love. A Goddess has not been carved out of collective, social, or cultural expectations. She does not embody any male judgment of what she should be. Being a Goddess represents the enjoyment of love, beauty, sensuality, eroticism, and sexuality. She holds a magnetism with an eclectic power for change and transformation. She is a creative fertility, a source of inspiration and life. Her sharp perception is focused on the here and now. She is a companion, a leader, and a friend, nurturing relationships with her wisdom, empathy, and compassion. The world needs all Goddesses, awakening and stepping forward, now more than ever.

IGNITE ACTION STEPS

Take a moment to breathe in what it means for you to be a Goddess. Move your feminine energy through your body. Use the vehicle that resonates with you. Paint, sing, play an instrument, dance. Listen to your Being, your feminine essence, your body. Here is my special tip for you: Awaken your Goddess with Belly Dance. The dance spins its magic and mystical healing powers to awaken your inner being, reconnecting parts of yourself that may have suffered disconnection. Whatever means you choose, by healing the rift between mind, body, and heart, you will be re-connected with your emotional center. You will be able to hear your inner voice and guidance reminding you what you truly want to express to the world.

Review your beliefs. Choose which ones you want to keep and which ones you can let go of. Ask yourself, are my beliefs empowering me? Or limiting me?

Look at how you talk to yourself. Be aware of self-limiting ideas, ways you dismiss yourself, discredit your accomplishments, and detach from your emotions.

It may take you some time. You may find resistance. You may feel that nothing you are trying is working. You may also feel people around you who would rather you stay the same, either afraid of losing you or afraid they can't keep up with you.

I encourage you to persevere. Look for the support of like-minded women. The world needs the energy of Goddesses more than ever!

Esther López – Spain
Coach & Trainer
Life & Business Coach, Health & Nutrition Coach
Wingwave® Coach, NLP & Hypnosis Master,
Psych-K® and Goal Mapping Practitioner
www.Smart-Change.es

INTEGRITY

MARIE MBOUNI, MD

"Be a Supercreator Goddess, a timeless multidimensional masterpiece."

It is possible to create the life that you desire despite what's happening, despite the reality that you are living in. Know that it is okay to dream. It is okay to pivot, to make your own definitions of what success means to you. My dream for you is that you fulfill the highest, truest potential of your expression as a magnetic feminine power. Be a supercreator goddess: inspired, loved, magnetic, fulfilled, and impactful. It's my honor and privilege to write this chapter and share my story with you.

A NEW ARCHETYPE OF THE GODDESS UNVEILED.

I was born in Cameroon, Africa, surrounded by the most beautiful stretch of rainforest, with the tropical green forming a living canopy overhead. Growing up as a girl child in a patriarchal community, I always felt like I never quite fit in — a brightly colored parrot standing out against the deep green of everyone else's leaves. I never took the easy path. When everyone said girls should not go to medical school, I didn't listen. I took the national exam and I passed, even though everyone told me that it wasn't done, that it wasn't worth trying. They said that I should just keep to my place and become someone's wife. But that was not my dream. I became a Medical Doctor in Anesthesiology and I spent 17 years taking care of people who are between life and death or experiencing extreme pain.

It was an incredible privilege that I was able to realize my dream. But the dream was not complete. I had shut down my feminine self and my spiritual side. I felt like I was not a human, as if I was not alive, but rather an automaton going through the same steps each day. I was overworking, pushing, in the monotony, too tired for any social life, struggling to get up again. After 17 years, I was burnt out and overwhelmed.

I had bought into the idea that success was about putting my head down, making sacrifices, and then one day retiring and starting to finally live my life. My day-to-day existence was always about trying to save time wherever I could, for example, balancing on one leg in the shower as I brushed my teeth and shaved my legs all at the same time.

I had bought into the culture of scarcity — the belief that suggests there is not enough to go around. Money, success, achievements, and even love are all limited. I had to do so much to earn them, and even then, there might not be enough for me. I had become hypercompetitive, comparing myself to others. The culture of adversity constantly hammered into my head the thought, "This is not enough. *I am* not enough." I found myself staying super busy so I could avoid the pain and the shame inside of me.

That deep feeling of unworthiness was pushing me to go above and beyond, trying to fill the void inside. I had become isolated from family and friends and a complete stranger to myself. I was not in touch with what I truly desired. I did not acknowledge my gifts and innate talents, and I underestimated my divine connection. I thought I had nothing more to contribute to humanity or the planet except my job.

My work had become my identity. I had no sense of my multidimensional potential.

On the outside, I looked like a complete success. Inside, however, my life felt utterly meaningless. I was going through each day without a clear vision, waking up only to go to a job that was slowly eating away my soul. Afterward, I would come back to an empty house day... after day... after day in a predictable routine. I had lost all sense of wonder and joy and felt unsupported, alone, and abandoned.

After many years of putting everything into my career, I wanted to take a couple of days off after coming home from a 26-hour shift. My time-off was approved, and I decided to go to a nearby beach town filled with cafes, little shops, and beautiful ocean views. It was the beginning of summer and I just wanted to feel the sun on my skin and visit with a long-time friend. Thirty minutes into my drive, my cell phone rang. I saw that the call was from the hospital and my heart started racing, my body feeling frozen, each heartbeat loud in my ears. I answered the call on my Bluetooth; the hospital was calling to rescind my days off. Patients were waiting on me and I had to come in.

Frustrated and looking forward to the mini holiday, I tried negotiating, but there was no compromise. If I didn't return to the hospital immediately, I would lose my job. Hearing those words, my entire body went still. I was frozen inside. I pulled my car over to the side of the road, engine still running, my friend sitting quietly in the seat next to me, and I felt the anger wash through me. My mouth fell open as I gasped in breaths of air, unable to breathe properly, each gulp a desperate effort to bring life-giving oxygen to my cells. The steering wheel felt cold and hard under my clenched fingers. In that moment of anger, the entire world had fallen away and everything had gone still. I realized I was just a cog in their wheel. They didn't care. And I didn't care to return to either.

I knew my patients were waiting, and I felt responsible for them, so I returned to the hospital: furious, powerless, and feeling shackled. After the initial rage came the anguish. The entire drive back, I cried, silent tears coming out of my eyes. Waves of defeat, followed by resentment… followed by fear and despair, helped find a decision already made inside of me: I was done.

The next day, alone in my house, I took stock of all that I was feeling and experiencing. I decided that it had to stop! I wanted to break free of my golden handcuffs, get out of my own way, and to end the hiding. My life had become so ruled by others and I had been completely denying the goddess within me. I made a vow to myself to reclaim my 'dreamself.' I did not know how this would happen; however I was committed.

I tried to leave my job in a responsible way by saving lots of money before departing. However, each time I did, something would happen and I would lose the money. I went into severe financial distress and was unable to cover my mortgage or car payments. Fear set in, along with the negative bank balance, and I felt tremendous stress. In denial, I avoided my mail, not wanting to see a bill or a letter from the bank. Eventually my house went into foreclosure. I was on the verge of being homeless. I would later learn that this 'dark night of the soul' is a part of the heroine's journey.

I only know that I felt numb. I had no energy or passion. Although I smiled a lot, I had lost my true internal joy. I was dead inside, slowly dying from not being the real me. I had relationships that were toxic to my soul. I lost myself. I shut down my gifts. I did not think I was good enough to be or share. I was in a prison, my soul's gifts were shackled and locked. I was letting myself disappear. Even with all this despair I remained committed to my spiritual awakening; I just didn't know the path yet.

Embracing my spiritual awakening and my innate gifts saved my life. I began remembering and reawakening to the spiritual powers I had been shutting down since my childhood; trying to 'belong.' At the time my belief was that I had to be like everybody else to be accepted and loved. Intuition was not talked about and my attempts at sharing my inner thoughts were always criticized and I was told to, "Shut up" by my elders.

My next step was forgiving myself and everyone else around me. This practice of deep, unconditional forgiveness creates alpha waves, which can transform your brain to function like a Zen monk. These alpha waves are linked to inspiration, genius-level intelligence, peak performance, balanced emotional capacity, and even increased immunity. As I started doing that practice, it brought me inner peace and resolve. It reinforced the fact that *I was the one* who needed to change. *I was the one* who had to take action. It wasn't about what *they* did; it was about what *I* was willing to do now that I had made the decision.

I started receiving messages, channelings, and transmissions from the Divine Source that I have a big mission in this life, that I came here for a purpose: to bring a message of liberation and empowerment, to bring heaven on earth. At first, my response was, "No. I'm a doctor. I don't know how this will fit in my reality. Who would listen to me?" But this guidance did not stop and I was feeling spiritual pressure.

I decided to release the fear of radical change from the mainstream path, the one that kept me asleep and numb. I needed to redefine what 'success' meant for me, and it was not more money and bigger stuff. It took me less than a year to ultimately unhook from a career I was devoted to for 17 years. I surrounded myself with inspirational people who saw me when I could not recognize myself, who believed in me when I could not see my way. They were the ones who guided me when I could not find the path.

As I continued to work on this journey, the voice of my calling and purpose became louder than any societal expectations, fears, or judgment. I was following my heart, my soul, my bliss. I started reawakening my multidimensional senses. Drawn by curiosity, I explored sacred plant medicine and the mystery teachings of ancient wisdom. I was connecting to guides, goddesses and light beings, sacred geometry, energetic patterns, cosmic practices, channeled symbols, things I had never seen or experienced before.

As I embraced my healing and my purpose, life started happening FOR me instead of TO me. I started becoming more peaceful, alive, vibrant, and magnetic. I began feeling like I had finally become the real ME. The things I wanted most in life arrived continuously. I was attracting healthier relationships into my life — and the toxic ones faded away. I went from being stuck in old patterns of invisibility, feeling off-purpose, and being a prisoner of my career to an enlightened goddess embodying my life's work!

After that intense spiritual initiation, I realized that all the hardships I had experienced were in preparation. I was being given codes that I was supposed to share with other women to usher the rise of the new feminine — to start a movement.

The new frontier is unlocking the feminine superpowers within us. It is the new paradigm. As women, we have lost our 'womb-maness.' We've been told how to behave by society. Told that if you want to be respected, don't smile too much. Don't wear dresses that are too this or too that. Don't walk a certain way. The codes that I was being given were about the remembrance of our power that was stolen and usurped by the patriarchy of the past, encasing our feminine powers in ice, out of balance with the masculine. Now, we're starting to thaw.

I was receiving that *We* as women have a new archetype, the Supercreator® Goddess archetype, where you reclaim your feminine goddess power and create a limitless future with powerful consciousness-based, energy and spiritual transformational technologies.

This archetype evokes those who DARE to believe that they deserve to have it ALL. Their life is not just about goals and outside achievement. Instead it is a harmonious life that is rich in meaning, with flowing prosperity, aligned with the soul's purpose. It is a deep connection to a Higher Power, God, Universe, and Source. That connection yields rich friendships, deep intimacy, alignment, creativity, and play, a full life where you thrive.

What previously was only accessible to the shaman, the alchemist, mystic, and the priestess became available to me. I knew I needed to guide women entrepreneurs to discover how to unlock their soul gifts by sourcing their innate wisdom. I assist them to that place inside where they know exactly what they need to fulfill their destiny and live their legacy this lifetime.

To receive this type of message is incredibly unique and rare. I am honored that *The Supercreator Goddess* is a movement, born from my journey. It is the new face of the divine feminine, with nine pillars representing the nine months of pregnancy to birth. Each pillar has gems of wisdom, transformation, and empowerment. Each includes a mantra and a mudra, with gem names to foster magic and beauty. Here are the fruits and harvest of that journey — a direct transmission for the Goddess.

- *Pillar One is Red Ruby Codes. This precious energy holds a deep wisdom of Earth. You learn Womb & Yoni Awareness and to release the Past.*
- *Pillar Two is Pink Diamond Codes, the frequency of unconditional love within. A love that is all-seeing, compassionate, and endless, the pure love which knows no boundaries and acts as a portal which unlocks the realms of miracles.*
- *Pillar Three is Golden Sheen Obsidian Codes, about Shadow Integration, the Inner Heroine, and surrender. The Shadow Self is the part of ourselves that we repress or deny.*
- *Pillar Four, Green Emerald Codes, is the frequency of the shapeshifter, embodiment, self investment. You are a reflection of the Goddess.*
- *Pillar Five, White Diamond Codes. The White Diamond purifies and acts as a transducer for the multifaceted energies of creation that are always streaming through you. You learn Clarity and Self Belief, to honor your intuition and inner Wisdom as well as Divine creativity.*
- *Pillar Six is Yellow Sapphire Codes. This radiant frequency empowers you to cultivate your Divine will in the most beautiful and sacred ways, a perfect alignment of the inner feminine and the inner masculine with Divine will. It encompasses Kundalini and Sexual Energy Activation Codes.*
- *Pillar Seven, Blue Sapphire Codes, is the energy of pure uncompromising truth and visionary leadership. Cosmic Egg Codes — Conceive YourSelf.*
- *Pillar Eight, Iridescent Pearl, the void of potentiality. The Iridescent Pearl is the wildcard which invites us to explore the darkest depths of the unknown, the alchemical journey of total transformation.*
- *Pillar Nine, Master Dow Crystal Codes. A Dow crystal is a combination of a channeling crystal and a transmitter crystal. It is a symbolic representation and attainment of quantum Intelligence, the knowledge, wisdom, and truth of the consciousness of the Supercreator Goddess.*

When you forget your innate wisdom and find yourself seeking answers outside of yourself, feeling overwhelmed, exhausted, and depleted by all the external striving and searching, know that it is possible to create the life you desire. You can set new foundations, disintegrate non-heart based guidance, and redefine rules, regulations, laws, habits, patterns, structures, and agreements that are limiting your free expression.

When you fulfill the highest, truest potential of your expression as a magnetic feminine power, you will feel yourself coming into wholeness and full alignment, fully ALIVE. With each dark night of the soul comes an opportunity for rebirth, a reclaiming of your soul's potential and awakening to a deeper meaning and connection in your life. May you find the Goddess you are and become your fulfilled, highest, truest potential — the ultimate expression of magnetic, feminine power.

IGNITE ACTION STEPS

I have a healing visualization and activation for you about Releasing The Womb and the Five Wounds of the Heart: Abandonment, Betrayal, Denial, Judgment, Separation.

We use the essence and mystical powers of the Rose and the power of the Breath. Place one hand on your heart, the other on the womb (the lower belly). Even if you have had a hysterectomy, your energetic womb is still present. Call in the violet Flame, surrounding you as if you are in an Eggshell: Safe, Secure, Protected. For each of the wounds below, vividly image an angelic rose of the indicated color. Breathe in its essence; let the unique color flood your whole body. Breathe out, release the wound. Say the mantra. Release the emotion. Then, spend a few minutes journaling.

- The Red Rose will allow you to release the wound of Abandonment. This heart wound sits at the Base Chakra. Say: "I See my beauty and perfection."
- The Yellow Rose will allow you to release the wound of Betrayal. This womb and heart wound sits at the Solar Plexus. Say: "I Embrace my vulnerability."
- The White Rose allows you to release the wound of Denial. This womb and heart wound sits in the Throat Chakra. Say: "I trust myself and the truth of my heart."
- The Pink Rose will allow you to release the wound of Judgment. This heart wound sits at the third Eye Chakra. Say: "I am enough, I forgive and accept myself."
- The Golden Rose will allow you to release the wound of Separation. This heart wound sits at the Crown Chakra. Say: "I am a Supercreator Goddess."

Marie Mbouni, MD – United States of America
Founder and CEO of Marie Mbouni Global
www.mariembouni.com

BEAUTY & MERCY

ANA CUKROV
AND IVANA SOŠIĆ
ANTUNOVIĆ

"Discover your Goddessness and let your magnificent uniqueness shine."

We encourage you to truly discover your divine calling. Then to live it. Fully. Proudly. Brilliantly. It takes courage and resilience to shed a light on your life, rediscover who you really are, and rebuild yourself all over again. We wish you to fall in love with yourself. To see who you are in a new light — pure, dashing, amazing, unique. As you go out and show the world what you've got, we hope you do it with a song in your heart, dance in your feet, and a smile on your face.

YES, IT'S TRUE... THERE'S A GODDESS IN YOU!

What if we are the true heroines of our lives? What if every feature of a goddess lives in you, lives in me? What if there is a reflection of eternity, beauty, courage, and kindness inside of all of us? What if your *goddessness* is in the core of your being, and no one and nothing is capable of taking it away from you?

With a certainty that you own that greatness, what would you do? How would you treat yourself and others? Would you keep trying to be that 'perfect' woman if you knew... really knew, you already are perfect the way you are? Would you give up that easily? Would you work as hard or would it be enough to just be yourself?

We would like to take you back to that place of inner wisdom, when each and every one of us remembers our origin is divine. For both of us, identical twins, mothers and self-explorers, the journey of rediscovering our inner goddesses was interesting and adventurous. We would love to share the highlights of this journey with you. The times in our lives when our self-awareness and innate self-dignity began to move into our awareness more and more. The amplitudes of perceived self-worth influenced our own feeling of dignity. There were moments that made a huge shift in our experiences in which we discovered our goddessness again. We are still on a path to reach the full, juicy feminine blossom of modern goddesses.

Feminine Blossom (Young Goddess)

There was a time when we used to stroll in our hometown main street, somewhere at the end of the last millenium. Those were our high school and university years. We would walk, heads high, two blond, tall, slim twins, feeling as though the world was at our feet. For no particular reason people seemed to smile at us, almost involuntarily, just when walking by. We didn't know at the time we were owning the feeling of being free and inspired — where you don't even acknowledge where it comes from — you just know that it exists. That feminine energy, still a mystery to us at that young age. We just remember enjoying it. It gave us the motivation to be the best students in our school, fueling our strength and optimism.

That feeling of *innate feminine glow* did not last forever. Somewhere along the way, life took its toll… and slowly, invisibly, insecurities and feelings of 'not-enoughness' crept in. We both gradually forgot that feeling of blissful femininity.

Learning About Life (Curious Goddess)

When we were eighteen, we knew how to shine. The young energy and beauty that girls have, multiplied with our double charm, intelligence, and friendliness, made it easy to glow. What we didn't know was how life worked. We hadn't yet discovered, one by one, all the layers of human consciousness, all that it takes to be a human. We hadn't yet peeled away the inner essence to discover the goddesses within. We were dancers and models leading a healthy lifestyle. We were aware of our bodies, but we weren't yet aware of the depth of our minds.

Curious about humans, eager to know everything, we both enrolled to study psychology. Intellectually, we discovered a lot about the human mind, emotions, and behavior. The next layer to uncover was spirituality. Raised in socialism, with no religious upbringing, we only stepped into faith in our 20s, when we both entered the Catholic Church. Prayer became a dear gift; community between brothers and sisters became a way of life. Having found our rich inner worlds, we also awakened to the divine dignity of each person — being a son or a daughter of God makes everyone feel completely worthy, without the need for external validation or success. It took many experiences before that knowledge for our own self-worth became a 'gut feeling', before it integrated throughout our whole beings. During this process of maturing we started to feel self-conscious both in body and feelings, brain and spirit.

Then life kept happening, with all its greatness, but also with its challenges. We both got married and delivered children, started jobs, took care of the household, and set aside our goddess involuntarily.

The Miracle of Life (Mother Goddess)

There's nothing as intensely goddessy as a 'mommy' experience. Some moments really opened our hearts and our eyes to connect with our mother goddess side.

Ivana: I remember intensely the moment I first gave birth. Having twins, it was a mixture of excitement, worry, gratefulness, joy, and hope. After 12 long hours of labor, my whole body hurting, not having much more strength... I knew the end was near. And then, finally — the time to push. My husband, standing behind my back, told me gently, "Open your eyes." So I did. What a rush! My newborn son, looking back at me! Locking my eyes with his, opened my soul — at that instant I saw the whole Universe in those beautiful eyes. To my surprise, there was wisdom and clarity, immense love in them. I realized my own divinity — my goddessness — the hugeness of being able to take a part of creating Life itself.

Ana: I didn't even realize how divine and special I was until my first daughter was born. At the very moment I first saw her, I understood why all the wise women in our lives looked at us with deep love and respect. This look signalled a kind of adoration that I had never understood before, unable as a child to connect my picture of myself, as young, fragile, submissive, and silenced with someone worthy of love and respect. But, at that moment, holding my little bundle, I was aware that each and every girl who comes to this earth has this goddessness within. There she was, a tiny angel, complete, defined, pretty, firm yet soft, giving and taking, glowing and resting, completely connected to the center of life and to us all.

As if that wasn't enough, the miracle repeated... twice... Now I have three blond goddesses to love and protect, lead and learn from, to grow with and admire.

The miracle of motherhood we witnessed through giving birth and raising all of our 10 children is delicious and, like a cake, unfolds in layers.

The first layer, the *Base*: the life itself, its holiness, its complete energy, a full circle, with every possible value included.

Then the *Cream*: that proud, holy feeling that comes from being able to co-create life.

The middle, the *Waffle*: re-birth of ourselves, a new understanding and acceptance of life.

All the *Decorations:* blissful situations, whatever makes us remember our divinity (music, dance, hugging, playing).

And the *Cherry* on top: hoping to become a grandmother sage and enjoy it even more!

Challenges Of New Roles (Serving Goddess)

Most of the time our everyday life consisted of boring, annoying tasks over and over again. Not at all goddess-like. To appreciate the usefulness and functionality of serving is one thing, but without self-love and self-nurture, it wore us out. Then some doubts would emerge and the crisis would come. Reaching for answers in Holy Scriptures helped. There is an immense dignity, almost a sanctity in serving family. Still, there was not much fun in that. Day by day, we kept forgetting that feeling of bliss, glow, spontaneity, and freedom. Our own goddessness was nearly forgotten.

Divine Inspiration (The Queen of the Angels)

God has been our guide and revelation of our inner divine dignity. And what about His feminine side? Being Catholic, we discovered the perfect image of a woman and a mother in the Virgin Mary. For us, she is the picture of femininity. Gentle, kind, loving, resilient, patient, brave, open, curious, accepting, and modest. The accepting way Mary says Yes to God astonishes us — she's ever so ready. She is willing to fulfill her destiny without hesitating. There is a willingness in how she accepts this baby from God, even risking her life and being abandoned. The diligence that she applies to doing her chores calmly and lovingly, mindfully, being in true peace inside. How she loves her Son and yet is willing to let him walk his own path, even when it tears her heart apart to see him suffer. The way she is open to love and serve her community later on and continues to Love humanity forever. For us, Virgin Mary is eternal inspiration and we both look up to her for guidance and strength. We pray to her daily.

Ivana: Twenty years ago, I asked Virgin Mary to bless my marriage, and she did. I often ask her for support to be the mother I want to be. When I was pregnant for the second time, I received her grace when I needed it the most.

Our twins were five when I got pregnant again. We decided to buy a house for our growing family. To get a loan from the bank, we needed to find the perfect place in one month, before I went on my maternity leave. We needed a miracle. Then the news came: we were expecting our second set of twins! We needed a double miracle! It needed to be available and affordable! Impossible, the real-estate agent said. Humanly impossible, I agreed. But, I believed that for God — nothing is impossible! So, every night I started praying with my kids to Virgin Mary. In twenty days, we found a perfect house, overseeing a beautiful bay and near to the sacrenage of Virgin Mary of Trsat, the pilgrims' destination for centuries. And there we have lived ever since. To keep a vivid reminder of this mercy, I had the urge to put an icon of Virgin Mary, a small mosaic-mural on my balcony-wall. I had a friend who made some mosaics before, so I asked her to do it. She said, "No way, I can't make Mary, I can only do fish or flowers!" So I let it be. A couple of months later, the same friend went on a pilgrimage to Fatima, Virgin Mary's big sacrenage. An incredible thing happened. She got up in the middle of the night, couldn't sleep… walking the streets of Fatima and in a shop she saw the already-made mosaic of Virgin

Mary! The next day, she came back, bought the icon, brought it back to our hometown, visited me, and put the icon on my balcony wall! So there She is — smiling upon me every day, reminding me of Her love and mercy!

Virgin Mary's divine model and inspiration gave us strength in fulfilling the demands of being (house)wives and mothers. We discovered the blessing of accepting and serving family. But we also discovered that there is more to motherhood than dignity and serving. We learned that a modern goddess gets to play a lot. Spending time with children, reading stories, running and hiding, molding or baking cookies, brought us back to that glowing, joyful place… that immense pleasure of living in the here and now.

Ana: I love my time at the beach. The sun kissing and caressing my face, a light wind playing with my hair, "Oh, that feeling of freedom." As my three-and six-year-old daughters are delightfully removing their toys out of their bag, I'm taken back in time… I remember sitting on the bow of our mother's boat, singing against the wind as we cut the waves… we must have been, what was it, 12?… then my eyes glaze across the bay… as I breathe deeply, surrendering to the breeze, another memory pops in… I remember my first kiss… there was a salty smell, a light breeze, and the Adriatic. God, how little it takes to bring back the soft, full, immense security of knowing who I am, how great I am!

U-Turn Back To Us (Mature Goddess)

Children grow up. Every day a modern goddess needs to adapt to their changing needs. From breastmilk and lullabies, to running around. From the phase of imagination, through logic and science, up to the irony and abstraction. In each phase, they keep us very busy. A modern mum does not have a lot of time for herself. With five children each, neither did we. Many books lay unread, places unseen, dresses never worn, parties never attended. Many personal accomplishments never reached. Still, at the end of the day, seeing our angels asleep, we know we are the richest queens on Earth!

Days followed one another. There was hardly any time for us. As menopause came closer, the perspective started to change. It made us turn inward, rethink our lives, feel grateful for many blessings, to enjoy ourselves more. We discovered our sacred right and obligation to take care of ourselves. To *own* our voices, honestly share them with the world and inspire others!

Gratitude Time (Wise Goddess)

We cannot thank all the goddesses in our lives enough. Many fantastic women in our birthline, different models and teachers, writers and dancers, doctors, trainers, and random women we've met along the way. We admired them and found out they admired us too. Let's honor them all and their amazing gifts: Our Grandma Emmanuela gave us the sense of beauty and refined aristocratic perfection. We cherish that immensely; it made us float through life with grace. Our Grandma Eufemia gave us strength, determination, traditional values, and a dose of matriarchal power. It pushed us through the hard times. Our Mom Zlatica gave us intelligence, playfulness, passion, sense of humor, and courage. We owe her our sensual, goddess-like self.

So, what is the advice, the gift we want to give other women? Our daughters? Our friends? Our neighbors? Our clients? Ourselves, every day again and again? How to get back to oneself and on the right track? On the track of discovering and fully living the luminous, shiny, brilliant, unique goddess you are? Slowing down to our own pace turned out to be helpful for us. Most modern goddesses live way too fast. The world is dominantly masculine, run by systems, achievement, competition, and speed. Female energy is gentle, kind, considering how to bring people closer together, interested in community, compassion, appreciation. To live as goddesses meant allowing ourselves to live by female rhythm and values.

Learn to listen to your inner voice... slowly but gradually move from living with trying to meet other people's expectations to living your own ideals and dreams. Please, as you walk that path, be extremely gentle and kind to yourself. The world might not be kind to you. Other people, with their own wounds, problems, and unawareness, will not always be respectful. We all grow up in the imperfect world so most of us carry a lot of burden. Unless we become conscious about it, we often go along hurting each other involuntarily. Unless we decide to evolve past the imperfect ways our parents raised us. We need to forgive and guide ourselves to heal our wounds. To surpass our soft spots. Underneath the surface, deep down in our core, we strive to thrive.

Spreading The Spark (Future Goddess)

Each day we discover a modern goddess within each of us. She is deep, juicy, full of layers. So, we are excited to see what's next. Maybe the best part is yet to come! We decided to light that sparkle and keep the flame of goddessness in ourselves, one another, our daughters, friends, neighbors, readers, and every woman we meet.

Ana: As I'm getting ready to edit this chapter, my little bundle, now 17-year-old daughter, is receiving a package. Her new skateboard just came; the one she was waiting for for years. And as I witness the glow on her face, all there is to do is be grateful for her liberty. I admire her awareness of what it is she needs at this moment in her life, what it is that makes her happy. I am feeling proud for having supported her in becoming the modern goddess she is.

Ivana: As I am completing this story, watching my daughter (Ana's niece) strolling on a catwalk in a fashion show, (as we once did) I enjoy knowing the circle is completed. All the feminine glow reveals in each generation. I feel grateful that another modern goddess is blooming.

We honor all of you and encourage you to discover your femininity. Fall in love with it. Wear it proudly. And never again go back to not accepting yourself. Wear your divine glow, worthiness, and goddessness. Show off your brilliant self and let the world know you're coming!

IGNITE ACTION STEPS

Nurture beauty: Look around. There's beauty in everything, there's beauty in you. Notice and admire it, create and spread it.

Nurture curiosity: Open yourself to new experiences, have fun learning new things.

Nurture enthusiasm: Enjoy life in its exploding splendor. At the very center of your life is you, the richest, fullest spring of every idea, sensation, emotion, and action.

Nurture kindness: Be kind and compassionate with everyone, including yourself!

Nurture mercy: Bless others, pray for them, send them your Love.

Nurture spontaneity: Just be. You are enough. Remember you have all the goddessness within. Let your magnificent uniqueness shine.

Ana Cukrov and Ivana Sošić Antunović – Croatia
Psychologists

GODDESS ACTIVATION IDEAS

On the pages that follow, you will find a series of activation ideas. Each suggestion holds words infused with wisdom, kindness, and a powerful desire to help you open your heart and your soul to the divine and sacred feminine energies that lie within you. We invite you to contemplate the words, do the work, and bring the power of grace and compassion into your day with love and joy.

There are as many ways to use the ideas as there are stars in the heavens. You might simply read them, letting their intent sink into your consciousness. You might cut them out and place them on the ground in front of you as you meditate, anchoring your practice in their presence. You might carry one in your pocket for the day, or tucked up against your skin inside your bra, letting the energies within entwine with your own body's energetic field. You might roll one into a tube and set it adrift in the world by balloon or in a bottle released in the ocean. You might light one on fire, watching as the flames transform the material words into smoke and energy. No matter how you choose to engage with these activating ideas, know that the intention behind them is to help you step out into the world as a modern goddess full of confidence, compassion, caring, and joy.

Light a candle and feel Divine Love fill your body, mind, and spirit. Hold a crystal and imagine your request come into being through each of your senses.

Embrace your darkness. Look deep within and see how you have been repressed, how you have repressed yourself, and when you have abandoned and forgotten your true nature.

Imagine a white light coming down through the top of your head to your heart. Let it fill you up before you send it out to the world. Feel the connection to all life.

Just be. You are enough. You don't have to do anything, please anyone, or meet any expectations. Being you is honoring the Goddess within.

Every woman has her own journey and her own inner Goddess. Do not give up on yours. Bring your Goddess to consciousness. Embrace her. Do what you are supposed to do. Love that!

Dive In. Listen. Nourish yourself in the stillness. Smile as you witness the magic and abundance around and within you.

Listen to the most beautiful songs. Close your eyes for a moment and smile, making sure that you can travel, dreaming! Expand your awareness and listen to the sounds of your heart.

Look inside; you will find every answer you
need there. Trust and respect yourself.

———————

Be willing to release your attachment to your beliefs when they
no longer serve you. What might be true for you today may not
be true for you in the future. Be open to discover new truths.

———————

If you were to step fully onto the path of the goddess, what would
you need to leave behind? What would you need to embrace?

———————

Review your beliefs. Ask yourself, are my beliefs empowering me?
Or limiting me? What old ways of being are you ready to let go of?

———————

Practice yoga, dance, or any other movement that will
bring you flow. It will boost the feminine energy around
you and open up your body and new possibilities.

———————

Discover your Goddexx. Identify how your ideals of the
masculine and feminine have been influenced by your
culture and society. Do they align with how you feel? Are
there parts of you that are resistant to your masculine
or feminine? Practice embracing that part of you.

———————

Bless in your heart the people around you; those you
love and those you struggle with. Pray for them. Send
them your Love. Envision them bathing in the Light.

———————

Know that you have the abilitiy to make anything possible. Sit with yourself, conjure up your greatest energy, and fuel that into your wishes, then trust they will come true.

Let loose the empowered and resilient spirit of the goddess within so you may inspire generations of girls and women, one life at a time!

Find your beautiful spot in nature where you can connect to the loving energy of Gaia, Mother Earth. Visually take in the sights of nature, listen to the sounds, and feel the energy. Appreciate that you are one with the creative feminine energy of Gaia.

Gaze into your mirror. Tell yourself 5 things you love about yourself, 5 things you forgive yourself for, and 5 things you promise yourself. Repeat every day.

Set the intention for one day to focus on listening. Prioritize listening rather than speaking. Listen deeply to the sounds that surround you. Go outside and listen to the sounds of nature. Witness what you feel and what you notice.

Be the queen of your queendom! Sit in a chair with your feet planted firmly on the earth. Sit tall, lengthen your spine, and lift your chin with confidence. Emanate energy out of your heart as you imagine you are sitting on your throne. Feel the power of your strong, full, clear, sovereign presence as you repeat, "I am whole unto myself."

Practice the sacred NO by setting boundies, trusting yourself, gaining clarity and discernment in all that you do. Your sacred NO gives you the gift to say YES to what you truly desire. Say 'Yes' to you!

———————

Apply healing touch. Lovingly massage your body and contemplate its beauty and wisdom. You can enjoy your massage in the shower using the type of oil that you love, or also in bed before sleep or upon awakening. Ignite your Goddess through Touch.

———————

Always ask yourself, "What is the gift of the situation I am in? Especially when you are in a tough or hard situation. Trust that your inner goddess will show you the silver lining.

———————

Radical self-love is essential. You deserve the same grace, love, thoughtfulness, and kindness you give to others. Take time to smile, dance, and sing to help fill your soul with light.

———————

As you move your body, notice which spaces feel tight and confined, reflecting where in your life your skin doesn't fit anymore. Take some time to dance in your new skin, witnessing the spaciousness you now have to be your true self.

———————

Be willing to receive it all! You have the clarity and power in your hands. Embrace your strengths and love your imperfections. Be present. Whatever happens, find gratitude and accept what is with goddess grace.

———————

Reach out to and connect with a caring friend who can guide you spiritually. Cultivate an open-hearted relationship with her, love her, trust her, and make her your sister, friend, or divine mother. Be inspired by her goddess wisdom and powerful shakti.

Honor yourself with the gift of time. Sit in front of a mirror and hold the parts of you that you struggle to love and accept. Hold them and speak love, giving thanks for what they have brought to your life. If it's something you need to let go of, have the strength inside to release it.

See your beauty inside and out. Don't compare yourself to anyone; there's only one of you. Embrace all your imperfections, especially the physical parts. Love the unlovable. There's a power in seeing beauty. You are a constant work of art in progress.

Repeat this mantra three times: "I honor virtue, it is all things. I respect the ways of the highest order. I release attachment to being right and make room for new ways of becoming more virtuous."

Make an anonymous donation. Be kind to a stranger. Give the gift of a smile to every person you meet today. Make someone else's life easier. Do something unexpected on behalf of someone else.

Let yourself feel. Breathe into resistance. Where can you switch your view to see the world through the lens of unconditional love and trust?

Ana Cukrov
- The Holy Bible
- Women That Love Too Much by Robin Norwood
- Letter to My Daughter by Maya Angelou
- Mamma Mia, the musical

Ana Paula Gomes
- Obstacle is the Way by Ryan Holiday
- Start With Why by Simon Sinek
- Trainings: Quantum Leap Program from Success Resources by T. Harv Ecker

Ambika Devi
- Harmonizing Prana, The Dance of Shiva and Shakti March 28 2012©Ambika Devi Masters Thesis
- Lilith, May 18, 2013©Ambika Devi, Mythologem Press

Caroline Oettlin
- www.we-are-eternal.love
- Gives you insights, basically future-oriented. You can get insights to different areas in your life. Pieter Riemens, Nadi Astrology & TCM Teacher: riemensp@gmail.com
- Air Yoga, Stephen Thomas, www.thesvarupa.com
- Antoine Solam-Cottebrune, www.coeursolam.com
- Santiago Rafael Pascual, Channeler and Akashic Records Master, www.lafam.org

Charlene Ray
- www.charleneray.com

Eliška Vaea
- 'I LOVE MY BODY' meditation FREE download at www.eliskavaea.com
- Yoni Wand self pleasure tool and other yums for your yoni: eshop section at www.eliskavaea.com

- Listen to my first poem and learn more about your body: www.youtube.com/c/EliskaVaea
- Bali blissed & blessed CHAKRA necklace and activation: www.bearthjourney.com

Esther López
- Mind Power Into the 21st Century by John Kehoe
- Quantum Warrior | The Future of the Mind by John Kehoe
- The Biology of Belief by Bruce H. Lipton Ph.D.

Ivana Sošić Antunović
- The Gift from the Sea by Ann Morrow Lindberg
- Little Women by Louisa May Alcott

Joann Lysiak
- Your Heart's Desire by Sonia Choquette

Katarina Amadora
- Quimera Ritual Dance
- Kaushik Ram, Hidden World
- Love Out Loud, Masterheart
- Isis Oasis, Geyserville, CA

Lauren Cuthbert
- Love out Loud by Nicole Gibson
- Eastern Body, Western Mind by Anodea Judith
- This is that by Anand Mehrotra
- Women who run with the wolves by Clarissa Pinkola Estes

Mayssam Mounir, MD
- www.doctormiso.com/awaken-your-goddess-challenge
- Conversations with God by Neale Donald Walsch
- Your sacred self by Wayne W. Dyer
- Ignite Your Health and Wellness by JB Owen

Rev. Priestess Anandha Ray
Contact anandharay.com or QuimeraRitual.Dance for information about ordination and the priestess training in the Iseum of Quimera or the "42 Ideals of The Goddess Ma'at Oracle Cards"

PHOTO CREDITS

Ana Cukrov - *Marie Kinkela*
Ana Paula Gomes - *Fernando Polo*
Ambika Devi - *Kersti Niglas*
Ariadna Cruz Groberio - *Ariane Decaroli and Adriane Cruz*
Charlene Ray - *Shonda Hilton Photography*
Eliška Vaea - *Denisa Sterbova*
Esther López - *Tomy Domínguez*
Hanna Meirelles - *John D. Russell*
Hannah Woebkenberg - *Kass Michelle Photography*
Ivana Sošić Antunović - *Marie Kinkela*
JB Owen - *White Willow Photography*
Joann Lysiak - *Mary Rafferty Photography*
Kerry Paton - *Laura Martin*
Lauren Cuthbert - *@Drishti_Studio*
Mayssam Mounir, MD. - *Paulius Staniunas*
Rev. Priestess Anandha Ray - *Robert Domondon*
Ruqaya Kalla - *Karen Harms*
Sedona Soulfire - *Carrie Meyer*
Yendre Shen - *Joep Olthuis*

Thank you

A tremendous thank you goes to those who are working in the background editing, supporting, and encouraging the authors. They are some of the most genuine and heart-centered people I know. Their devotion to the vision of IGNITE, their integrity, and the message they aspire to convey is of the highest possible caliber. They all want you to find your IGNITE moment and flourish. They each believe in you and that's what makes them so outstanding. Their dream is for your dreams to come true.

Editing Team: Alex Blake, Andrea Drajewicz, Jock Mackenzie, Nicole Arnold, and Chloe Holewinski

Production Team: Dania Zafar, Peter Giesin & JB Owen

A special thanks and gratitude to the project leaders, Hanna Meirelles and Katarina Amadora, for their support behind the scenes and for going 'above and beyond' to make this a wonderful experience by ensuring everything ran smoothly and with elegance.

A deep appreciation goes to each and every author who made Ignite The Modern Goddess possible — with all your beautiful stories embracing this powerful idea of the modern goddess found within each and every one of us.

To all our readers, we thank you for reading and loving the stories; for opening your hearts and minds to the idea of Igniting your own lives. We welcome you to share your story and become a new author in one of our upcoming books. Your message and your Ignite moment may be exactly what someone needs to hear.

Join us on this magical Ignite journey!

Leading the industry in Empowerment Publishing,
IGNITE transforms individuals into
INTERNATIONAL BESTSELLING AUTHORS.

WRITE YOUR STORY IN AN IGNITE BOOK!!

With over 400 amazing individuals to date writing their stories and sharing their Ignite moments, we are positively impacting the planet and raising the vibration of HUMANITY. Our stories inspire and empower others and we want to add your story to one of our upcoming books!

If you have a story of perseverance, determination, growth, awakening and change... and you've felt the power of your Ignite moment, we'd love to hear from you.

Go to our website, click How To Get Started and share a bit of your Ignite transformation.

We are always looking for motivating stories that will make a difference in someone's life. Our fun, enjoyable, four-month writing process is like no other — and the best thing about Ignite is the community of outstanding, like-minded individuals dedicated to helping others.

Our road to sharing your message and becoming a bestselling author begins right here.

YOU CAN IGNITE ANOTHER SO JOIN US TO
IGNITE A BILLION LIVES WITH A BILLION WORDS.

Apply at: www.igniteyou.life
Inquire at: info@igniteyou.life

Find out more at: www.igniteyou.life